THE PAPUAN LANGUAGES OF NEW GUINEA

CAMBRIDGE LANGUAGE SURVEYS

General Editors: B. Comrie, C. J. Fillmore, R. Lass, R. B. Le Page,
J. Lyons, P. H. Matthews, F. R. Palmer, R. Posner, S. Romaine,
N. V. Smith, J. L. M. Trim, A. Zwicky

This series offers general accounts of all the major language families of the
world. Some volumes are organized on a purely genetic basis, others on a
geographical basis, whichever yields the most convenient and intelligible
grouping in each case. Sometimes, as with the Australian volume, the two
in any case coincide.

Each volume compares and contrasts the typological features of the
languages it deals with. It also treats the relevant genetic relationships,
historic development, and sociolinguistic issues arising from their role and
use in the world today. The intended readership is the student of linguistics
or general linguist, but no special knowledge of the languages under
consideration is assumed. Some volumes also have a wider appeal, like that
on Australia, where the future of the languages and their speakers raises
important social and political issues.

Already published:
The languages of Australia *R. M. W. Dixon*
The languages of the Soviet Union *Bernard Comrie*
The Mesoamerican Indian languages *Jorge A. Suárez*

Forthcoming titles include:
The languages of Japan and Korea *M. Shibatani and Ho-min Sohn*
The Chinese language *J. Norman*
The languages of South-East Asia *J. A. Matisoff*
Austronesian languages *R. Blust*
Slavonic languages *R. Sussex*
Germanic languages *R. Lass*
Celtic languages *D. MacAulay et al.*
Indo-Aryan languages *C. P. Masica*
Creole languages *J. Holm*
Romance languages *R. Posner*

THE PAPUAN LANGUAGES OF NEW GUINEA

WILLIAM A. FOLEY

Australian National University

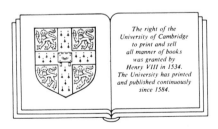

The right of the
University of Cambridge
to print and sell
all manner of books
was granted by
Henry VIII in 1534.
The University has printed
and published continuously
since 1584.

CAMBRIDGE UNIVERSITY PRESS

Cambridge
London   New York   New Rochelle
Melbourne   Sydney

Published by the Press Syndicate of the University of Cambridge
The Pitt Building, Trumpington Street, Cambridge CB2 1RP
32 East 57th Street, New York, NY 10022, USA
10 Stamford Road, Oakleigh, Melbourne 3166, Australia

First published 1986

Printed in Great Britain by Bath Press, Bath, Avon

British Library cataloguing in publication data

Foley, William A.
The Papuan languages of New Guinea.
(Cambridge language surveys)
1. Papuan languages
II. Title.
499'.12   PL6601.A/

Library of Congress cataloguing in publication data

Foley, William A.
The Papuan languages of New Guinea.
(Cambridge language surveys)
Bibliography.
Includes index.
1. Papuan languages. I. Title. II. Series.
PL6601.F65 1986   499'.12   85-30942

ISBN 0 521 24355 6 hard covers
ISBN 0 521 28621 2 paperback

SE

To the people of Papua New Guinea,
whose kindness and hospitality
during my stays in their beautiful
country have made these such rich
experiences for me.

CONTENTS

MAPS

PREFACE

In some respects this book may seem premature. Papuan languages are probably the most poorly known in the world; of over 700 languages in more than sixty language families, no more than fifty languages or less than ten per cent are in any sense adequately documented. For some languages little more than a name is available, and for many others only a brief word-list. Indeed, entire language families are often represented by no more than a brief word-list.

Yet, in spite of these difficulties, I believe that this book will be both useful and timely. First, I hope it will encourage other professional linguists to work in the Papuan field, the incredible richness of which I hope this book will demonstrate. Secondly, as Papuan languages number over 700 or nearly twenty per cent of the world's total, it is important that they be considered in the ongoing search for language universals and generalizations in linguistic typology. As Papuan languages are poorly represented in the general linguistic literature, linguists working in these areas have had little access to information on them. It is hoped that this book will remedy the problem. Finally, the processes of language contact and linguistic diffusion are present in New Guinea to an extent probably unparalleled elsewhere on the globe. Consequently, I believe this book will be of interest both to sociolinguists interested in the social dynamics of language contact and to comparative linguists worried about the effects of such extensive language contact on the smooth applicability of the comparative method.

A book on Papuan languages presented special problems in organization. With over sixty distinct language families, on the order of relatedness of Romance or Germanic, it was not viable to organize this book along the lines of genetic groupings. Nor, given the tremendous linguistic diversity in rather small geographical areas like the Sepik River area or Madang Province, did it seem profitable to organize the text around geographical groupings. Rather, I decided the most advantageous course was to organize most of the material along typological lines. Although Papuan languages are extremely numerous and quite diverse, there are in fact many phonological and grammatical features which reappear in language after language. It is these features which I have highlighted in this book: what phonological and grammatical features are common in Papuan languages, and what patterns of variation are found? This is the 'unity in diversity' theme, a principle which I think is useful to bear in mind in Papuan linguistics.

This book has been written at a fairly elementary level, assuming only as background a single course in descriptive linguistics. Basic linguistic concepts such as morpheme, clause or phrase are assumed, but more complex notions are defined and exemplified when introduced. The only possible exceptions to this are sections 7.2 and 7.4, which non-comparative linguists may find rather rough going. I suggest that readers not specifically interested in the ins and outs of Papuan comparative linguistics skip these sections, confining themselves to the other three sections of Chapter 7. Educators and others not interested in the specifics of Papuan languages, but desiring just an overview of the language situation in New Guinea, would do best to concentrate on Chapters 1, 2 and 8.

This book owes much to many people. I would like to thank for their useful comments the following: Bob Dixon, Harold Koch, Jack Golson, Tony Diller, Buck Schieffelin, John Haiman, Bernard Comrie, Nick Evans, Mark Durie, Bronwyn Eather, Karl Franklin and Phil Staalsen. Most important of all, I wish to thank my editor, Eugénie Henderson, without whose help this book would have been much the poorer. Thanks also go to Val Lyons, who drew the maps, and to Rosemary Butt, who saved me most of the job of checking the text. Finally, my greatest thanks go to the person whose hard work and quiet forbearance made what you hold in your hands a concrete reality: Mrs Ellalene Seymour, who typed the whole manuscript from my handwritten drafts and made what seemed to be an innumerable series of corrections.

My work on Yimas and other languages of the Lower Sepik family has been supported by the Australian Research Grants Scheme, Grant A176/15655. My thanks for this support.

Finally, simple thanks is inadequate to express my debt to the Yimas people, who opened their language and their lives to me, and to the people of Papua New Guinea, to whom this book is dedicated.

W. A. Foley
Canberra, Australia

ABBREVIATIONS USED IN GLOSSES

A	actor, subject of transitive verb
ABL	ablative
ACC	accusative
ALL	allative
BEN	benefactive
CAUS	causative
CAUSE	causal
CL	nominal class
CLASF	classifier
COMP	complementizer
CONT	continuative
CONTRAST	contrastive
COP	copula
CUST	customary
DA	different actor
DAT	dative
DECL	declarative
DEL SEQ	delayed sequence
DEM	demonstrative
DEP	dependent
DER	derivational morpheme
DIFF	different referent
DIM	diminutive
DL	dual
DUR	durative
EMP	emphatic
ERG	ergative
EXCL	exclusive

EXT	extended aspect
F	feminine
FAR PAST	far past
FUT	future
HABIT	habitual
HORT	hortative
IM PAST	immediate past
IM SEQ	immediate sequence
IMP	imperative
INCL	inclusive
INF	infinitive
INSTR	instrumental
INTENT	intentive modality
IRR	irrealis
LIKELY	likely
LOC	locative
M	masculine
NCAUS	noncausal
NOM	nominalizer
NR FUT	near future
NR PAST	near past
NSG	nonsingular
OBL	oblique
OTHER	person/number other than 2SG, 1PL
Q	question
PART	partitive
PAST	past
PAUC	paucal

PERF	perfective/completive	SG	singular
PL	plural	SIM	simultaneous
POSS	possessive	SOV	subject–object–verb
POT	potential	SPAN	span sequence
PRES	present	STATE	stative
PRESUP	presupposition	SUB	subordinator
PRO	pronoun	SVO	subject–verb–object
PROG	progressive	TP	topic marker
PURP	purposive	TR	transitivizer
REAL	realis	TRIAL	trial
REC	recipient	U	undergoer, object of
REF	referential		transitive verb
RM FT	remote future	UNREAL	unreal
RM PAST	remote past	VB	verbalizer
S	subject of intransitive	WISH	optative
	verb	1	first person
SA	same actor	2	second person
SAME	same referent	3	third person
SEQ	sequential	I-XI	Yimas nominal classes

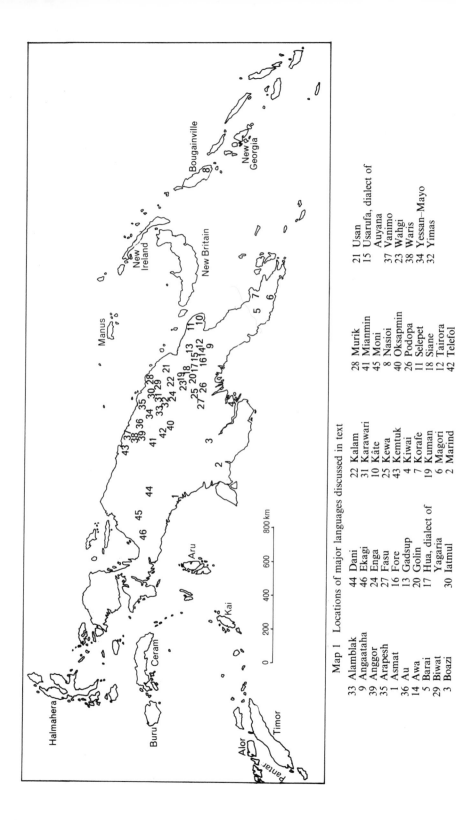

Map 1   Locations of major languages discussed in text

33 Alamblak	44 Dani	22 Kalam	28 Murik	21 Usan
9 Angaataha	46 Ekagi	31 Karawari	41 Mianmin	15 Usarufa, dialect of
39 Anggor	24 Enga	10 Käte	45 Moni	Auyana
35 Arapesh	27 Fasu	25 Kewa	8 Nasioi	37 Vanimo
1 Asmat	16 Fore	43 Kemtuk	40 Oksapmin	23 Wahgi
36 Au	13 Gadsup	4 Kiwai	26 Podopa	38 Waris
14 Awa	20 Golin	7 Korafe	11 Selepet	34 Yessan–Mayo
5 Barai	17 Hua, dialect of	19 Kuman	18 Siane	32 Yimas
29 Biwat	Yagaria	6 Magori	12 Tairora	
3 Boazi	30 Iatmul	2 Marind	42 Telefol	

1

Introduction

1.1 Papuan languages: what are they?

One-third of the world's total number of languages are spoken in the Pacific basin. Excluding mainland Asia and the Americas, the Pacific basin contains approximately 1,500 languages, which fall into three general groupings: Australian, Austronesian and Papuan languages. The Australian languages, spoken by the aboriginal people of Australia, numbered around 200 at white contact. Since then they have declined to only about 100 actually spoken today, and even many of these are endangered. The Austronesian languages constitute the largest language family in the world, with over 600 languages, spread from southeast Asia to Easter Island and New Zealand. With the exception of Australia and most of New Guinea and a few islands close to it, all of the land areas in the Pacific basin are occupied by speakers of Austronesian languages.

The Papuan languages occupy those areas of New Guinea and adjacent islands not claimed by Austronesian languages. Their most westerly position is eastern Indonesia: northern Halmahera, Alor and Pantar, two small islands west of Timor, and the mountainous interior of eastern Timor. Their territory then extends east, occupying the great bulk of mainland New Guinea, as well as areas of the offshore islands New Britain, New Ireland and Bougainville. The territory of Papuan languages terminates in the New Georgia archipelago, in the western Solomon Islands, although there is some debate concerning the genetic affiliations of the languages of the Reef and Santa Cruz islands, which lie between the Solomon Islands and Vanuatu (Lincoln 1978; Wurm 1978). Because of its immense size compared to the other islands, it is on the mainland of New Guinea that the overwhelming majority of Papuan languages are found. Almost all the languages discussed in this book come from this area. See Map 2 for the distribution of the Papuan languages.

The term 'Papuan languages' must not be taken in the same sense as 'Austronesian languages'. While all Austronesian languages are genetically related in one family, in the sense that they all descend from a common ancestral language

1

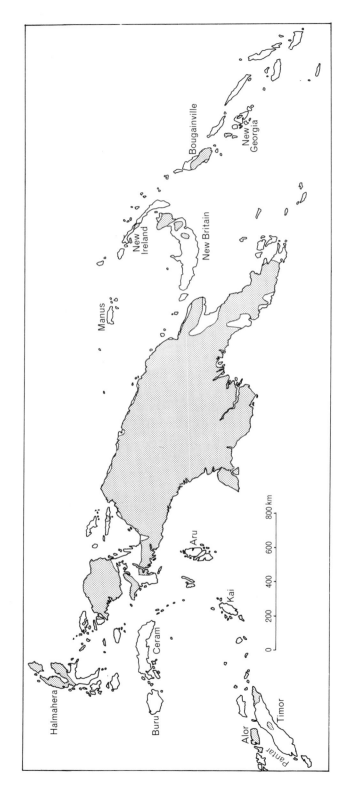

Map 2 Location of Papuan languages in the Pacific

called Proto-Austronesian spoken some 6,000 years ago, this is definitely not the case for Papuan languages. Papuan languages are not all genetically related. They do not all trace their origins back to a single ancestral language. On the basis of present knowledge, they belong to at least sixty different language families, all with their own common ancestral language. Section 7.3 discusses the major families of Papuan languages, and Map 6 in that section presents their geographical positions. In many ways, the alternative term 'non-Austronesian languages' is to be preferred for Papuan languages, as this highlights their purely negative characterization, i.e. that they are the languages of the Pacific which are *not* Austronesian. However, as the term 'Papuan' is in widespread use and is also the general term for the people of New Guinea, I will stick with it here. It is important to remember that, when a language is termed 'Papuan', this claims nothing more than that a language is not Austronesian. More specific terms such as 'Ok language' or 'Gorokan language' are necessary to indicate substantive genetic links for Papuan languages.

Papuan languages number some 750, making New Guinea and its environs the linguistically most complex area in the world (Wurm 1982). As mentioned above, these are organized into upwards of sixty distinct language families, with wider relations not yet conclusively demonstrated. Undoubtedly, with more careful and complete comparative work, this picture will become simpler; a number of families will probably combine into larger families, as Romance, Germanic and Slavic combine into the Indo-European family. But our present state of knowledge of most of these families is still much too incomplete for wider relationships such as these to be proposed with any great confidence. Some hypotheses concerning wider relationships are advanced in Wurm 1982, but almost all of these remain to be confirmed by careful comparative work. At this point in our knowledge, I believe it is wise to be conservative: there are upwards of sixty Papuan language families plus a number of Papuan languages, probably a couple of dozen, which are isolates, i.e. not demonstrably related to any other language.

1.2　New Guinea: the land, its people and its history

The land area of New Guinea is geologically of very recent formation, and the entire area is still seismically very active. Earthquakes and active volcanoes are common. New Guinea occupies the northern edge of the Australian continental plate, where it adjoins the Pacific plate, and its seismic activity is a direct result of this position.

All of the Papuan-speaking areas, New Guinea and its environs, lie in the tropics. But, that having been said, it must not be imagined that all Papuan speakers occupy the same ecological zone. New Guinea, because of its immense size (it is the second largest island in the world), presents a number of different environments. There is a fundamental contrast between highland and lowland zones. A spine of high mountains stretches the entire length of New Guinea, the highest mountain of which, Mt Jayawijaya, stands at over 5,000 metres. These highlands provide a year-round temperate climate in an otherwise tropical land. In many areas these mountains open up to large grassy valleys which, thanks to sophisticated agricultural techniques, support dense populations.

The lowland areas are generally more sparsely populated and have a constant hot and humid climate. The lowlands present two ecological zones, tropical rainforest and swampland. The tropical rainforests contain a great abundance of plant and animal life which has provided the mainstay of Papuan diets for many millennia. The swamplands result from the rivers which drain the northern and southern sides of the central cordillera. Some highlands, and especially border highlands areas, are among the wettest in the world, with over 200 inches a year in some places. This water drains into rivers which cascade down from the highlands and join the great rivers of New Guinea. Because of the very flat nature of the terrain of much of lowland New Guinea and the poor drainage of its soil, huge expanses of alluvial swamp generally surround these river areas. The five major rivers of New Guinea are the Mamberamo of the northwest, the Sepik and Ramu of the northeast, the Fly of the southeast and the Digul of the southwest. Map 3 (pp. 6–7) is a physical map of New Guinea which summarizes this information.

New Guinea has probably been inhabited by Papuans for 40,000 years or more (see sections 8.1 and 8.2). The people of New Guinea are basically Australoids, although there is a great deal of local variation. Papuans are dark-skinned, from a light reddish brown to black, and frizzy-haired. In fact, the word 'Papua' comes from a Malay word for 'frizzy-haired' (Chowning 1977). The great majority of Papuan groups are sedentary villagers, but in a few remote areas there were, at least until recently, nomadic hunter-gatherer bands. Some of these sedentary village dwellers, especially those of the highland grassy valleys, are heavily dependent for subsistence on agriculture, with yams, taro or sweet potatoes as the main crops. Other groups, mainly rainforest or swampland dwellers, are predominantly hunter-gatherers. In much of the drainage area of the Sepik and Ramu Rivers, for example, the villagers subsist mostly on fish taken from the rivers and swamps, and sago, a starch drawn from a palm tree which grows wild in these extensive swamps. The diets of many of the agriculturally dependent groups are particularly deficient in meat protein. Domesticated pigs provide some protein, but as they are usually only killed during festival times, their effect on the diet is minimal.

Although human habitation in New Guinea extends back some 40,000 years, recorded history is only very recent. For a pleasant, very readable history of New Guinea up to the 1960s, see Souter 1963. Europeans first set eyes on New Guinea in the early sixteenth century, during the first period of colonial expansion of the

European powers. The name 'New Guinea' was conferred in the sixteenth century by a Spanish navigator, Ortiz de Retes, probably because he fancied the dark, frizzy-haired natives he encountered resembled those of the Guinea coast of west Africa. For the next 300 years, European ships continued to sail the waters around New Guinea, but there was little actual contact with the indigenous population. This no doubt resulted in some part from the hair-raising tales circulated among the sailors concerning the grisly headhunting and cannibalistic raids that were inflicted on some of the more unfortunate crews who went ashore on the island. But also it was a function of the fact that the European colonial powers had more substantial fish to fry elsewhere, in the Americas, Africa and Asia.

All this began to change in the late nineteenth century. Although the Dutch, taking advantage of a questionable claim by the Sultan of Tidore, one of their vassals, claimed the entire western half of New Guinea in 1848, they largely ignored it, as they had far more profitable territories in the large western islands of Indonesia, especially Java. Interest by Germany, which was late in joining the colonial game, in the eastern half of the island caused Great Britain in 1884 to claim the southern half of eastern New Guinea, which was later named Papua. This prompted Germany in the same year to claim the northern half, as well as the large offshore islands of New Britain, New Ireland and Bougainville. New Britain and New Ireland were named the Bismarck Archipelago in honour of the chancellor of Germany and the German half of eastern New Guinea, Kaiser Wilhelm's Land, after the emperor.

With New Guinea now neatly carved up by the colonial powers, development as these powers saw it could take place. West New Guinea continued to suffer from Dutch neglect until 1900, when continued raids by Marind Anim headhunters into British Papua caused the British government to complain. After this, the Dutch East Indies government began a period of extensive exploration of West New Guinea, but little commercial development followed, as they were still far more interested in the fabled riches of the East, in Java and Sumatra, than in their swampy and headhunter-infested New Guinea holdings. The Dutch capital of Hollandia remained a sleepy backwater, and this situation lasted until after World War II.

More intense change occurred in the eastern half of New Guinea. The British, and later the Australians, to whom sovereignty over Papua was transferred with Australian independence at the beginning of the twentieth century, undertook an extensive programme of exploration and pacification. The capital of Papua was Port Moresby, and this became the centre of the small amount of commercial development in the territory.

The most intense commercial development occurred in the German section of New Guinea. The Germans alienated much land and began large-scale copra

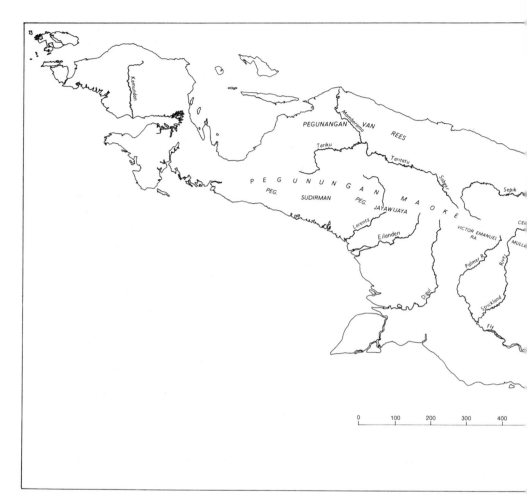

Map 3   Physical map of New Guinea

plantations in the Rabaul area of New Britain. Rabaul became the capital of German New Guinea. German exploration of their territory was equally intense; by World War I most of the Sepik and Ramu Rivers had been explored and mapped.

With World War I, the scene in New Guinea changed. Australian troops quickly overran the small garrisons of Germans, and after the war the League of Nations awarded control of former German New Guinea to Australia. This was known as the Mandated Territory of New Guinea and was administered from Rabaul. Between the two world wars, Australia extended government control over large

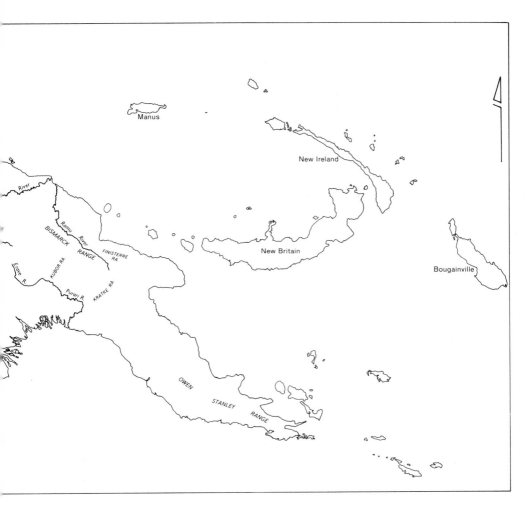

areas of eastern New Guinea, and commercial development intensified in coastal areas. After World War II the two Australian territories were joined as the Territory of Papua and New Guinea, and administered from Port Moresby.

World War II left the Dutch empire in Indonesia in ruins. As a final departing act, the Japanese recognized independence for Indonesia, something young nationalist intellectuals had been struggling for since the 1920s. The president of the new republic was Sukarno. The Dutch refused to recognize Indonesian independence, and a bloody civil war ensued. But in the end the Dutch were forced to concede, and in 1949 Indonesia became an independent state. West New Guinea was withheld from the new republic and remained a Dutch colony. As the last remaining bastion of the Dutch colonial empire in the East, it now became the centre of Dutch energy and finances. Huge sums of money were spent in the development of West New Guinea from 1949 to 1962, but it continued to remain a sore point in relationships with Indonesia, as Sukarno repeatedly claimed it was an integral part of Indonesia. In 1962 Sukarno undertook military campaigns to oust the Dutch. The campaigns were a disaster, but in the end international opinion forced the Dutch to yield. In 1963 sovereignty of West New Guinea under the new name 'West Irian' was transferred to Indonesia under United Nations trusteeship. There was to have been a plebiscite of the people of West Irian to determine whether they wished to become independent or join Indonesia. This was never held. Rather, the Indonesian government selected around 1,000 delegates to do the voting for the entire population. They voted to join Indonesia without a single dissenting vote. In 1969, western New Guinea became Irian Jaya, the easternmost province of Indonesia, with its administrative capital at Jayapura, formerly Hollandia.

The post-World War II history of eastern New Guinea is far less eventful. Commercial development in the Territory of Papua New Guinea intensified, especially after the central highlands areas were really opened up in the 1950s. Port Moresby continued to grow, to become a town of over 100,000 today, as did the secondary centres of Lae, Mount Hagen, Goroka, Wewak and Rabaul. In 1973, self-government was conferred, and in 1975 the new independent nation of Papua New Guinea was born. Since independence, Papua New Guinea has been a politically stable but economically fast-developing nation. A complex system of roads is being developed to counteract the very real problems in communication and transport presented by the topography of the country. The people of Papua New Guinea are being drawn together in a way impossible in the many previous millennia. The present political boundaries of New Guinea are presented in Map 4 (pp. 10–11).

1.3 The nature of Papuan languages

As already pointed out, New Guinea is linguistically extremely diverse, with 1,000 languages in a land area of some 900,000 km^2 or one language in every 900 km^2. This is a language density unparalleled elsewhere, and in some areas, such as the Sepik–Ramu basin, the density is much greater than that, as much as one in every 200 km^2. 750, or seventy-five per cent, of these languages are Papuan.

The reasons for this extreme linguistic fragmentation are threefold. First, a time depth of 40,000 years for human habitation in New Guinea would allow ample time for the natural processes of language change and diversification to produce a great plethora of languages. Assuming a single immigrant community speaking a single language and a language splitting into two every 1,000 years – both conservative assumptions – this alone would result in 10^{12} languages in 40,000 years. Even New Guinea has nowhere near this astronomical number of languages; but this model does provide a glimpse of the order of magnitude of language change that 40,000 years can produce.

The second major cause of extreme language diversity in New Guinea is the nature of the terrain. Most of New Guinea is difficult country indeed, steep, forest-covered mountains with precipitous drops, swirling rivers, dense, nearly impenetrable rainforests and endless tracts of swampland. The terrain thus poses some genuine barriers to human social interactions and would certainly favour, rather than inhibit, linguistic diversity.

Finally, certain cultural attitudes of Papuan speakers need to be considered. These are discussed in detail in section 2.2; I will only summarize here. Papuans have conflicting attitudes toward their languages, viewing language traits as trade items to be borrowed as one sees fit for reasons of prestige and novelty, but also as indispensable badges of a community's unique identity. The inherent contradiction in these views results in languages converging toward each other only so far, and the remaining differences between them being accentuated. This simultaneous process of convergence and divergence results in a high linguistic diversity remaining intact, if not actually being increased.

Given the very high number of Papuan languages, one would expect them to exhibit an equally wide range of structural features. While Papuan languages are typologically very varied, it is also true that there are a number of significant generalizations that can be made about their structural types. This illustrates the 'unity in diversity' principle which is so important in understanding New Guinea. While New Guinea languages and cultures are certainly very diverse, there are a number of common themes which reappear again and again throughout the island. These general cultural traits are discussed in section 2.1; here I will only consider some general linguistic features. Chapters 3–6 will flesh out the outline below by providing much more detailed discussions of common linguistic features of Papuan languages.

Phonologically, Papuan languages are characterized by relatively simple phonemic systems. In fact, the language with the smallest phonemic inventory in the world is a Papuan language – Rotokas of Bougainville, with six consonants and five vowels (Firchow and Firchow 1969). The typical Papuan vowel system contains five vowels, /i, e, a, o, u/. Consonantal systems contain at least three places of articulation – labial, dental/alveolar and velar – but often add a palatal as well. Unlike Australian and Austronesian languages, Papuan languages generally have a different number of stops and nasals; commonly only two nasals, /m/ and /n/, are

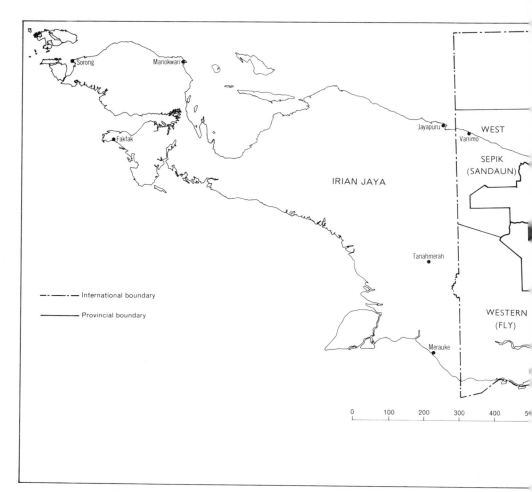

Map 4   Political map of New Guinea

present. In the Sepik area, however, languages are often found with the same number of distinctions in place of articulation for stops and nasals. Papuan languages usually have a single liquid; a /r/–/l/ contrast is uncommon.

On the grammatical level, Papuan languages are almost universally characterized by verb-final word-order. They are commonly classified as SOV, but, as the order of nominals is often quite free, it seems more judicious to claim them simply as verb-final. Exceptions to this generalization are the Torricelli languages, and languages which have undergone Austronesian influence. Both of these groups have SVO word-order.

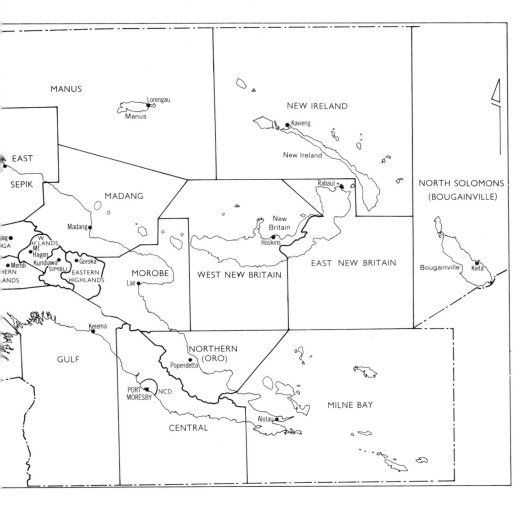

Closely related to the verb-final word-order is a typological distinction in verb types according to inflectional possibilities. Many Papuan languages distinguish between dependent and independent verbs. Independent verbs have a full range of inflectional possibilities, including subject agreement, tense, mood etc., and occur sentence-finally. Dependent verbs occur before the independent verb, and are generally reduced in their inflectional possibilities. They take their specifications for the missing inflections from those on the final verb. Consider the following example from Yimas of the Sepik area:

marɨmp-ɨn awŋkwi-mp-i   *antɨ-nan . yampara-mp-i ama-sɨpan-ɨt*
river-OBL   down in water-SEQ-DEP ground-OBL stand-SEQ-DEP 1SG-bathe-PERF
'I went down into the river, stood on the ground, and washed'

The independent verb occurs in final position and is inflected for person and number
of the subject, *ama-* 1SG, and tense-aspect, *-ɨt* PERF. The two dependent verbs which
precede it are not inflected for these categories, but take their specifications for
them from the independent verb, so they too are perfective in tense-aspect and have
1SG subjects. The dependent verbs are uniquely inflected; they occur with a suffix
-mp, which indicates the temporal relation between them and the following verb as
sequential, and *-i*, which marks them as dependent. These suffixes may never occur
on independent verbs. Many Papuan languages, notably those of the highlands,
have far richer morphological systems for dependent verbs than does Yimas.

Papuan languages are commonly characterized by quite complex morphologies,
especially in the verb. Morphology is generally on an agglutinative pattern. For
verbs, subject agreement is nearly universal and object agreement is very common.
Many Papuan languages also have constructions which permit agreement for
indirect objects as well. Commonly, Papuan languages have suppletive verb stems
for common verbs, according to the number of the object, as in Barai *abe* 'take it', *ke*
'take them' (Olson 1981). Tense and mood are almost always indicated by verbal
suffixes, as would be expected in verb-final languages. True voice alternations, such
as passive verb forms, are unknown.

The morphology of the other major part of speech, nouns, is much simpler. Often
the only inflectional category for nouns is case, and even that may only be of
secondary importance, as in some Sepik area languages. Number is rarely signalled
on nouns, but may be specified by the verbal agreement affixes. A number of
languages have gender distinctions in nouns; this may vary from a simple two-
gender system, masculine and feminine, as in Alamblak (Bruce 1984), to a full noun-
class system with over a dozen classes, as in Yimas.

Pronominal systems in Papuan languages are highly variable in the number of
distinctions in person and number, and may be highly abbreviated. A singular and
plural is almost always distinguished, and a dual is common as well, but some person
distinctions may be neutralized. For example, second and third persons may not be
distinguished in the dual and plural. A distinction between exclusive and inclusive
first-person forms is uncommon.

1.4 Sketch history of research in Papuan languages
With the possible exception of South American Indian languages, Papuan
languages were the last group of languages in the world to be investigated, and

remain today the most poorly known. The north coast of New Guinea, especially the Irian Jaya half, remains probably the most poorly known linguistic area in the world; for many languages of this region the only documentation is a small word-list. The first recording of a Papuan language in New Guinea was a small vocabulary of Kamoro, a language of the south coast of Irian Jaya, taken down in 1828 by a passenger on a Dutch vessel. With the colonial annexation of New Guinea, linguistic investigations intensified, largely carried out by missionaries. This basic pattern – the study of Papuan languages largely by missionaries – continues today.

Nationals of each colonial power (naturally enough) concentrated on research in their own area. Although German sovereignty over part of New Guinea ended in 1918, a number of German missionaries stayed on in the Mandated Territory and continued their linguistic research, notably in the Sepik area. In Papua, the name of S. H. Ray looms large in the annals of linguistic research. While his own periods of fieldwork in New Guinea were limited, Ray published many articles over a period of forty years, often systematizing and disseminating the work of missionaries in the area. In West New Guinea, missionaries (especially the Dutch priest Drabbe) are almost exclusively responsible for the quite detailed knowledge we have of these Papuan languages, especially in the southern coastal area.

The most important event in the history of New Guinea linguistic research was the establishment in the mid-1950s of the Summer Institute of Linguistics, Papua New Guinea branch. Around 1970 a branch of the Summer Institute of Linguistics was formed in Irian Jaya as well. This institution is a group of missionary linguists who study native languages with a view to the preparation of literacy materials and a native translation of the bible. The overwhelming majority of descriptive linguistic studies of Papuan languages have been provided by SIL workers. Most of the references at the back of this book are by authors working within SIL. Without their exemplary efforts, our knowledge of Papuan languages would be much poorer indeed, and this book would certainly not have been possible.

Most comparative work in Papuan languages has been undertaken at the Australian National University, and the name of S. A. Wurm is most prominent in this area. He and co-workers at the ANU have provided the linguistic mapping of many previously unknown areas of New Guinea, and have proposed a detailed classification of Papuan languages, based largely on the evidence of lexicostatistics. The publication *Pacific Linguistics*, which is issued from Wurm's department, remains by far the single most important publication vehicle for work dealing with Papuan languages. In the past twenty years, Wurm has suggested wider and wider interrelationships among Papuan languages. At this stage these remain hypotheses and conjectures, because detailed comparative work according to the rigorous methods of comparative linguistics (see Chapter 7) has yet to prove these links. They are bold hypotheses, indeed, and future research may prove Wurm right. But I have chosen here to follow a more conservative course, and have accepted as proven only the low-level family groupings in Wurm's classification, groupings of languages of clear genetic affiliation. A recent and detailed presentation of Wurm's views may be found in Wurm 1982.

2

Language in its social context

2.1 The nature of traditional New Guinea society

As pointed out in Chapter 1, the key word in understanding New Guinea is diversity. This is readily apparent in the great variety of social systems and customs found there. In spite of this diversity, there are some general patterns in the organization of New Guinea societies that may be adduced, and this will be attempted here. Some areas of New Guinea are still very poorly known ethnographically, so it is possible that some of the general traits discussed here are contradicted in those areas; but they do seem to hold in many widely separated cultural areas in New Guinea.

New Guinea societies are small, the hamlet or the small village being the normal settlement pattern. In a survey of the population of villages in Irian Jaya, De Bruyn and Pouwer (1958) showed that over ninety per cent of communities had populations under 300, and more than half had populations under 100. Small communities are equally the rule in Papua New Guinea, although the percentage of communities under 100 would probably be smaller. Exceptions to this rule are few, but large villages (500–1,000 inhabitants) are found among the Iatmul of the Sepik basin (Bateson 1936) and among the Asmat of Irian Jaya (De Bruyn and Pouwer 1958).

A major factor favouring the small size of New Guinea communities is the difficult ecological conditions in which many communities are situated. Leeden (1956, 1960) highlights this point in discussing the culture of two societies of the interior of northern Irian Jaya. This area is indeed difficult terrain, with boggy marshland alternating with mountainous country covered in dense rainforest. The people subsist on sago, a high-starch, nutritionally deficient carbohydrate extracted from the pith of the sago palm, and whatever game or fish they can gather, the game being minimal. As seems to be true throughout New Guinea, pigs are domesticated but do not serve significantly in supplementing the diet. Clearly, the terrain imposes severe constraints on these cultures, and we are not surprised to learn that one community has sixty-eight members, and the other seventy-one, with a population density in the area of one person for every 2.25–4 km² (Oosterwal 1961). Such marginal conditions for human settlement are common in many areas of New Guinea, and help to account for the small size of the communities.

But this cannot be the whole story. Even in areas where the environment and the technology of the people could support much larger communities, such as the highland areas, they are not found: instead, the small village, hamlet or even individual homestead are the preferred settlement patterns. Highlands peoples have developed elaborate horticultural techniques for their staple, the sweet potato, which provides them with a reliable, reasonably nourishing diet, albeit a protein-deficient one. Being malaria-free, the high grassy valleys and mountain slopes where the highlanders live are relatively healthy, as witnessed by the high population densities of the highlands in comparison to the lowlands. But this high population has not resulted in large communities; in fact, in the Western and Southern Highlands Provinces of Papua New Guinea, individual family homesteads are the norm. So we are dealing with more than ecological causes for the small size of New Guinea communities. There seems to be a strong aversion among New Guinea societies to large communities, and we need to investigate the factors that contribute to this aversion.

New Guinea societies are characterized in the main by a considerable flexibility of structure (Pouwer 1960; Brown 1962). They are basically egalitarian, with no institutionalized means for transmitting power and authority. At birth all men are equal, ideologically at least. This principle has been expressed as the value of 'equivalence' by Read (1959). He defined this as the view that 'satisfactory (stable and amicable) relationships rest on the recognition, on the part of those related, of an essential parity' (Read 1959: 429). This principle is an important leveller of social differences. Gifts have to be repaid in kind; they are a debt which must be discharged to redress the balance. People should be amenable to persuasion, and should follow the course of action which is agreed by the general consensus of the community.

This is an important principle as well in inter-community relations. The traditional ceremonial exchanges, such as the *moka* (Strathern 1972), which are such a pronounced feature of highlands traditional life, are guided by it. These elaborate exchange ceremonies cement good relations between different communities and must be repaid in kind by the receiving communities at a later date. In some societies, even in traditional warfare, this principle played an important role. In these cases the aim in warfare was not generally to eliminate the opposition, but to score a few points with a few injuries or deaths, and then withdraw. This would then be revenged by the enemy at a later round. Ultimately, no-one won absolute victory; this endless round of tit-for-tat killings and injuries perpetuated itself. This is vividly documented by the film *Dead Birds*, which deals with traditional Dani warfare in the central highlands of Irian Jaya.

This value of equivalence results in consensus being the basic governing principle in village government. Mead's (1935) description of the Mountain Arapesh is a vivid case study of this principle in action. This is a 'cooperative society', in which members perform their share of group tasks to accomplish ends for the general good. There are no political units or political structure, and no moral or legal sanctions for antisocial acts, save the general disapproval of the community. People are expected to be gentle, unacquisitive and cooperative for the general welfare of the community. In such a society of equals, oriented toward cooperative, cheerful social action, some members of the community are seen, from the ego's viewpoint, as having a greater call upon ego's cooperative labour than others. Closer affinal and agnatic relations have a greater right to his labour than distant relatives. The practical result of this is to put severe limits on the size of communities of this type. Larger communities would contain many members unrelated or only distantly related to ego. His sense of responsibility for cooperative action with these people would be proportionally much less than with his close relations, and, given that these latter would be constantly using his services, he would seldom, if ever, act in cooperative tasks with these other members. There would, then, in such communities, be little sense of solidarity between unrelated members, and the preference for small communities, consisting largely of agnatically or affinally related members, seems natural in this context.

There is yet another factor to be considered here, albeit one not operative in the Mountain Arapesh context – one of the purest examples in New Guinea cultures of the principle of equivalence as the basis for social organization. Read (1959) contrasts with the principle of equivalence an opposing principle, that of 'strength'. Strength refers to personality traits exemplified in certain abilities and skills. Read (1959: 427) defines the strong man, the ideal masculine type, in these terms: 'he is a person who is aggressive, a warrior, a man inclined to swagger and boast, who displays a marked awareness of his individuality and is jealous of his self importance . . . strength is correlated with wealth'. Strength is the acquisition-oriented, self-directed value in New Guinea cultures in contrast to the gift-oriented, other-directed value of equivalence.

Although the outcome of warfare is governed by the equivalence principle, its actual performance is a major arena in which to demonstrate strength. Bravery and aggressiveness are indications of strength. Exchanges also are deeply imbued with the strength value. They place the recipient under an obligation to the donor, which demonstrates the latter's superiority. The great ceremonial exchanges in the highlands are institutionalized activities, where groups can demonstrate their strength in opposition to other groups. The elaborate finery of the dancers, as well as the competitive performance of the dances themselves, testify to the fact that these are activities in which the giving group is demonstrating its prestige and pre-eminence.

The strength value provides a second governing principle for New Guinea societies, that of coercion. People are moved to action by the physical or oratorical power of a dominant member of the community. Some of this function of coercion is inherent in the kinship system: for example, fathers have power over children and older brothers over younger brothers, husbands have power over wives. But some power differentials are strictly economic in base. Men of greater wealth are able to use that wealth to get numbers of men indebted to them, and then to use that indebtedness to get them to take their side in village disputes. Wealth, by itself, does not confer status in New Guinea societies, but the intelligent use of that wealth in manipulating others is a major factor in acquiring status. As a case in point, among the Ekagi of the Irian Jaya central highlands (Pospisil 1966), a miserly wealthy man who does not share his wealth with less fortunate members of the community through loans and exchanges is despised, and his miserliness is considered adequate grounds for his execution.

It is readily apparent that the twin governing principles of New Guinea societies, consensus and coercion, are inherently contradictory, and the tension between these two underlies some of the interesting variations among New Guinea cultures. The Mountain Arapesh (Mead 1935), which we have already discussed, exemplify the situation in which the consensus principle is overwhelmingly dominant. The opposite situation, in which coercion is overwhelmingly dominant, is represented by the Biwat, as discussed by Mead (1935), and called by her the Mundugumor. In a society dominated by the coercion principle and lacking any institutionalized forms for its administration, such as a secret police force, there can be no general community at all, and this is true of the Biwat as Mead describes them. There are no villages or hamlets among the Biwat, but rather we find individual polygamous households, dominated by a patriarch and surrounded by his wives and children who live in an atmosphere of mutual distrust. These households are not grouped into villages, but are found as individual palisaded compounds at points in the bush. Within the nuclear family there is little solidarity; the social customs turn fathers against sons, mothers against daughters and brothers against sisters (see Mead's description for details). What social control exists does so by dint of superior wealth or physical force.

An independent variable which adds to the diversity of New Guinea cultures along these lines is sex. Among the Mountain Arapesh and Biwat, the social character among both men and women is very similar (Mead 1935), but the Iatmul (Bateson 1936) are an interesting contrast in this regard. The Iatmul are situated on the middle

Sepik River between the Mountain Arapesh and the Biwat. Their easternmost village is less than fifty kilometres from the Biwat country. There are great differences between the social character of men and women among the Iatmul. Iatmul men are much like the Biwat, aggressive and quick to violence. Relations between men are characterized by competition and frequent brawls. Social control is by means of force. Nothing demonstrates this so amply as the fact that, traditionally, Iatmul men could wear homicide honours (certain bodily decorations) for killing a co-member of the village, so weak were the institutionalized forms of social control. However, among the Iatmul, unlike the Biwat, social relations among relatives and in the nuclear family are generally good, characterized by exchange and mutual aid.

The social character of Iatmul women is quite different. It is they who provided the requisite social cohesion to the village. They emphasize cooperation in social activities, in food gathering and child rearing. The women dominate the economic life of the village, and within the household they wield considerable authority by virtue of this economic power, although they still submit to the ritual and greater physical power of the men.

Iatmul society, then, is a complex interaction of our twin principles – coercion and consensus. Each applies to specialized domains: coercion dominates relations between unrelated men, and between men and women, while cooperation dominates relations between related men and between women. This kind of pattern is possible because Iatmul villages are often large: Tambunum, the largest, has around 1,000 inhabitants. Social control in such large villages is to some extent provided by the men's cults, associated with the men's ceremonial house, as it is the competitive attitude of the men which is the greatest threat to social cohesion (see Tuzin 1974). Kin links here are not extensive enough to establish a society based on consensus, especially given the cultural ideology (at least the masculine version thereof) which emphasizes strength. The tension inherent in such a situation may suggest instability, and this is indeed the case; Iatmul villages are highly prone to fission, and the breaks generally follow kinship lines. Yimas society, a Sepik group south of the Iatmul, further supports this viewpoint. It is similar to the Iatmul in cultural values and in the social character of men and women, but lacks any important role for the men's cult of the ceremonial house. Social control is achieved by kin links and, consequently, it is much smaller, with about 250 members in the village.

Some highlands societies have achieved a delicate balance between the opposing forces, coercion and consensus, in the institution of the big man, an institution that most Sepik and other lowland societies lack. It is the big man who wields the true power in highlands societies, and he must realize in his own personality a careful blending of the two forces. The big men are expected to be strong warriors, large contributors to the ceremonial exchanges (thus demonstrating their wealth) and skilful, persuasive orators. In their bearing they demonstrate the qualities of strength, by behaving aggressively and exhibiting a strong awareness of their individuality and self-importance, acting as if they expected others to follow. Yet, simultaneously, they must manifest the ideal of equivalence in their attempt to dominate others; they must also recognize the others' right to parity. They must appreciate the views of others and show recognition of their rights. The big men achieve a degree of social control through the skilful use of oratory. In their bearing and style they exhibit their dominance, their strength. Yet they use their oratory according to the principle of equivalence; rather than dictating a course of action, they guide the opinions of the group in order to achieve a final consensus. The persuasiveness of the big men's oratory is also backed up by their economic power. Through the skilful use of their wealth in loans and exchanges, they build up a large reservoir of indebtedness on the part of other members of the community, and this acts as a strong inducement in getting their own views accepted as the consensus of the group as a whole. Posposil's (1966) discussion of Ekagi big men highlights this economic base of the big men's power.

The role of the big man is not transmitted from father to son, but is acquired by the initiative, skill and intelligence of the individual. Potentially any man can become a big man. This form of social control is contingent on the smallness of the communities, depending as it does on an individual's skilful manipulation of face-to-face interactions with fellow villagers. There is no institutionalized use of force to back up the big man's decisions: his power depends largely on his own resources. Clearly, the domain of that power has practical limitations, and that determines the size of communities. Villages often have several big men who cooperate in the administration of power. Overt rivalry between big men produces great stress in these societies, and may lead to severe village factionalization (Posposil 1966).

From all that has been said about the fundamental organizing principles in New Guinea societies, it might seem that the ideal form of community would be the autonomous family unit. It has already been mentioned that this was the settlement pattern among the Biwat; and it is also found in the Western and Southern Highlands Provinces of Papua New Guinea, among such people as the Huli, who live on family homesteads. But this ideal would ignore one fundamental fact about traditional New Guinea: the hostility that often existed between communities. Warfare was an endemic and pervasive fact of traditional New Guinea life, and one needed allies to wage war. Among the Biwat, warfare and the ceremonials connected with it was one of the few unifying forces which welded a community out of individually hostile family units (Mead 1935). And in other societies, too, it was warfare which galvanized a disjointed body of individuals who happened to live in the same place into a true community with coordinated actions.

It is immediately apparent that warfare would put great stress on these small communities, especially those which already find themselves in a precarious position on marginal lands. The loss of only a few men could spell disaster for the survival of the community. This fact is correlated with two widespread traits of New Guinea societies. First there is their well known loose structure or openness (Leeden 1960; Pouwer 1960; Langness 1964; Watson 1970). This refers first of all to the fact that kinship in many New Guinea societies is not reckoned strictly on a unilineal descent basis, either patrilineal or matrilineal. Brown (1962) claims that the descent groups could be interpreted as cognatic (descent reckoned on both patrilineal and matrilineal basis), but with a patrilineal bias. This provides ego with greater flexibility in determining the kin group to which he belongs, and if for some reason affiliation with one group becomes untenable, he can take up with another. But the actual situation is even more fluid than this. We often find shifting of groups to areas which is unwarranted by the rules of descent. This may result from a serious defeat in war, so that the remaining population takes refuge with another group. If the refugee group remains, it will in time become fully integrated within the descent system of the host group as a lineage. The group may or may not retain links with its former territory. Yimas village exemplifies this well: of the six descent groups in the village, only one is autochthonously associated with the land; all the rest are immigrants, and constitute a large majority of the population. This situation, with its constant fragmentation and realignment of groups, results in the residential group being the primary basis of the community. In Yimas and other languages, the name of the descent groups is based on the village name for the plot of land on which their houses or ceremonial house stands, emphasizing the correlation of groups with the land. The residential group has a core of descent-related individuals, and immigrant groups are integrated into that system.

The exigencies of war and the need for allies play a significant role in the second widespread trait, the importance of exchanges and trade. We have already discussed how exchange manifests the importance of the equivalence principle in intra-community relations, but it is equally important in this regard in inter-community relations. By maintaining friendly relations with neighbouring groups, bolstered with elaborate ceremonial exchanges, communities can build up a system of alliances in war. But the exchange motive goes far beyond the simple need for allies in warfare. It is the fundamental principle in interpersonal and intergroup relations. Interpersonal relations outside the village are so structured by exchange activities that people generally think of them primarily in terms of their exchange potential. To take an enlightening example, Mead (1935) reports that the Biwat regarded their eastern Dimiri neighbours with contempt, and as rightful victims of their headhunting raids. But they claimed they were careful not to kill all of them because if they did, there would be no one left to get pots, mosquito bags or baskets from!

The importance of exchange has given rise to a pronounced trading consciousness in many New Guinea cultures. This pervades all aspects of the culture, and results in a premium put on the new, and on things brought in from the outside. Mead (1938) was so struck by this that she referred to the Mountain Arapesh as 'an importing culture'. We may term this an 'other-directed' consciousness, and it may be the psychological correlate of the social principle of equivalence. This orientation may lead to a very rapid turnover of cultural traits, as documented by Mead (1938) for the Mountain Arapesh. But just as the social principle of strength opposes equivalence, there is also a 'self-directed' consciousness opposing the 'other-directed'. 'Self-directed' consciousness puts a premium on the status quo, and the customs and values of the in-group or community. Just as strength and equivalence interact in complex ways in New Guinea societies, 'other-directed' and 'self-directed' are important opposing forces in shaping the patterns of New Guinea cultures. Let us consider the Iatmul again (Bateson 1936). The 'other-directed' consciousness is a very significant force here (as in all Sepik societies I know); and, well situated as they are on both banks of the middle Sepik river, the Iatmul have been the receivers of wave after wave of innovations. But unlike the Mountain Arapesh, for whom the new simply replaces the old, the Iatmul have developed a very elaborate and rich culture by specializing and adapting the innovations as features or rites for specific social groups, without jettisoning the older features or rites, which are simply assigned to other groups. The new forms are simply grafted onto the old ones with some readjustments, resulting in increased richness in cultural form. The 'self-directed' consciousness preserves the status quo, but there is enough flexibility through the 'other-directed' consciousness to permit new forms to enter the cultural system. Just as Iatmul social organization is a blend of strength/coercion and equivalence/consensus, Iatmul culture is a complex interplay of the 'self-directed' and 'other-directed'. Further, the richness of Iatmul culture and society is typical of that of New Guinea as a whole.

2.2 **Languages and social groupings**

In the introduction to her ethnography of the Mountain Arapesh, Margaret Mead wrote of the Sepik basin:

> Each local community, sometimes only a hamlet, sometimes several hamlets, occasionally three or four villages, presents an aggregation of widely diffused traits peculiar to it. From this narrow vantage ground

> each individual sees the behavior of the members of neighbouring
> communities as becoming steadily more diversified from his own as the
> distance increases between the communities involved. Each commu-
> nity is a center of many lines of diffusion, which cross and re-cross in
> arbitrary ways, variously determined by the topography of the
> country, the natural resources, the immediate state of feuds and
> alliances, all only partly interdependent factors.   (Mead 1938: 151)

While admitting that the Sepik may be an extreme case, this statement may be
taken as characteristic of New Guinea as a whole. In the highlands, as well as in Irian
Jaya, cults, dances, artistic styles, horticultural techniques, patterns of material
culture, are also diffused over wide areas. The same is true of vocabulary items and
patterns of linguistic structure, and because of this tendency, the application of the
comparative method to the Papuan languages is often rendered extremely
problematic. This will be discussed in detail in Chapter 7.

This extensive diffusion is a direct manifestation of the trading, 'other-directed'
consciousness. At the same time, in keeping with the 'self-directed' consciousness,
the village or hamlet is viewed as the centre of the social world, and outside it other
communities are viewed as being increasingly different from it. They are the 'other'.
The inherent tension between 'self-directed' and 'other-directed' consciousness is
often expressed in the differences in solidarity between communities with shared
linguistic allegiances. The Karawari language of the Sepik basin is spoken by around
2,000 speakers in about ten villages. Dialect differentiation is not great, but there is
little feeling of a larger community composed of the villages speaking Karawari.
Some Karawari villages have rather closer cultural links to villages speaking other
languages than to those speaking Karawari. Salisbury (1962) makes a similar claim
for the Siane, a language group of the Papua New Guinea highlands:

> They are a congeries of culturally similar tribes, having no conscious-
> ness of an overriding political unity . . . the same general culture, with
> local variations, continues both to east and west of the Siane, with no
> sharp discontinuities, and with non-Sianes attending Siane ceremonies
> and vice-versa. Interaction between Siane and non-Siane is also the
> rule, and a statistical analysis of the marriage pattern indicates that
> marriages are random as between Siane and non-Siane.
>
> (Salisbury 1962: 1)

A similar situation is found for Iatmul. Iatmul villages often raided and headhunted
in other Iatmul villages (Bateson 1936), the shared language being no hindrance to
these raids. And, further, the Iatmul-speaking village Aibom has closer ties to the

three Chambri-speaking villages geographically near to it than it has to the other more distant Iatmul villages. Mead (1935) reports something of the opposite situation for the Biwat. The Biwat claimed that it was forbidden to eat someone who spoke the Biwat language. However, it would not do to carry this taboo too far. A group of Biwat speakers was separated from the main group living on both banks of the Yuat River, and inhabited two hamlet clusters in the bush country to the west. As their way of life began to diverge from that of the river groups, the latter tried eating one of them. As the diners suffered no ill effects, both groups were then free to eat each other.

As villages often do not recognize any solidarity with other villages of the same language, but more often form ties with geographically closer villages regardless of the language spoken, frequent shifting of linguistic boundaries is a common feature of New Guinea language groups. Like other cultural artifacts, language is a trade item. Villages on the border between two language groups may shift their linguistic allegiance if their shifting cultural and economic links would seem to warrant this. Some border villages may be so precariously balanced culturally and linguistically that it is difficult to determine their affiliation. Some individuals and families are bilingual; other speak only one of the two languages. Mead (1938: 159) mentions the case of Ulap village on the border between the Arapesh and Abelam languages. These two languages are structurally very different and belong to different language families. Neither the Arapesh, nor the Abelam, nor the inhabitants of Ulap themselves were sure of their affiliations.

In a shifting situation like this, small language groups may be gradually assimilated and disappear entirely. In the early 1950s Moraori (Boelaars 1950) of southern Irian Jaya was spoken by only about forty people, and the tribe was surrounded by the numerically much larger and culturally aggressive Marind tribe. All Moraori were bilingual in Marind, and Marind influence on the language was extensive (Drabbe 1954). It is now likely that Moraori is extinct, or nearly so. A similar situation obtains when a refugee group takes up residence with a friendly host group speaking a different language. If the refugee group remains with the host group, it will gradually give up its own language. Newman (1965) reports that a group of Chimbu speakers fled to the Upper Asaro and gave up speaking Chimbu in favour of Upper Asaro. Even if the refugee group returns to its home territory, a shift of linguistic boundaries is possible. Salisbury (1962) reports how a group of Chuave speakers took up residence as refugees with Siane speakers. They remained for a while, learned Siane, and then returned to their own territory. As they viewed Siane speakers as the most powerful tribe in the area, this language was regarded as more prestigious than Chuave. Consequently, when they returned to their own territory and rebuilt their villages, they continued speaking Siane. The boundary between Chuave and Siane is a major linguistic break, the two languages being at best only distantly related.

Rather more common than wholesale abandonment and adoption of languages is the less drastic effect of language convergence. The language of a prestige group in an area will influence those of less prestigious groups. The prestige of the Iatmul has resulted in that language influencing lexically and structurally the languages of adjoining groups. Such language convergence does not require extensive bilingualism, merely enough bilingual speakers to innovate and propagate the adoptions. These can then be spread through the community by other monolingual speakers.

But the situation may be more complex than the Iatmul case would suggest. Let us consider the language convergence between Yimas and Alamblak, contiguous but unrelated languages (discussed in greater detail in section 7.5). On the whole the languages are quite different, but still there are a large number of striking similarities between them, both lexically and structurally. The social situation seems to be that Yimas is the more prestigious language. This is indicated by the fact that there is a pidginized form of Yimas which is used as a trade jargon in the area, in contacts with the Alamblak, and with speakers of the also unrelated language, Arafundi, spoken up-river from Yimas village. In spite of this social situation, the direction of linguistic influence is from Alamblak into Yimas. Yimas has many Alamblak loan words, even for basic vocabulary, like *taki* 'stone'; and, further, some of the verbal morphology is calqued on Alamblak patterns. The explanation for this anomaly may be found in the marriage patterns. As Yimas seems to have always been a very small community (present population around 250), some marriages have been exogamous. Strong trade and marriage links have been maintained with the Alamblak-speaking village of Chimbut. Wives acquired from Chimbut must, in their acquisition of the Yimas language, have introduced some Alamblak vocabulary and structures. As Yimas children of both sexes until the age of ten spend much of their time with their mother and relatively little with their father, they would be more influenced in the acquisition of their native language by their mother, and by this means Alamblak features would have diffused into Yimas, in spite of the higher prestige of Yimas. Given the small size of many New Guinea communities, the role of exogamous marriages as an instrument of language change may be quite important, and is deserving of a much fuller study; Salisbury (1962) pointed out the importance of exogamous marriages for the multilingualism of the Siane.

The extensive diffusion of linguistic features is found throughout New Guinea, and has resulted in the formation of a number of linguistic areas (Emeneau 1956). The features diagnostic of these linguistic areas may be phonological, morphosyntactic or often both. As phonological features we may cite the widespread presence of central vowels and palatal consonants in unrelated languages of the Sepik basin and adjoining areas, or the presence of nasalized vowels in languages of the Southern Highlands and Great Papuan Plateau of Papua New Guinea. On the morphosyntactic level, we find the example of a two-gender system with a similar semantic basis in sex and shape spread throughout much of the Sepik basin and adjacent northern Irian Jaya, into the centre of the island around the Star Mountains, and down into the southern part of Irian Jaya. This is a huge diffusion area, covering well over 100 languages.

Perhaps the most famous example of language convergence in the New Guinea area is that between Papuan languages and Austronesian languages. The Austronesian languages which penetrated into the New Guinea area belong to the Oceanic subgroup, and languages belonging to this subgroup are characterized by verb-medial word-order and the use of prepositions to mark the semantic functions of oblique nominals. Papuan languages contrast, in that they favour verb-final word-order and the use of postpositions. Many Austronesian languages of New Guinea such as Mekeo, Motu, Gedaged and Adzera have been influenced by Papuan languages to the extent that they too now employ verb-final word-order and postpositions. For case studies of this kind of influence, see Capell 1976b or Dutton 1976. Gedaged of the Madang area even has dependent or medial verbs of the type widespread in Papuan languages, as discussed in Chapter 1. Adzera of the Markham Valley has been so heavily influenced by the adjoining Papuan languages that it betrays its Austronesian affiliation only in some basic vocabulary and a few morphemes. In at least one area of New Guinea, in the eastern Bird's Head, the opposite situation appears to obtain. Here the Papuan languages have verb-medial word-order (Voorhoeve 1975b), presumably by diffusion from the adjoining Austronesian languages of Sarera Bay.

This exuberant diffusion of traits, and the resulting linguistic and cultural convergence means that each community has become a sink of traits of the entire linguistic and cultural area. Consequently, there is often no correlation between the cultural patterns and the linguistic affiliations of communities. For example, the southernmost groups of Arapesh speakers are culturally very similar to the adjoining Abelam group (Tuzin 1977), in spite of the fact that the languages are in structure radically different and completely unrelated. On the other hand, while the language of these southern Arapesh is very similar to that of the Mountain Arapesh described by Mead (1938), the cultures are strikingly different. Communities must thus be viewed as foci in areal networks of cultural and linguistic patterns. Each community constructs its identity by drawing on the available pool of cultural and linguistic traits.

A question that might arise here is why, with all the tendencies toward cultural and linguistic convergence, does not a homogeneous culture and unifying language emerge from all the diversity? Of course, the sheer size of New Guinea and the imposing geographical barriers prohibit this on any large scale, but we might inquire why such a development has not occurred in, for example, the Sepik basin, with its main arteries – the Sepik River and its many lesser tributaries – providing easy access to the communities in the area. Such a development would be the logical outcome of the 'other-directed' consciousness, but it ignores the importance of the 'self-directed' consciousness view, which regards one's own customs and language as best and others as inferior. This is an equally important consideration in New Guinea, and the interaction between these two accounts for the pattern of 'unity in diversity' which is so typical of New Guinea; the centrality and value of one's own community and its language is an important theme in New Guinea cultures. To illustrate this with one linguistic example, let us consider Chambri, a language spoken on the southern shores of a lake south of the Sepik River and related to Yimas. There are three Chambri villages, which might be more aptly termed hamlets, as they are very close together, stretched out along the shore of the lake. The members of each village have regular contact with members of the other two villages, but one of the villages, Wombun, speaks a dialect of the language which is rather different from that of the other two. The differences are manifest on the phonological, lexical and morphosyntactic levels, with the latter being especially pronounced. The proclitics to the verb which mark the person and number of the subject and object are different for certain combinations in the Wombun dialect, and there are many other such differences. In spite of the small size of the Chambri language groups (about 1,000 speakers) and the close spatial proximity of the villages, the Wombun people have preserved a dialect different from that of the other villages (comparative evidence indicates that the Wombun dialect is more conservative than that of the other two villages). This is correlated with the feeling of the Wombun people of their uniqueness as a subgroup within the larger Chambri-speaking group. And such feelings on a wider scale throughout New Guinea must be partially responsible for the dazzling diversity we find here, in spite of the pervasive tendency toward convergence. Chambri language and culture has itself undergone extensive influence from Iatmul, the prestige group in the area.

In recent times the delicate balance between the 'self-directed' and 'other-directed' modes of consciousness has been upset by the introduction of Western culture and artifacts. Tok Pisin, the trade jargon developed through contact with Western culture and later spread as a *lingua franca* through many parts of northern Papua New Guinea, is seen as an avenue by which to acquire the goods of this culture. This force has given the 'other-directed' consciousness the upper hand, with the result that in certain areas the vernacular indigenous languages are being abandoned in favour of Tok Pisin, which is being acquired as a first language. This is occurring not just in urban areas, but also in rural areas. Murik, a language of the lake country west of the mouth of the Sepik river and related to Yimas and Chambri, is dying, and is not spoken by younger people in the villages. It is being replaced by Tok Pisin. Other groups resist this trend, the 'self-directed' consciousness still being strong. Iatmul is alive and doing well in its villages, and I have often been struck by the frequency with which the Iatmul speakers speak their language, even in an urban context such as Port Moresby. The reason for the different fates of Murik and Iatmul might be sought in the grammatical structures of the languages. Murik, like its sisters Yimas and Chambri, is a very complex language morphologically, and presumably a difficult one to acquire, while Iatmul is a reasonably easy language, almost isolating by Papuan standards. However, I believe that it is the mental attitude of the speakers, rather than the structure of the language, which is the most important variable. To support this view, we can contrast Yimas and the neighbouring village, Ambonwari, speaking the closely related language Karawari. Ambonwari is a much more traditional village culturally than Yimas. The cults of the men's house are still active and initiations of boys are still regularly performed, whereas these have ceased in Yimas since World War II. The Yimas are much more outward-looking, and now make regular expeditions to the provincial centre Wewak to acquire goods for their three trade stores. Ambonwari has just acquired a trade store. Tok Pisin is extensively used in Yimas, even in conversations between native speakers of Yimas, and is the language of choice for speakers under twenty, especially males. The Yimas language is not dying yet, but I did notice on a recent field trip in 1982 that few children under six could speak or understand Yimas. The situation in Ambonwari is radically different. Karawari is still the language of choice in the village, and all children appear to be acquiring it. Tok Pisin is reserved for special situations, and for talking to outsiders. Yimas and Karawari are closely related languages, of very similar structure, and the differences in linguistic usage in the two villages must be attributed to different cultural attitudes. Such differences in cultural attitudes may account for the Murik versus the Iatmul case. Iatmul culture is a strongly integrated, 'self-directed' one, with great stress placed on the high value of all things Iatmul. The culture of the Murik, on the other hand, was traditionally oriented towards trade. The Murik often functioned as middlemen in the distribution of certain highly valued items, such as masked dances, in order to facilitate the selling of their own local products, such as ornaments of shells, baskets and grass skirts (Mead 1938: 175). Their canoes sailed along the north coast of New Guinea around Wewak, selling their material and ceremonial wares to the people of the coast. This is a very different cultural emphasis from that of the Iatmul. It is very outward-looking and 'other-directed' in contrast to the more integrated, 'self-directed' culture of the Iatmul. These differing cultural emphases may account for why the Murik are now abandoning their language in favour of that language of the outside, Tok Pisin, while the Iatmul are proudly clinging to theirs. Detailed sociolinguistic studies along these lines are desperately needed in New Guinea, as the rural communities become more and more integrated into the modern world.

2.3 Multilingualism in vernacular languages

As mentioned briefly in the previous section, multilingualism is a common feature of New Guinea communities. Multilingual competence may be in a regional or national *lingua franca* or one or more adjoining vernacular languages. I will discuss the cases of *lingue franche* in the next two sections of this chapter; here I will restrict myself to multilingualism in vernacular languages. For a general survey of multilingualism in Papua New Guinea, see Sankoff 1977.

Multilingualism is reasonably common in New Guinea language communities, though its extent within the community depends on its overall size. Small or very small language groups are much more likely to exhibit extensive bilingualism. Yelogu, a Ndu language related to Iatmul, is spoken in a small village of sixty-three inhabitants (Laycock 1965). All speakers are bilingual in their own and the distantly related language Kwoma, which has several thousand speakers. In the highlands, there is a similar situation with the Binumarien language group (Oatridge and Oatridge 1973). Now only 117 strong, this group was once larger, but its population has been reduced due to tribal fighting and prolonged residence in the malarious Markham valley. Many of the men among the Binumarien are competent in one or more of the three adjoining languages – the related Tairora and Gadsup, and the unrelated Adzera.

With larger language groupings, bilingualism may be more selective, restricted to border communities or to individuals, generally men, with extensive outside contacts through trade or exogamous marriage contracts. In the latter case, multilingualism may be viewed as an index of status, correlated as it is with a higher economic position in the community. The restriction of bilingualism to border villages is noted by Berndt (1954) with regard to the Eastern Highlands of Papua New Guinea. Usarufa, a small language group of around 1,000, is surrounded by the much larger and distantly related languages, Fore and Kamano–Kanite, each with over 10,000 speakers. Bee (1965) claims that most adult Usarufa speakers can speak Fore and Kamano–Kanite, but few Fore and Kamano–Kanite speakers can speak Usarufa, and these, as Berndt (1954) asserts, are restricted to border communities.

A rich case study of multilingualism within a larger language grouping is provided by Salisbury's (1962) study of a highlands group, the Siane, numbering some 15,000. Siane speakers in the area of study are bilingual in the (at best) distantly related language, Chuave, the population of which numbers around 8,000. The village Emenyo, in which Salisbury carried out the study, is close to the border between the two languages, and bilingualism within the village is extensive, involving both men and women. Many Chuave women have married into Emenyo, and close trading links are kept up with the Chuave-speaking communities across the border. Further, within the Siane context, there is a distinct prestige associated with multilingualism, which is regarded as a desirable accomplishment. There are many indications of this in the culture: the use of foreign languages in Siane songs (none of the songs Salisbury recorded were in Siane), as well as the ubiquity of translations from one language into the other on formal occasions as a means of showing off language proficiency, even if such translations are unwarranted for reasons of comprehension. At least one very important man spoke Chuave on almost all occasions within his own Siane-speaking village. He presumably regarded this marked linguistic behaviour as consistent with his high social standing.

With the exception of multilingualism in women acquired from other communities through exogamous marriage patterns, as in the Siane example above, it is generally the case in New Guinea that multilingualism is a male affair. The nature of women's roles in New Guinea societies is such that they tend to have few sustained contacts outside the village, and hence encounter few situations which would encourage multilingualism. Conrad (1978a), writing of the rules determining language choice among the May River Iwam of the upper Sepik area, states flatly that women do not speak to outsiders, thus obviating any need for multilingual proficiency. And Litteral (1978) writes of the Anggor (also an upper Sepik group, but not closely related to the Iwam), that multilingualism was extremely limited or nonexistent among women, except for those of Amanab birth who had married into Anggor villages by exogamous marriage arrangements. This attitude toward women and language skills is pervasive in Anggor society, so that girls do not actively learn Tok Pisin, in contrast to boys, and the older males attempt to restrict the access of married women to the literacy classes. Whether such restrictions are common throughout traditional New Guinea is not known, as no-one has extensively studied the question of women and multilingualism.

2.4 Indigenous *lingue franche*

Because of the very large number of small language communities, in many areas of New Guinea *lingue franche* have long been used in inter-group communication before knowledge of Tok Pisin became widespread in the area. Among the different language groups of the middle Sepik, a simplified form of Iatmul was used as a trade language (Mead 1938). Iatmul speakers rarely had any knowledge of the languages of neighbouring groups. Similarly, along the Arafundi River, a trade jargon derived from Yimas was developed to communicate with the neighbouring Arafundi, an unrelated language and one completely different in structural type. However, a number of Yimas also control the Arafundi language, resulting in a symmetrical arrangement of language use, rather than the asymmetrical Iatmul case. Other indigenous languages which functioned as *lingue franche* in pre-contact times were the Austronesian languages, Motu of the central Papuan coast, Suau of the southwest tail area of Papua, and Dobu of the islands off eastern Papua.

With European contact and the resulting economic and missionary activity, a great need arose for *lingue franche* in the New Guinea area. When the different missionary organizations first arrived in New Guinea, they were immediately faced with the daunting task of communicating their message to speakers of widely different language backgrounds. Given the small numbers of missionary staff, the need for a missionary *lingua franca* was immediately apparent. The various missions chose different indigenous languages as *lingue franche* for the areas within their spheres of influence. Some of the languages selected were Papuan, and others were Austronesian. The factors which largely determined the selection of a language as a missionary *lingua franca* were its size and its proximity to the mission station, with the latter being generally more important. The early missionaries translated religious materials into these languages, and used such translations to propagate their message. Later the missions started schools and used these languages as the medium of instruction, so that the number of second-language speakers of these languages, and their use as secular *lingue franche*, grew quite rapidly in the first half of the century. All this came to an abrupt end around 1960, when the Australian administration prescribed English as the medium of instruction in all accredited schools; and since then these languages have been declining in use.

The Papuan languages which were selected as missionary *lingue franche* were Boiken of the Sepik area, Gogodala and Kiwai of the Fly River area, and Kâte of the Huon Peninsula. The Catholic Church in the early part of this century attempted to use the Ndu language Boikin, with the second largest number of speakers in northeast New Guinea, as the *lingua franca* of this area, which was one of extreme linguistic diversity (Z'graggen 1977). This attempt failed, as the local people resented having to learn another local vernacular which they in no way regarded as superior to their own. Furthermore, the Catholic missionaries themselves were divided on the issue, many preferring to exploit the growing knowledge of Tok Pisin. In the end, this sentiment won the day, and in 1930, Tok Pisin was made the *lingua franca* of the mission.

In the Western Province, Gogodala was used as a *lingua franca* for the Fly River area by the Evangelical Church of Papua (Neuendorf 1977), and Island Kiwai has been employed by the London Missionary Society in the Fly Delta since the 1880s

(Wurm 1977a). The use of both of these languages has been declining recently as religious materials become more available in the other vernacular languages of the area. Any secular use they might have is met by Hiri Motu (see below) or by English.

The Papuan language which has gained the widest currency as a *lingua franca* is Kâte. Originally spoken by a population of 680 in the mountains to the northwest of Finschhafen on the Huon Peninsula, it spread throughout the Huon Peninsula and into the central highlands as a result of missionary activities. The missions set up schools in this area in which Kâte was the medium of instruction. With the banning of such schools around 1960, the importance of Kâte began to fade, but today there are still around 75,000 people with an active knowledge of the language and a further 40,000 with a passive knowledge (Renck 1977b). The majority of these speakers are in the Huon Peninsula area, where the language is still used for religious purposes, but rarely in secular contexts, as Tok Pisin is widely known. The language has almost entirely vanished from the central highlands, its functions as a *lingua franca* being taken over by Tok Pisin. Also, because of the large size of many language groups in the highlands, in many cases vernacular languages are viable for missionary use.

The indigenous language which has been most successful as a *lingua franca* is undoubtedly Hiri Motu. Strictly speaking, this is not an indigenous language, but a pidginized version of the indigenous Austronesian language Motu, which developed in the contact situation of speakers from diverse language backgrounds, especially members of the police force, coming together in the Motu-speaking milieu of Port Moresby around 1900 (Dutton and Brown 1977). The name 'Hiri Motu' is taken from an earlier trade jargon used by the Motu and the Papuan-speaking tribes of the Papuan Gulf on the annual trading expedition of the Motu to this area. The Motu name for this journey was *hiri*. However, this trade jargon is not the ancestor of the present day Hiri Motu, which took form independently in Port Moresby in the early colonial period, although it may have played a role in the formation of Hiri Motu (Dutton and Brown 1977). As increasing areas of Papua came under administrative control in this century, Hiri Motu spread as a contact language and an unofficial *lingua franca* in these areas. It is now one of the official languages of Papua New Guinea, along with Tok Pisin and English. It has wide currency in the provinces corresponding to the old administrative districts of Papua, and may be spoken by as many as 200,000 people.

Hiri Motu is spoken in two basic varieties (Dutton and Brown 1977), one spoken essentially in the Central Province by native speakers of Austronesian languages, and the other spoken elsewhere, largely by native speakers of Papuan languages. The former variant is closer to the vernacular language Motu of Port Moresby than the latter, which represents a more radically pidginized form. This is understandable, as the vernacular languages spoken in the Central Province are

Austronesian languages very similar in structure to the vernacular Motu. For example, the central dialect generally follows the Motu pattern of indicating the inalienable possession of body parts and kin terms (at least as an option) and, like Motu, has verbal suffixes which indicate the person and number of the direct object. The non-central dialect diverges in both these features (Dutton and Brown 1977):

	Motu	Central Hiri Motu	Non-central Hiri Motu
		lau-egu tamana I-my father	
'my father'	*tama-gu* father-my		*lau-egu tamana* I-my father
		tama-gu father-my	
			oi lau itaia you I see
	na ita-mu	*lau ita-mu*	
'I saw you'	I see-you	I see-you	
			lau itaia oi I see you

In the following sketch of the major differences between Motu and Hiri Motu we will discuss the non-central dialect, as this has wider currency. The linguistic sketch is adapted from Dutton and Brown 1977.

Hiri Motu is phonologically simple like most pidgin languages, and has the following phonemic system, in which the symbols represent their usual English value, except that /r/ is a flap:

```
p   t   k
b   d   g            i                    u
    gw                     e       o
m   n                          a
f   s   h
v
    r
    l
```

In certain dialects of Hiri Motu some of these oppositions may not be maintained, especially those of /r/ and /l/, /f/ and /p/, /b/ and /v/. Some varieties lack /h/ entirely, and the contrast in voicing in the stops may be neutralized. This system differs from that of Motu in that the voiced velar stop /g/ corresponds to both the stop phonemes /g/ and the fricative /γ/ of Motu. Further, the free fluctuation between /l/ and /r/ in most varieties of Hiri Motu neutralizes the phonemic opposition between them in Motu: Motu *lau* 'I', *rau* 'leaf', Hiri Motu *lau* 'I, leaf'.

Grammatically, Hiri Motu is characterized by a good deal of morphological simplification in comparison to Motu proper, particularly in the verbal morphology. Motu has a larger number of affixes and clitics which indicate tense: these are replaced in Hiri Motu by the independent words *vadaeni/vada* for past tense and *dohore/do* for future:

Motu: *bai-na-ita-la*
              FUT-I-see-it
Hiri Motu: *dohore lau itaia*
              FUT   I   see
              'I will see it'

Motu also has suffixes indicating durative action, in the past *-va* and in the present *-mu*. These are not found in Hiri Motu, but a periphrastic verbal construction involving *noho* 'stay' must be used:

Motu: *na ita-ia-mu*
              I   see-it-PRES DUR
Hiri Motu: *lau itaia noho*
              I   see   stay
              'I am watching it'

Motu has a number of different negative forms depending on the tense and person and number of the subject. Hiri Motu has the invariable negative *lasi*, occurring after the verb:

Motu: *asi-na   ita-ia*
              NEG-I   see-it
Hiri Motu: *lau itaia lasi*
              I   see   NEG
              'I did not see it'

Motu: *basi-na   ita-ia*
              FUT-NEG I see-it
Hiri Motu: *do   lau itaia lasi*
              FUT I   see   NEG
              'I will not see it'

Perhaps the most striking differences in the verbal morphology between Motu and most dialects of Hiri Motu concern the verbal suffixes which indicate the person and number of the direct object. These are a common feature of the Austronesian languages of the Oceanic group, and are well developed in Motu:

> (*ia*) *e ita-gu*   'he saw me'
> he   3 see-me
> *na bata-ia*   'I hit him'
> I   hit-him
> (*idia*) *e utu-mui*   'they cut you (PL)'
> they   3 cut-you (PL)

In most dialects of Hiri Motu these suffixes are absent, and the object is placed either before or after the verb, which ends in -*a* as a marker of transitivity:

> *lau itaia oi*
> I   see   you

A similar simplification of a typical Oceanic Austronesian feature is found in the nominal possession system. Motu, like most Oceanic languages, has a system of noun classes which are realized in the possessive morphology: inalienable versus alienable versus edible:

> *adava-gu*   'my spouse' (inalienable)
> spouse-my
> *lau-a-gu*   *aniani*   'my food' (edible)
> I-EDIBLE-my food
> *lau-e-gu*   *ruma*   'my house' (alienable, inedible)
> I-INEDIBLE-my house

No distinctions are made in Hiri Motu; one construction, that involving -*e-gu*, the alienable, inedible class, is used for all nouns.

Lexically, Hiri Motu is ninety per cent drawn from Motu, but it shares with other pidgin languages the feature of being much restricted *vis-à-vis* the source language. A single form often carries a much wider range of meanings in Hiri Motu than in Motu proper. For example, the Motu verb *atoa* means 'put or set something', while the corresponding Hiri Motu word of the same form may mean, depending on context, 'to contribute funds, to put, to put on (clothes, paint), to place' (Dutton and Brown 1977). Because of this reduction in vocabulary items and resultant wide range of meanings, circumlocutions are often used in Hiri Motu to express more specific ideas, especially in the domain of more technical vocabulary. The language does not lack expressive power, but often more words are required to communicate the message than in the corresponding Motu sentence.

2.5 Intrusive *lingue franche*: Tok Pisin, English, Malay

Tok Pisin, English and Malay were introduced into New Guinea through colonization. English and Malay were the languages respectively of the Australian and Dutch (and later Indonesian) administrations. Tok Pisin, in one sense, is not an intrusive language, but grew up in the post-contact situation of east New Britain, around Rabaul. However, as eighty per cent of its vocabulary is of English origin, it can be regarded as an intrusive language.

Tok Pisin or New Guinea Pidgin is one of the three official languages of Papua New Guinea. It is the *lingua franca* with by far the largest number of speakers, around one and a half million, and this number is rapidly increasing. It is most widely known in the area of the old Mandated Territory of New Guinea, the area for which it has served as the main *lingua franca* since the turn of the century; but it is now rapidly spreading into Papua. In many areas of the Sepik basin, Madang Province, New Britain and New Ireland, knowledge of Tok Pisin is almost universal, with only older women or very old men ignorant of it. Creolization of Tok Pisin is beginning to occur on a wide scale in most urban centres of Papua New Guinea, although the number of first-language speakers of Tok Pisin is still below 100,000. This number can be expected to grow with increasing urbanization.

Tok Pisin is one of a family of English-based pidgins spoken in the Pacific. It is closely related to Solomon Islands Pidgin, Bichelamar of Vanuatu, and Queensland plantations Pidgin (Dutton 1980). The earliest history of Tok Pisin is not fully documented, but some reconstruction is possible. It appears that some form of jargon consisting of unstable varieties of broken English was spoken in New Guinea, and especially in New Britain and New Ireland, before the arrival of the German colonialists in the late nineteenth century. Mühlhäusler (1977a) reports that the size of the vocabulary was between 200 and 500 words, and that the grammatical structures exhibited great variation and instability. Stabilization occurred with the arrival of the Germans. They pacified large areas and created conditions for indigenous peoples to communicate across tribal boundaries. Furthermore, in the plantation areas developed in New Britain and New Ireland there was an urgent need for a common language, and Tok Pisin quickly assumed this role. It is important to note that at this point the superstrate language was German, not English, and·the substrate language, the native language of many of the plantation workers, was Tolai or one of the closely related New Ireland languages. Consequently, both of these languages were influential in the development of Tok Pisin. The lexicon of Tok Pisin today is ten per cent Tolai and four per cent German in origin; and much of the grammatical structure of Tok Pisin is closely related to Tolai (see Mosel 1981), and presumably derived from it. With the extension of

German control to the northern half of mainland New Guinea, Tok Pisin spread as a contact language. As Tok Pisin was now spoken by speakers of very diverse language backgrounds, the importance of Tolai began to decline, and further developments in the grammar were language-internal, independent of any substrate language (Mühlhäusler 1977a). The German colonial administration frowned on the use of Tok Pisin and tried to discourage it, but the language thrived in spite of official antipathy. After World War I, the Australian administration of the Mandated Territory of New Guinea pursued a similar line, but was no more successful than the Germans. Tok Pisin continued to spread, primarily as a result of the practice of recruiting villagers from remote areas to work on plantations and then repatriating them, so that today in many areas of the old Mandated Territory it is almost universally known. What differentials we find in the command of Tok Pisin in a given community are correlated with age and sex. In more recently contacted areas, older people may not know Tok Pisin simply because of its recent introduction. In other areas, women, and especially older women, may not know Tok Pisin, as it is the men who were contracted as plantation workers and who, in addition, have most of the extra village contacts. Among the Anggor (Litteral 1978) of the upper Sepik area, even today girls are not actively learning Tok Pisin in contrast to the boys. This reflects earlier, pre-contact attitudes in the community towards what were the proper language skills for women.

Mühlhäusler (1977b) distinguishes three current varieties of sociolects for Tok Pisin. First there are the bush varieties, spoken in remote areas where Tok Pisin is used infrequently, such as areas of recent development in the central highlands and elsewhere. These varieties are characterized by heavy first-language interference. (See the description of Tok Pisin as spoken by a highlands group, the Usarufa, in Bee 1972.) The most widespread variety of Tok Pisin is the rural variety. This is a predominantly lowland variety in the old Mandated Territory, and is the standard used for Tok Pisin publications such as *Wantok* newspaper. Rural Tok Pisin is the most stable of varieties, due to the fact that it is the major means of communication for speakers of widely divergent language backgrounds. This factor favours conservation, so as not to impede understanding, as does the isolation of these speakers from the anglicizing influences emanating from the urban centres. Finally, the urban varieties of Tok Pisin are those found in the towns as well as those spoken by speakers with a fair command of English. Urban varieties of Tok Pisin are in a diglossic relationship (Ferguson 1959) with English, so that English influences are evident throughout, especially in the phonology and lexicon, but also in the grammar. The overriding influence of English as the target language gives rise to instability in these varieties of Tok Pisin, and to communication difficulties between speakers of rural and urban varieties. The absence of any official standardization of Tok Pisin contributes in no small measure to this confusion. Any standardization of Tok Pisin will have to take the rural variety as the base, given its much wider distribution and the restricted access of its speakers to English, but some additions to its lexicon, probably by loans from urban varieties of Tok Pisin (and ultimately from English) will probably be necessary, although calques using exclusively rural Tok Pisin forms are a possibility worth investigating.

In presenting the following summary of Tok Pisin, I will be describing the rural variety; a sketch of its grammar can be found in Mihalic (1971). Tok Pisin has a simple phonemic system:

p	t	k		i			u
b	d	g			e		o
m	n					a	
	s	h					
	l						
	r						
w	y						

The opposition between /l/ and /r/ is commonly neutralized in rural dialects of Tok Pisin, and many dialects lack /h/ entirely. The voiced stops may not occur word-finally.

Syntactically, Tok Pisin parallels English and Tolai in having verb-medial word-order. Subject and object are morphologically unmarked. A preposition *bilong* indicates possession and benefactive nominals, and *long* marks all other oblique cases. Nouns are morphologically invariable, but plurality can be indicated by preceding them with the pronoun *ol* 'they': *ol meri* 'they woman', i.e. 'women'.

Tok Pisin follows Tolai and other Oceanic Austronesian languages in having a fundamental distinction in its verbs between transitive and intransitive forms. In most cases transitive verbs are indicated by the suffix *-im*, while intransitive verbs are unmarked:

bagarap	'be ruined'	*bagarap-im*	'ruin something'
op	'be open'	*op-im*	'open something'
singaut	'call out'	*singaut-im*	'call someone'
skrap	'to itch'	*skrap-im*	'scratch something'
win	'to win'	*win-im*	'beat someone'

Aspect and tense are indicated in Tok Pisin by a set of verbal satellites. Durative aspect is expressed by a periphrastic verbal construction involving *stap* 'stay' and perfective aspect with *pinis* 'finish'.

> *em i kaikai pinis/i stap*
> he   eat   finish/stay
> 'he has eaten/is eating'

Tense is indicated by a set of particles including *bin* for past tense and *bai* or *baimbai* for future. A number of preverbal bases are used to express modal notions: *laik* 'will', *inap* 'able to', *ken* 'be permitted to'.

In interclausal syntax Tok Pisin predominantly uses juxtaposition; the dearth of conjunctions in a text is a characteristic feature of Tok Pisin discourse. The language does possess the subordinating conjunctions *sapos* 'if', *taim* 'when' and *olsem* 'as', and the coordinator *na* 'and'. The order of clauses is generally iconic with the order of the events in time, and a causative relation between these events is not generally signalled formally, but is determined by inference, as in this example (Wurm 1977b):

> *mi kaikai planti kaukau   pinis, mi no hangre*
> I   eat   many sweet potato finish I   not hungry
> 'I've eaten so much sweet potato, I'm not hungry', *or*
> 'because I've eaten so much sweet potato, I'm not hungry'

In areas where knowledge of Tok Pisin is extensive and has been so for more than a generation, the language has exerted significant influences on the lexicon and grammar of vernacular languages. In the most extreme cases it may oust the vernacular language altogether, as in the Murik situation, discussed in 2.2. In less extreme cases, heavy borrowing from Tok Pisin is found, even in the area of basic vocabulary. In many Papuan languages, for example, the Tok Pisin numerals have replaced the native ones; and other basic vocabulary items may be affected as well. The younger speakers of the Angoram language on the lower Sepik River often simply do not know the native words for many basic vocabulary items, including flora and fauna. The Tok Pisin equivalents have completely replaced the original items. Many Papuan languages borrow Tok Pisin verbs, but nativize these by combining them with native verb-roots or affixes. The central highlands language Hua (Haiman 1980) uses the transitive form of the Tok Pisin verb in combination with the auxiliary verb *hu-* 'do', which carries all the verbal affixes: *bekim-hu* 'reciprocate', *bihainim-hu* 'follow', *pasim-hu* 'close'. Abelam, an Ndu language of the Sepik related to Iatmul, has borrowed Tok Pisin verbs on the same pattern, again with the verb 'do' (Abelam *yə*): *brukim marit yə* 'commit adultery', *hadwok yə* 'work hard', *poto yə* 'take a photo' (Laycock and Wurm 1977). These Hua and Abelam verbs would inflect normally in these languages, with the verbal affixes occurring on the supporting native verb. Yimas sometimes borrows the Tok Pisin root directly, without the need for a supporting native verb. The verbal affixes are simply added directly to the Tok Pisin root:

> na-ka-**kirapim**-ɨt
> it-I-start-PERF
> 'I started it'

In addition to borrowing vocabulary items, many Papuan languages borrow grammatical constructions from Tok Pisin. I will illustrate with two examples of such borrowing into Yimas. The formation of a negative verb from a positive one in Yimas is a complicated affair, involving alteration of the form and the position of certain verbal affixes. Many younger speakers do not know this method of negation, but negate a verb by merely placing a particle *ina* before it. This is clearly a borrowing from Tok Pisin *i no*, but these speakers were totally unaware of its origin, regarding it as a native Yimas word until I pointed out its similarity to the Tok Pisin negative. Now let us consider a bit of Yimas interclausal syntax. Yimas parallels many other Papuan languages in lacking subordinating conjunctions. Most subordinate clauses have the same form; the verb occurs with a dependent verb marker -*mp* which is followed by the oblique case marker -*n*. Conditional clauses (i.e. *if* clauses) are not distinguished formally from temporal clauses (i.e. *when* clauses). The difference resides in the choice of tense and mood markers. An irrealis suffix or a potential mode prefix on the embedded verb will normally be found in a conditional clause, while a realis tense suffix, like a remote past tense suffix, will indicate a temporal clause. This method of forming conditionals has a serious potential weakness. The meaning of conditionality does not reside in any one morpheme, but is the result of the interaction between the tense/mood morpheme and the embedding morpheme. This system may be disfavoured in the context of language acquisition. This weakness has been resolved by the borrowing into Yimas of the Tok Pisin conjunction *sapos* 'if', which is a single morpheme, unambiguously expressing a conditional meaning.

English, together with Hiri Motu and Tok Pisin, is one of the three official languages of Papua New Guinea. In all provinces it runs second in number of speakers to the other two *lingue franche*, a close second in Papua to Hiri Motu, but a rather poor second to Tok Pisin in the old Mandated Territory. The number of second-language speakers of English is probably around half a million, but very few Papua New Guineans speak it as a first language. English is the language of instruction in all government schools, so younger people in many rural villages have a smattering of it, although it is rarely used at that level. In Yimas village, more than thirty young people have completed six years' schooling, exclusively in English, but I have never heard it used spontaneously among themselves, Yimas vernacular or Tok Pisin being preferred. This preference also applies when they speak to me, even though English is of high prestige and my native language. This preference arises simply from the fact that English is viewed as a remote, foreign language, belonging to the arenas of official business, far removed from the affairs of the village.

Within Papua New Guinean society, English is the language of the elite, associated with government and business circles. It is viewed as the key to socioeconomic advancement of the individual – hence the importance still placed on the use of English in government schools. Within the urban centres, English is viewed as a neutral instrument of social intercourse, while the use of Tok Pisin or Hiri Motu implies solidarity between the interlocutors. In Port Moresby especially, but also in other urban centres, conversations with a stranger should be initiated in English (assuming his appearance is such that he is likely to be a speaker of English). Initiating such a conversation in Tok Pisin or Hiri Motu could be regarded as a slight, implying that the addressee is of lower socioeconomic status or of poor education, and hence not familiar with English. Solidarity cannot be rightfully asserted between strangers, so the normal principle determining the selection of Tok Pisin or Hiri Motu is invalid. These conversational rules apply much more strictly to white expatriates than to Papua New Guineans, given that in most situations of contact they have much less claim to solidarity with Papua New Guineans.

Within Irian Jaya, the official language is Malay or, more precisely, the standardized version of Malay used as the national language of Indonesia, and called Bahasa Indonesia. This is the language for all government and official business, and is the language of instruction in schools, except for some vernacular mission schools. There are some trade jargon varieties of Malay in Irian Jaya which spread through earlier trading contacts with other Indonesian islands, but these never played a major role as *lingue franche* for speakers of different language backgrounds. Dutch, the language of the earlier colonialists, was of little importance in Irian Jaya, as it was the policy of the Dutch administration to encourage the use of Malay as a *lingua franca*, and schooling under the Dutch was in that language. The number of Irianese who know Malay is not known, but is probably not large, especially in remote areas, as government education in many rural areas is not yet widespread. The sociolinguistic interaction between Malay and the vernacular languages in the rural areas has not yet been researched, but this would be a project well worth undertaking in the near future.

2.6 Specialized speech styles

Specialized speech styles have been reported from many areas in the world. Haas (1944) reports on grammatical differences in the forms of the Koasati language spoken by men and women. In Australia especially, a good deal of anthropological and linguistic research has been devoted to the forms of language used in songs, and to the special language styles used when addressing affinal relatives (Dixon 1977; Haviland 1979) or among initiated men. For a general introduction to the form and use of these language styles in Australia, see Dixon 1980: 47–68).

Similar patterns of linguistic behaviour can be found in the New Guinea area. While I know of no New Guinea community which has a distinct language style for speaking to affinal relatives parallel to the Dyirbal case in Australia discussed by Dixon (1971), very many have a system of taboos for words homophonous with, or close in form to, the names of affinal relatives. Among the Yimas, there is total prohibition against uttering the name of the father or mother of one's spouse. Franklin (1967) reports that when a Kewa man marries he is given a new name, frequently by his wife. His original name must then be avoided in the presence of his wife's brothers, who must address him by the new name bestowed by the wife.

Other contexts require still different word taboos. While hunting, the Yimas prohibit the uttering of words denoting the animals being hunted, for fear that the latter will hear the hunter's plans and conceal themselves. Laycock (1969) reports a similar prohibition and rationale among the Buin of Bougainville. Clans among the Kuman are also said to have secret languages which are used in hunting expeditions (Laycock 1977a). The justification provided here is that men of other clans must not learn of the hunters' plans.

An elaborate system of word taboos and consequent lexical replacement is described for the Kewa by Franklin (1975c). This is associated with religious cults devoted to powerful spirits providing healing to the sick. Nouns denoting items associated with the cult's activities are tabooed and replaced by new lexical coinages. These new words must not be spoken outside the area by non-cult members, and the unfortunates who do commit this error are subject to heavy fines.

The semantic factors which determine the new coinages are rather diverse. One of the principles used is antonymy, so that *inumakua* 'young unmarried girl' means 'boy' in one cult argot. In other cases metonymy is operative: *sapi* 'sweet potato' is replaced by *modomapuaa* from *modo* 'sweet potato mound' plus *ma-puaa* 'it was caused to go'. *Wabala* 'tree oil', a very important item in the curing techniques, is replaced by *reponaipaa*, which means in the standard language 'tree sap'. In one dialect of Kewa, *ipa* 'water' is replaced by *utyali* 'casuarina tree seedling'. Casuarina trees grow in abundance near streams. In still other cases, the semantic principles underlying the replacement are metaphorical in base: *mena* 'pig', an important item in the cults' activities, becomes *kuga*, normally meaning 'the sound of a river in flood or many pigs eating'. *(K)ana* 'stone', also an important cult item, becomes *yaaragala*, from *yaa* 'sky/cloud' plus *ragala* 'high dispersed cloud'. Other substitutions have no clear semantic basis: *repali* 'fish' to *ainya* 'it remains there', *sogo* 'tobacco' to *walia* 'he will look for it', or *ro* 'corpse' to *saapu* 'path'. There may be some motivation for these replacements in the mythology or cultural beliefs of the people, but they do seem unusual from a general semantic point of view.

Special languages like the avoidance language of Dyirbal (Dixon 1971), in which there is lexical replacement on a massive scale, are also found in New Guinea. The cases described are associated with the annual gathering of pandanus nuts, and are reported in the highlands areas of Papua New Guinea. Pawley (1975a) conjectures that pandanus nuts may have played a much greater role in the diet of these people a few centuries ago, and a specialized language used for its gathering would be a historical remnant of that earlier situation. Also, the pandanus trees grow in the deep forest in areas inhabited by nature spirits and wild animals, a place dangerous to human activities. Pawley mentions that this may be a factor in the use of the Kalam pandanus language, and Franklin (1972) claims that control of the forces in this wild area is the primary motivation for the use of the Kewa pandanus language. Franklin (1971) states that the pandanus language should never be used outside the area where the trees are located. These pandanus languages do not differ phonologically from the standard languages; the deviations are primarily lexical, although Kewa does exhibit some grammatical differences as well.

The Kewa pandanus language is discussed in Franklin (1972). The vocabulary and grammar has been restricted and regularized, but its relationship to the standard languages is readily apparent. The nature of the vocabulary reflects the restricted items and actions talked about on these expeditions. Individual words cover a much wider range of meanings in the pandanus language, and generally correspond to several words in the standard language; for example:

(a) *yoyo*, a reduplicated form of *yo* 'leaf', has the referents 'hair', 'ear', 'breast' and 'net bag', all of which correspond to distinct words in the standard language. The common meaning here seems to be hanging protrusions from the body, like a leaf from a tree.

(b) *yadira*, meaning 'nose stick' in standard Kewa, covers 'nose', 'eye', 'seed', 'face' and 'head' in the pandanus language. The core here may be association with the eyes. In the standard language 'seed' is *ini repena*, literally, 'eye tree'.

(c) *palaa* 'thigh' or 'branch' in standard Kewa, means 'tree', 'firewood', 'fire', 'root', as well as any reference associated with trees. The semantic commonality here is clear enough; even in standard Kewa 'fire' and 'tree' are both *repena*.

(d) *maeye* 'crazy' covers 'pig', 'marsupial' and generally any kind of animal other than a dog. These are opposed to the rational world of man and, perhaps, dogs.

Often pandanus language words are coined from compounds of standard language words:

(a) *aayagopa*, from *aa* 'man' plus *yago* 'fellow man, namesake' plus *pa* 'make', has the referents 'man', 'skin', 'knee' and 'neck'. Many expressions in the pandanus language are built on this term: *ni madi aayagopa-si* I carry man-DIM means 'my father'.

(b) *aaugiasi*, from *aa* 'man', *ugia* 'break into' and *-si* DIM, means 'boy', 'child', 'young man'.

(c) *kadusupa*, from *kadu* 'nose', plus *su* 'ground', plus *pa* 'make', covers all creatures which crawl along the ground like snakes, lizards and certain insects.

(d) *lupa*, from *lu* 'hit' and *pa* 'make', refers to actions, such as hitting, killing or eating, which affect an object adversely.

(e) *mupa*, from *mu* 'take' and *pa* 'make', covers 'get', 'walk', 'go', 'come', 'stand', i.e. verbs involving a motion component.

(f) *mumudusa*, from *mu* 'take', plus *mudu* (of unclear meaning, but perhaps *mudu* 'chief'), plus *sa* 'put', refers to resting actions, like sleeping, resting or sitting.

The Kewa pandanus language also exhibits a considerable simplification in the grammar in comparison to the standard language. Standard Kewa has two verb-stems for 'give', one when the recipient is third person and the other when he is first or second. The pandanus language uses one verb-stem in both these contexts, a reduplication of the stem for 'say'. The morphology of the tense system is also simplified in the pandanus language. In standard Kewa there are two sets of tense suffixes, one used with verbs which express actions done for the speaker's benefit and the other set used elsewhere. Only the latter is used in the pandanus language. There are also significant differences in the suffixes indicating the person and number of the subject, as the following paradigms demonstrate:

English	Standard language	Pandanus language
'I am . . .'	*ni pi*	*ni mupi*
'you are . . .'	*ne pi*	*ne mupa*
'he is . . .'	*nipu pia*	*aayagopa mupia*

'we (2) are . . .'	*saa pipa*	*saa mupapana*
'we all . . .'	*niaa pima*	*niaa mupapana*
'they are . . .'	*nimu pimi*	*aayagopanu pupipa*

In the pandanus language *aayagopa* 'man' replaces the third person singular pronoun *nipu* 'he'. The dual or plural pronouns are formed by adding the collective suffix *-nu* to this base. Still another simplification in the pandanus language is that the verbal suffixes which function like conjunctions to indicate different semantic relations between clauses, such as causation, are lost. Simple juxtaposition of clauses serves as the primary clause-linkage device in the pandanus language.

Many Papuan languages also have special language styles for use in songs. The most detailed study of the language of songs is Voorhoeve's (1977) paper dealing with Asmat, a language with 40,000 speakers in southern Irian Jaya. The Asmat possess an elaborate culture, centred on ceremonial houses and recurrent feasts, and the singing of songs constitutes an integral part of these feasts. A special language style is used in these songs, again involving lexical replacement. The Asmat distinguish in their songs two kinds of words: *arcer* and *ta-poman*. *Arcer*, which normally means the mainstream of a river or the most important chief among a number of headmen, denotes, when applied to song language, a word from everyday speech in its literal meaning. Opposed to it is *ta-poman* from *ta(w)* 'speaking, word' and *poman* 'opposite side', which is a word used in the song language with the same denotation as its *arcer*, but which in everyday language may have a very different meaning. Given an *arcer* term X, then a *ta-poman* of X is Y used metaphorically to denote the same referent as X, or a special 'poetic' word with the same meaning as X. The *arcer* word *ese* 'carrying bag' has the word *cem* 'house' as its *ta-poman*, while the *arcer* word *mu* 'water' has as its *ta-poman* the 'poetic' word *okom* 'water'.

Asmat songs acquire their particular character from the rule that the *arcer* of the song should be replaced in subsequent verses by their *ta-poman*, as in this example (Voorhoeve 1977: 29):

> *yewer amis si eme si emare:*
> tree sp. top still it-is still it is
> *minar eke fufu yano:*
> tree sp. fruit crunchy-crunch sound
> 'the top of the *yewer* tree is still;
> the sound of the *minar* fruit being eaten'

Minar is the *ta-poman* of *yewer*, so it replaces it in the second line.

As mentioned above, there are two types of *ta-poman*: metaphorical and 'poetic'. Metaphorical *ta-poman* fall into two groups: those which form an *ofew* 'kin group'

and those which do not. *Ofew* is a kin term denoting the group of one's brothers and
first or second cousins. Terms belonging to the same *ofew* are interchangeable, and
can be freely substituted for each other in songs. Within an *ofew* set of terms, one
term is senior (in Asmat terms, the 'older brother') and is mentioned first, i.e.
functions as *arcer*. Then the 'younger brothers', the *ta-poman*, are mentioned,
according to their relative ranking. For example, the *ofew* of the dog has *yuwur* 'dog'
as *arcer*, and the *ta-poman sun* 'wallaby', *foc* 'possum', *nayir* 'marsupial type', *yiwir*
'flying squirrel', *mupir* 'water rat', *poco* 'rat', *pirow* 'big mouse', *pea* 'mouse'. The
relative ranking within this set of *ta-poman* is not known. The common feature
uniting *arcer* and all *ta-poman* in this *ofew* set is that they are all furry animals. The
pig does not belong to this *ofew*, but is classified with human beings. Other sets of
ofew are:

pandanus group:

ar:	*manim*	'pandanus tree'
t-p:	*epnam*	'young pandanus tree'
t-p:	*amuw*	'kind of tall reeds'
t-p:	*yua*	'tall grass'
t-p:	*tuwus*	'kind of plant'

sun's group:

ar:	*yow*	'sun'
t-p:	*yesir*	'morning star'
t-p:	*pir(si-*	
	mit)	'moon'

Other sets of *arcer/ta-poman* do not form *ofew* groups. The basis for the pairing of
terms may be similarity of shape:

ar:	*apan*	'many-pronged arrow'
t-p:	*cecerei*	'opening flower'
ar:	*as*	'faeces'
t-p:	*peke*	'lump of clay'
t-p:	*minuk*	'hard lump of clay'
t-p:	*pow*	'soft mud'

or similarity of function:

ar:	*ese*	'plaited carrying bag'
t-p:	*cem*	'house'

and some pairs are associated through metonymy:

ar:	*cen*	'vagina'
t-p:	*men*	'sharp edge'
t-p:	*pim*	'edge, rim'
ar:	*ser*	'fish species'
t-p:	*makpin*	'ripples on the surface of the water' (often caused by *ser* swimming close to surface)

The 'poetic' *ta-poman* do not correspond to words in the ordinary language, but exist only in the songs as *ta-poman* to the ordinary language *arcer*. These *ta-poman* do not presuppose the prior use of their *arcer* in the songs; they may be used at the first mention of their referents. In fact, some of them seem to be used to the exclusion of their *arcer*. Some of these 'poetic' *arcer/ta-poman* sets are 'cassowary' (ar: *pi*, t-p: *sap*); 'crocodile' (ar: *ew*, t-p: *osama*); 'moon' (ar: *pir*, t-p: *manam*); 'woman' (ar: *cowuc*, t-p: *yuwar*); 'water' (ar: *mu*, t-p: *okom*); and 'sago' (ar: *amas*, t-p: *mama*). Some of these *ta-poman* seem to be borrowed from neighbouring languages; see Voorhoeve 1977 for details.

3

Phonology

3.1 Vocalic systems

Phonology is the study of the distinctive sound segments in a language. All speakers of all languages can produce a wide range of different sounds phonetically, but many of these differences are not significant within the system of the language, i.e. are not phonemically contrastive. Consider the following variants of what is generally regarded as a voiceless velar stop in English, a /k/:

$$[k^h] / [k^h\Lambda t] \quad cut$$
$$[\underline{k}^h] / [\underline{k}^h iyp] \quad keep$$
$$[q^h] / [q^h \mathfrak{d}fiy] \quad coffee$$
$$[k] / [skay] \quad sky$$

All speakers of English recognize the voiceless velar stop in these words as the 'same sound', regardless of the fact that they are all phonetically rather different. They are all different realizations of a single distinctive sound /k/, or, in more technical terms, allophones of a phoneme /k/. These allophones are never contrastive, as each occurs in a different environment. The phoneme /k/ with its allophones can be summarized as follows:

$$/k/ \quad [k^h] / \# \_\_\_\_ \text{ non-low back vowel}$$
$$[k^h] / \# \_\_\_\_ \text{ front vowel}$$
$$[q^h] / \# \_\_\_\_ \text{ low back vowel}$$
$$[k] / s \_\_\_\_$$

This important distinction between phonetics and phonology, between sounds and phonemes, can be illustrated in Papuan languages by a vowel system rather common in Sepik area languages. At first impression these languages seem to have seven vowel phonemes, as follows:

(1)   i   ɨ   u

            e   ə   o

               a

There is a large amount of evidence that the Ndu languages like Iatmul (Staalsen 1966) or Abelam (Laycock 1965) actually have basic vowel systems consisting of a three-way contrast in height among central vowels:

(2)   ɨ

        ə

           a

The front and back vowels of system (1) are analysed as allophones of /ɨ/ and /ə/ in Iatmul under the following rules:

/ɨ/ → [i] / ____y,ɲ
    [ɪ] / y,ɲ____
    [u] / ____w
    [ɔ] / w____
    [ɨ] / elsewhere

Examples of these rules are [lɨkəndɨ] /lɨkəntɨ/ 'it's here', [nduw] /ntɨw/ 'man' and [yuwiy] /yɨwɨy/ 'grass'.

/ə/ → [e] / ____y,ɲ
    [ɛ] / y,ɲ____
    [o] / ____w
    [ɔ] / w____
    [ə] / elsewhere

Examples of these include [ndow] /ntəw/ 'shrunken', [məriy] /məliy/ 'mud flats'.

    /a/ → [a] / everywhere

Contrast with above examples: [mariy] /maliy/ 'rat' and [yɛtuwrɨndɨ] /yətɨwlɨntɨ/ 'he walks'.

    Yessan–Mayo (Foreman and Marten 1973), a non-Ndu language up-river from Iatmul, is very similar, but adds the fourth vowel /ɔ/, resulting in:

(3)   ɨ

        ə

           ɔ

          a

with the following allophonic rules:

/ɨ/ → [i] / ____y   [tiy]   /tɨy/   'bed'
    [ɪ] / y____   [wiyɪ]   /wɨyɨ/   'hornet'
    [u] / ____w   [tuw]   /tɨw/   'torch'

[ɒ] / w___	[wɒs]	/wɨs/	'skin'
[ɛˠ] / ___#	[mɛˠ]	/mɨ/	'tree'
[ɨ] / elsewhere	[kɨᵐp]	/kɨb/	'bat'

/ə/ → [e] / ___y	[ŋgey]	/gəy/	'cockatoo'
[ɛ] / ___l,r	[ɛlïᵐbuw]	/əlïbïw/	'cane'
[o] / ___w	[owkuw]	/əwkïw/	'sugarcane'
[ɛˠ] / ___f, t, s	[nɛˠf]	/nəp/	'blood'
[ʌ] / elsewhere	[aŋgʌ]	/agə/	'rest'

/ɔ/ → [ɒ] / Cʷ	[kʷɒkʷɒ]	/kʷɔkʷɔ/	'chicken'
[œ] / ___y	[wœy]	/wɔy/	'yam'
[ɔ] / elsewhere	[sɔk]	/sɔk/	'dry'

/a/ → [a] everywhere	[ak]	/ak/	'man'
	[aᵑgʌtaᵑgʌ]	/agətagə/	'hurry'

Minimal pairs for the four contrasts are [uwk] /ɨwk/ 'over there', [ʌk] /ək/ 'over there', [ɔk] /ɔk/ 'water' and [ak] /ak/ 'then'.

In all languages with vowel systems of this type, as well as in many other Sepik area languages, the /ɨ/ phoneme has certain functions not shared by the other vowels. In these languages it functions as a linking vowel breaking up non-permissible consonant clusters. Consider the following Yimas examples of this phenomenon:

> *am-* 'eat' + *-t* PERF > *amɨt*
> *kantɨk* 'with' + *-n* class I concord marker > *kantɨkɨn*
> *nam* 'house; + *-n* OBL > *namɨn*
> *kɨsak* 'cut' + *-ntut* FAR PAST > *kɨsakɨntut*

The basic question here is what the status of [ɨ] is in such languages. Are all [ɨ]s to be analysed simply as transition vowels, inserted to break up certain consonant clusters, or are some [ɨ]s really phonemically present and others transition elements?

Pawley (1966) argues the former case for Kalam: that all [ɨ]s are transition vowels between consonants. Phonetically, Kalam has no consonant clusters, except at morpheme and word boundaries. This can be easily verified in Kalam because at these positions the initial and final allophones of the consonants occur:

> [korɸaᵑgɨp] / kot#pagp/ 'the stick is broken'
> [korɨbaᵑgɨp] /kotp#agp/ 'he spoke at the house'

The string of phonemes for these two examples is the same, but the phonetics of each is different. This is because the phrase-medial /p/ in the first example is word-initial, and is therefore realized by the word-initial allophone [Φ], while the /p/ in the second example is word-final and realized by the final allophone [b]. The position of the word boundary is clearly delineated, then, by the allophones of the phonemes involved.

Although Kalam words lack consonant clusters phonetically, Pawley analyses the language as having extensive consonant clusters at the phonemic level, with the consonants phonetically separated by a nonphonemic transition vowel. He also analyses the language as having three phonemic vowels, /e/, /a/, /o/. The general transition vowel is [ɨ], but if the next syllable contains one of the three phonemic vowels, or either of the phonemic semivowels, then the transition vowel is phonetically the same by vowel harmony. So:

∅ →	[o] /__ Co	[koŋgon] /kgon/	'garden'
	[ʌ] /__ Ca	[yʌɣam] /ykam/	'arrow'
	[e] /__ Ce	[ᵐbenep] /bnep/	'a man only'
	[u] /__ Cw	[muluk] /mlwk/	'nose'
	[i] /__ y	[ⁿbiyant] /byad/	'my husband'
	[ɨ] / elsewhere	[kɨⁿdɨl] /kdl/	'sinew'

Kalam is also analysed as completely lacking high vowels. The phonetic high vowels [i] and [u] are viewed as syllabic allophones of /y/ and /w/. So: [yaⁿt] /yad/ 'I', but [ᵐbim] /bym/ 'down valley'; [woⁿk] /wog/ 'garden', but [kur] /kwt/ 'stick'.

In this analysis, vowels occur initially and medially, but never finally (/e/, /a/, /o/ are never found in this position). Consonants are unrestricted in their distribution. This analysis results in many vowel-less words, as [ɨ] is the most common vowel phonetically. The claim that the language lacks phonemic high vowels, i.e. that [i] and [u] are /y/ and /w/, is supported by two pieces of evidence. First, it has been established above that, while consonants are unrestricted in their occurrence, vowels (/e/, /a/, /o/) may not occur finally. However, all three vowels [i], [u] and [ɨ] occur finally, thus indicating that they are not in fact vowels phonemically speaking, but consonants, or transition elements. Secondly, this analysis simplifies the statement of morphophonemics. The negative morpheme in Kalam has two forms: *m-* before the vowels /e/, /a/, /o/, and *ma-* before consonants. /y/ and /w/ always select the latter:

/ynb/ 'it is cooked'	/maynb/ 'it is not cooked'
/wkp/ 'it is cracked'	/mawkp/ 'it is not cracked'
/pkp/ 'it has struck'	/mapkp/ 'it has not struck'
/owp/ 'he has come'	/mowp/ 'he has not come'

Comparing this analysis of Kalam with the earlier one of Iatmul, note that the phonetic vowels [i] and [u] are assigned to different phonemes in the two languages:

/y/ and /w/ in Kalam and /ɨy/ and /ɨw/ in Iatmul. Thus, Kalam [suw] 'to bite' is analysed as /sw/, but Iatmul [nduw] is analysed as /ntɨw/. These two analyses can be reconciled if the Kalam analysis is accepted and the [ɨ] of Iatmul is assumed to be inserted to break up the consonant cluster. By this analysis Iatmul [nduw] is /ntw/, not /ntɨw/. [ɨ] is inserted between /t/ and /w/ in /ntw/ and then undergoes the normal allophonic rules to become [u]. This suggests that, at least in clusters /ɨy/ and /ɨw/, the /ɨ/ is not really phonemic, and that perhaps an analysis of Iatmul [ɨ] as always being transitional, along the lines of Kalam, is warranted. If this is the case, then Iatmul could be argued to be a two-vowel language:

ə

a

or even perhaps a one-vowel language with /a/, plus a length distinction. This latter analysis is especially tempting, as /a/ is noticeably longer phonetically than the other Iatmul vowels.

The Kalam and Iatmul vocalic systems illustrate the important distinction between phonetics and phonology, between sounds and phonemes. Depending on how one treats these languages, [i] could be a phoneme in its own right or an allophone of /y/ or /ɨ/. The choice depends on the careful analysis of the overall phonological and morphological pattern of the language, as well as on the theoretical predispositions of the analyst. This can often make comparison of phonemic systems across languages quite deceptive. In the following typological sketch of vocalic systems, and later sketches of consonantal systems in Papuan languages, I will be comparing phonemic systems. To do otherwise would make the exposition far too complex, but it is important to realize that similar phonemic systems can often disguise quite different inventories of sounds, and vice versa.

The basic vowel system in Papuan languages is the usual five-vowel system:

(4)

Languages with this pattern are extremely common: Barai (Olson 1981), Chuave (Swick 1966), certain Danɨ dialects (Bromley 1965), Kunimaipa (Pence 1966), Baining (Parker and Parker 1974) and Orokaiva (Larsen and Larsen 1977). This basic system is extended in two very common ways to form a six-vowel system. The first method of extending the system is to add an extra low back rounded vowel /ɔ/ to form:

(5)   i   u

         e   o
            a   ɔ

This pattern is general in the languages of the Huon family like Kâte (Pilhofer 1933) and Selepet (McElhanon 1970a). Other languages with this system are Samo of the Western Province (Shaw and Shaw 1977), Abau (Bailey 1975) and Pawaian (Trefry 1969).

An even more common six-vowel system is that created by the addition of a second higher central vowel to the basic system:

(6)   i   u

         e   ə   o
               a

The height of the second central vowel can vary from [ɨ] to [ʌ], with [ə] being the most common realization. Languages of this type are common throughout New Guinea and include many languages of the Papua New Guinea highlands, such as Fore (Scott 1978) and Kewa (Franklin 1971), Asmat (Voorhoeve 1965), Biangai (Dubert and Dubert 1973), Kamasau (Sanders and Sanders 1980b), Chambri and Nimboran (Anceaux 1965). The Yimas vowel system is a collapsed variant of (6) in which there is no height distinction in the front and back vowels, resulting in a four-vowel system. Some highland languages with this system can be further analysed as a three-vowel system with a length distinction, as /i/, /ə/ and /u/ are phonetically short vowels while /e/, /o/ and /a/ are long. It could be argued that [e] = /i·/, [a] = /ə·/ and [o] = /u·/, resulting in an underlying three-vowel system plus distinctive length.

The rarest type of six-vowel system is that involving the addition of a front vowel. Two subtypes are attested; one involving the addition of a lower high front vowel /ɪ/, as in Nii of the Chimbu family (Stucky and Stucky 1973):

(7)   i   u
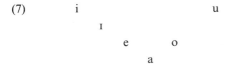
            ɪ
         e   o
               a

or the addition of a lower mid vowel [ɛ], as in Boazi of the Marind family (Voorhoeve 1970a):

(8)   i   u

         e   o
            ɛ
               a

Seven-vowel systems are not uncommon and are formed in two ways. They may involve the addition of extra front and back vowels:

Vowel system (9a) is found in a number of Dani dialects (Bromley 1965), as well as in Weri of the Kunimaipa family (Boxwell and Boxwell 1966). System (9b) is found in Awa of the Eastern Highlands (Loving 1973a). A more common seven-vowel system is the typical seven-vowel system of Sepik languages discussed above, with a three-way contrast in vowel height in the central vowels (system (1)). This system is very common among Sepik languages, such as Iatmul (Staalsen 1966) and Alamblak (Bruce 1984). It is also found in Kobon (Davies 1980a), in the Angan languages such as Baruya (Lloyd and Healey 1968), and in the Torricelli languages Yil (Martens and Tuominen 1977) and Ningil (Manning and Saggers 1977). The problems in analysing the vowel systems of Sepik languages such as Iatmul as having seven distinctive vowels have already been discussed.

The final seven-vowel system is that of Sentani (Cowan 1965), which adds an /ə/ to system (8):

(10)   i   u

        e   ə   o

            ε

            a

The earlier Sentani vowel system was like that of (9b), but the missing back vowel shifted to /ə/, to result in (10) (Cowan 1965).

Vowel systems with more than seven vowels are extremely rare in Papuan languages. The Sko languages along the north coast in the border area between Irian Jaya and Papua New Guinea are eight-vowel languages, as in Vanimo (Ross 1980):

(11)   i   u

        e   ə   o

            ε   ɔ

            a

Languages with more than eight distinctive vowels are unattested.

3.2 **Consonantal systems**

The phonemic systems of consonants in Papuan languages are in general relatively simple. There are no Papuan languages with consonantal systems of the order of complexity of, say, Caucasian languages or languages of the Athabaskan family, and almost all Papuan languages have inventories of consonantal phonemes simpler than that of English.

The basic consonantal system of Papuan languages, of which more complicated systems are simply variants and elaborations, is typified by Fore and other languages of the Eastern Highlands of Papua New Guinea. The consonantal phonemes of Fore (Scott 1978) are as follows:

(12)   p   t   k   ʔ
            s
        m   n
        w   y

Similar systems can be found in Awa and Usarufa (McKaughan 1973). Given such a small inventory of distinctive consonants, it is not unexpected that some phonemes have a wide range of allophonic variation in many New Guinea languages. This is especially true of the stops. A pervasive feature of Papuan languages is the tendency to weakening and voicing of the stops between vowels. This phenomenon is called lenition by linguists who study phonological changes. The Fore stops have the following allophones intervocalically:

/p/   /t/   /k/
[b ~ β]   [r ~ l]   [g ~ γ]

All stops are intervocalically voiced and, further, tend to be continuants. The realization [γ] for /k/ is extremely widespread in those Papuan languages which do not have a phoneme /g/ or /ɣ/. A /ɣ/ phoneme is not common in Papuan languages, but is found in some languages of the Sepik area, especially those of the Torricelli group. The interrelationship between /t/ and the liquid consonants [r] and [l] is also a common feature of Papuan consonant systems, but Fore is unusual in having no distinctive liquid phoneme, both [r] and [l] being allophones of the phoneme /t/. Other Papuan languages do have a distinctive liquid, but generally [r] and [l] are free or conditioned variants of this one phoneme. In those languages like Yimas, in which /r/ and /t/ are distinct phonemes, there is very often a morphophonemic alternation between the two:

            tɨkɨt 'chair'   *tɨkɨr-ɨŋkat* 'chairs'
            yakut 'net bag'   *yakur-ɨŋkat* 'net bags'

In Yimas /r/ and /t/ are almost in complementary distribution, with /t/ in initial and final position and before /n/, and /r/ elsewhere; but there are enough cases of intervocalic /t/ to establish the existence of separate phonemes. Finally, the lenition of /p/ to [β] is also quite common, but rather less so than the other two cases, because a considerable number of languages have a phoneme /v/ with [β] as one of its allophones. Unlike the lenition of /t/ and /k/, the lenition of /p/ may be found also in initial position, although in this position the fricative is voiceless. Fore and Kalam (Pawley 1966) both have [Φ] as a word-initial allophone of /p/.

Papuan languages are generally not rich in fricative phonemes although, as we saw above, they can be quite common phonetically in the language. A few, like Yimas, can be said to be lacking fricative phonemes entirely. Yimas does have a sound [s], but this is best analysed as an allophone of the palatal stop phoneme /c/. Beyond this fricativeless system, Fore represents the most basic Papuan system with the single fricative /s/ and, again, this is a quite widespread feature of Papuan languages.

All Papuan languages have at least the nasal sounds [m] and [n], but in a few Papuan languages the phonemic status of these can be in question. In Rotokas (Firchow and Firchow 1969) and Asmat (Voorhoeve 1965) the nasals are in complementary distribution with the corresponding homorganic voiced stop. These phonemes could be analysed as voiced stops with nasal allophones or as nasals with stop allophones. But, given the almost universal presence of nasals in the consonant systems of the languages of the world (see Ferguson 1966), the latter solution seems preferable in these ambiguous cases.

The problem of the phonemic status in different languages of the semivowels /y/ and /w/ is much too complicated to discuss here. These semivowels are present in all Papuan languages, but their phonemic status varies widely according to the phonetic features of the individual languages and, to some extent, according to the analyst's preferences in analysing diphthongs and other complex vocalic nuclei. In Fore and a number of other languages, e.g. Asmat (Voorhoeve 1965), Hua (Haiman 1980) and Vanimo (Ross 1980), /y/ has fricative allophones which clearly suggest that it is a consonant and not a nonsyllabic vowel. In Vanimo (Ross 1980) the /w/ also has a fricative allophone [β], but spirantization seems less common in Papuan languages with /w/ than with /y/. I have already discussed the role of semivowels in the Sepik vowel systems in the previous section.

The glottal stop phoneme occupies a unique position in Fore phonology. Although a common phoneme in highlands languages, it is less frequent in other Papuan languages. In Fore, it can only occur intervocalically or preceding any other consonant except itself and /s/. The explanation for the restricted distribution is found in the phonotactic patterns of Fore. Only nasals and the glottal stop may close a syllable in Fore. The syllable-final glottal stop is the neutralization of the contrasts between the three voiceless stops /p/, /t/ and /k/ which may not occur in syllable-final position.

With regard to the phonetic forms of its words as opposed to its syllables, Fore has applied an even more rigid constraint. No consonants at all are allowed in word-final position: words must end in vowels. This constraint, combined with the above rather different constraint on the form of syllables (and morphemes), has given rise to a very interesting system of morphophonemic alternations in Fore and other Eastern Highlands languages like Usarufa (Bee 1973) or Gadsup (Frantz 1973). In these languages, morphemes or words end in nasals or the glottal stop; but when the words are uttered in isolation, the nasals and glottal stop disappear because of the phonetic constraint on the forms of words. When morphemes are uttered in sentences or phrases, the individual words are vowel-final, but the final nasals or glottal stop in the basic morphological form of the word induce morphophonemic changes on the initial segment of the next word. Compare the following three examples from Fore (Scott 1978):

(a)   *teʔté ma-we*
       red   soil-DECL
       'it is red soil'

(b)   *ka:sá: ʔma-we*
       new   soil-DECL
       'it is new soil'

(c)   *tunú mpa-we*
       black soil-DECL
       'it is black soil'

Note that the three adjectives all end in vowels, but that the noun *ma* 'soil' takes on a different form following each adjective. After *teʔté* 'red' the noun is unchanged. This adjective in its basic morphological form actually ends in a vowel, and so it induces no change in the initial of the following noun. But compare *ka:sá:* 'new'. Here the noun *ma* 'soil' has the form *ʔma*; the initial consonant is pre-glottalized. This is because this adjective in its basic morphological form ends in a glottal stop, i.e., it is actually *ka:sa:ʔ* 'new'. Finally, compare example (c) with the adjective *tunu* 'black'. Following this adjective, the noun has the form *mpa*, this alternation arising from words which actually end in nasals. This is perhaps not immediately apparent from the Fore form, but the corresponding construction in Usarufa (Bee 1973) will result in a geminate nasal cluster, i.e. *mm*, and in Gadsup (Frantz 1973) this construction will result in a simple nasal through degemination. The consonantal phonemes of

Fore are affected as follows (note that /s/ remains unaffected):

	/p/	/t/	/k/	/m/	/n/	/y/	/w/	/s/
after /ʔ/	ʔp	ʔt	ʔk	ʔm	ʔn	ʔy	ʔw	s
after nasals	ʔp	ʔt	ʔk	mp	nt	nt	nk	s

When the following word would normally begin with a vowel, then /ʔ/ initiates that word if it follows /ʔ/, and /nk/ does so if the word follows a nasal. Because of the rule which requires homorganic nasal stop clusters in Fore, it is impossible to determine which nasal, /m/ or /n/, actually terminates the morphemes. The contrast between /m/ and /n/ is neutralized in this environment, so I will indicate the presence of a final nasal simply by N.

(a) *yaga:* 'pig' ends in a vowel, so no changes:

       yaga: tára-we
       pig   two-DECL
       'there are two pigs'
       yaga: + *-ánto-wé* > *yagá:ntowé* (with vowel coalescence)
       pig   small-DECL
       'it's a small pig'

(b) *koʔ* 'net bag' ends in /ʔ/:

       ko   *ʔtára-we*
       net bag two-DECL
       'there are two net bags'
       koʔ + *ánto-wé* > *koʔántowé*
       net bag small-DECL
       'it's a small net bag'

(c) *tuN* 'axe' ends in a nasal:

       tu   *ʔtára-we*
       axe two-DECL
       'there are two axes'
       tuN + *-ánto-wé* > *tunkántowé*
       axe   small-DECL
       'it's a small axe'

Usarufa, to the north of Fore and genetically related to it, has the following system of consonantal alternations:

	/p/	/t/	/k/	/m/	/n/	/y/	/w/	∅(__V)
after /ʔ/	ʔp	ʔt	ʔk	ʔ	ʔn	ʔy	ʔw	r
after N	ʔp	ʔt	ʔk	mm	nn	ʔk	ʔk	n

(a) *waa* 'man' ends in a vowel:

> *waa* + *-ma* NOM > *waamá*
>
> *waa* + *-e* DECL > *waaé*

(b) *wáá?* 'noise' ends in /?/:

> *wáá?* + *ma* NOM > **wáá?ma* > *wáá?a*
>
> *wáá?* + *-e* DECL > *wááre*

(c) *waa*N 'possum' ends in a nasal:

> *waaN* + *-ma* NOM > *waamma*
>
> *waaN* + *-e* DECL > *waane*

The basic Papuan system of consonantal phonemes presented in (12) above (p. 55) and exemplified by Fore can be extended in three ways: by filling in the gaps, by adding further places of articulation, or by adding new manners of articulation. Abau of the upper Sepik region (Bailey 1975) has the same number of consonantal phonemes as Fore and basically the same system, with a few rearrangements.

(13) p   k
      m   n
          s   h
          r
      w   y

In Abau the phoneme consisting of alternates [r] ~ [t] is best analysed as /r/, as this is the allophone in the widest range of environments, in contrast to Fore, which favours /t/. Other than this, Abau differs from Fore in having the glottal fricative instead of the glottal stop. Somewhat elaborated from the Fore or Abau systems is the system found in Sentani (Cowan 1965), spoken near Jayapura:

(14) p   t   k
      f   h
      m   n
          l
      w   y

In this language there is a distinct liquid phoneme; it is no longer an allophone of /t/, and varies in realization between [l] and [r]. The /h/ replaces the /s/ and corresponds to /s/ in the western dialects of the language. The /f/, which has both bilabial and labiodental allophones, is an additional phoneme, but one which fits neatly into the basic system already established by simply filling an available gap. Ningil of the West Sepik (Manning and Saggers 1977) has nearly reached saturation point by filling in the gaps of the basic system:

(15) p   t   k   ʔ
      f   s   γ
      m   n   ŋ
          l
          r
      w   y

In this system each stop has its corresponding fricative and nasal, filling in three gaps of the basic system. Further, not only is the liquid phoneme distinct from the /t/, but there are two distinct liquids: an /r/ and an /l/.

Papuan consonantal systems often differ from the basic system in employing additional places of articulation. The most common additional position is the palatal one, and this is exemplified by the Yimas consonantal inventory:

(16) p   t   c   k
      m   n   ɲ   ŋ
          r   l
      w   y

While the previous consonantal systems already discussed do possess a palatal sound /y/, in those systems it is best viewed as an apical semivowel, in the same basic series as /t/, as there are no other palatal consonants. Yimas has a full complement of palatal consonants. The system is more or less symmetrical; each stop has its corresponding nasal. There are no fricative phonemes, [s] being perhaps the most common allophone of /c/ but always potentially replaceable by a palatal stop articulation. Yimas has two contrastive liquids: an apical /r/ which varies between a lateral and a flap articulation, and an /l/ which is palatal lateral [ʎ]. Systems like Yimas, containing palatals, a symmetrical arrangement of stops and nasals, and a contrast between an apical and a palatal liquid, are not uncommon in the Sepik and its fringe areas. Languages with such systems include Abelam (Laycock 1965), Kobon (Davies 1980a) and Enga (Lang 1973). Other languages may have less elaborate systems, with a palatal stop and semivowel, but no nasal or liquid, like Asmat (Voorhoeve 1965):

(17) p   t   c   k
      f   s
      m   n
          r
      w   y

or a stop, nasal and semivowel, but no liquid, as in Kewa (Franklin and Franklin 1962):

(18)   p   t   c   k
                b   d   g
                m   n   ɲ
                     s
                     l
                     r
                w   y

There are no known cases of a language with a palatal stop, liquid and semivowel, but no palatal nasal.

Other languages extend their consonantal systems by adding an extra series in the velar area. A good number of languages have a labiovelar series, as in Kâte (Pilhofer 1933):

(19)   p   t   k   kp
                b   d   g   gb
                f   s   h
                v
                    ts
                    dz
                m   n   ŋ
                     r
                     y

In Kâte the labiovelars are stops with simultaneous double closure, but in other languages with this series they may simply be velar stops with a secondary labiovelar articulation, as with English /kʷ/. Certain languages of the Marind family have a uvular series, as in Boazi (Voorhoeve 1970a):

(20)   p   t   k   q
                b   d   g
                ᵐb ⁿd ᵑg ᴺG
                f   s
                v   z
                m   n
                    l
                    y

The most common additional distinctive phonetic feature employed in extending consonantal inventories beyond the basic system is that of voicing. In a great many Papuan languages, including some of those whose systems were illustrated above, the voiced stops are obligatorily pre-nasalized. Some languages such as Fore and

Yimas have pre-nasalized voiced stops that are best interpreted as clusters of a nasal and homorganic voiceless stop rather than as a unit phoneme. This analysis is justified in Fore by the fact that such clusters do not occur word-initially except as a result of the morphophonemic process involving the final nasals of the previous word. In Yimas such pre-nasalized voiced stops are extremely rare word-initially, and the only examples involve [mb]. The stops in these clusters also vary freely between voiced and voiceless allophones, suggesting that these are clusters of nasal and stop rather than unit-voiced stop phonemes with pre-nasalization. Finally, Yimas has a number of heterogeneous nasal-plus-stop clusters like /mk/, /np/, /mt/, which arise by morphophonemic rules of vowel deletion. The function of these rules is to produce clusters of nasal-plus-stop, which is a favoured phonological pattern in the language. All this strongly supports the analysis of the Yimas pre-nasalized stops as clusters of nasal and the corresponding voiceless stop. In languages like Kewa (Franklin and Franklin 1962), Kalam (Pawley 1966) or Barai (Olson 1981), in which the pre-nasalized voiced stops are simply the realization of the voiced stop phonemes, such restrictions are not found. The voiced stops occur word-initially, medially and finally, and are not generally the result of morphophonemic processes. Further, the stops do not vary freely with voiceless allophones, although such may be a conditional variant in restricted environments, as in Kalam (Pawley 1966), in which the pre-nasalized voiced stops are devoiced finally.

A good number of Papuan languages have plain voiced stops without pre-nasalization. Kâte (system (19) above) is an example of this. Similar languages include Urii (Webb 1974), Golin (Bunn and Bunn 1970), Telefol (Healey 1964a) and the Gorge dialect of Dani (Bromley 1965). Other dialects of Dani have a three-way contrast in stops in the bilabial and dental positions: a voiceless aspirated stop, a pre-nasalized voiced stop and an implosive voiced stop (Bromley 1965), as in the Wodo Valley dialect of Dani:

(21)
p	t	k	k^w
^mb	nd	^ng	^ngw
ɓ	ɗ		
m	n		
	l		
w	y		

Other languages also have a three-way contrast in stops, but without implosives. Boazi (system (20) above) exemplifies this. There is a contrast between voiceless stops, voiced stops and pre-nasalized voiced stops. Voicing is also an operative distinction in the fricative system. Kamasau (Sanders and Sanders 1980b) of the Sepik area has a similar three-way contrast in stops.

Perhaps the most unusual set of phonemes in Papuan languages are the laterals found in a number of languages of the Chimbu family. Although some languages of this family like Golin (Bunn and Bunn 1970) have only one lateral /l/, other languages are rather richer in this regard. Kuman (Piau 1985) has an /l/ and a laterally released velar affricate /gɬ/, voiceless finally [kɬ], voiced elsewhere [gɬ]. Nii (Stucky and Stucky 1973) seems to be the most elaborate. It has a three-way contrast in laterals: a simple dental lateral /l/; a dental lateral fricative, voiceless finally [ɬ] and voiced elsewhere [ɮ]; and a velar lateral fricative, also voiceless finally [ʞ] and voiced ~ elsewhere [ʟ̝]. These fricatives may not occur initially in Nii, and this applies as well to the laterally released velar affricate in Kuman.

3.3. Suprasegmentals

Tonal systems have been reported for a number of Papuan languages, but on the whole these seem better analysed as pitch-accent systems rather than as genuine tonal systems. The vast majority of such Papuan languages have a single contrast between high and low tone, and this suggests a pitch-accent system with a contrast between accented syllables and unaccented ones. I will consider the Fore tone pitch-accent system here as an exemplar of this type.

Scott (1978) gives the following minimal pairs in Fore (the standard orthography for Fore is now used; orthographic a = /ə/ and a: = /a/):

asiyúwe	'I stand up'	*asíyuwe*	'I peel (it)'
napa:wé	'(it is) my father'	*nápa:wé*	'(it is) my marriageable cousin'
naya:né	'(it is) my hair'	*nayá:né*	'(it is) my kidney'
aiwé	'(it was) yesterday'	*áewé*	'(it is) he'

The accented syllables are distinguished from the unaccented syllables by their higher pitch, which may be either level or falling. Each Fore morpheme has its basic accent patterning. The accent of words containing these morphemes results from the combination of these basic accent patterns. A morpheme may be accented on one syllable, or it may be completely unaccented. A single morpheme may have two accents, but never in adjoining syllables. A morpheme may also induce an accent on a following syllable. For example, the verb root *asi'* 'stand' is an accent-inducing morpheme, as indicated by the accent following the morpheme. Combining this verb root with other morphemes:

$$asiyúwe < asi' \text{ 'stand'} + -u \text{ 1SG} + -e \text{ DECL}$$

the accent will fall on the first syllable of the following morpheme. In many cases this induced accent is the only distinction between otherwise homophonous forms:

-*ake* 'name':   *nakewe* '(it is) my name'
-*aké* 'ear':   *nakewé* '(it is) my ear'

In addition to morphemes of this kind, there is another class of accent inducing morphemes which place the accent on the next but one syllable, as does *keʔpe:* ' 'sand', as well as a class of morphemes which cancel any accent which would otherwise occur on either or both of the next two syllables. For examples see Scott 1978: 48.

As morphemes build into words, various constraints rule out certain potential patterns of accents. For example, only two adjacent accents are permissible. When three or more would otherwise occur, the second and alternate accents are lost:

> *yabúne mpáentuwé* 'I got my sugarcane'
> *yabú* 'sugarcane' + -*né'* N 1SG POSS,
> *máe* 'get' -*nt' '* RM PAST + -*u* 1SG + -*e* DECL

Also, no word may commence with two accents. If this would otherwise be the case, the first accent is lost:

> *maeʔtáye* 'he got (it)'
> *máe* 'get' + -*ʔtá* PAST + -*e* DECL

For descriptions of the pitch-accent systems in other Papuan languages (often analysed as tone systems), see Franklin 1971 on Kewa, Bailey 1975 on Abau, Huisman and Lloyd 1981 on Angaataha, and Healey 1964a on Telefol.

The languages with the most elaborate accent systems, which, with more detailed analysis, might turn out to be true tone systems, are those of the Kainantu family in the Eastern Highlands. Awa (Loving 1973a) has four contrasting pitches: high (*nó* 'breast'), low (*nò* 'house'), falling (*nô* 'taro') and rising (*pǒ* 'fish'). There are problems with treating this as a true tonal system, although it appears at first to be a good candidate. The rising tone is rare, and quite restricted in its distribution; and further, in polysyllabic words many of the potential pitch patterns are simply unattested, much like the constraints on pitch patterns in Fore. It seems likely, then, that Awa too has a pitch-accent system, with the contour pitches being a combination of accented or unaccented vowels, so that *nô* 'taro' is actually *nóò*, vowel length being non-contrastive in Awa. In any case, a detailed study into the suprasegmental system of languages like Awa and other members of its family is needed.

4

Nominals

4.1 Nominals: nouns versus pronouns

Nominals may be defined as those word-classes whose function is to refer. By this I mean that words like *Wewak, wind, chair, Harry, love, I, they, that* are employed in discourse by speakers to introduce props, objects and entities relevant to the progression of the discourse or to trace those previously introduced. These words accomplish this because by the conventions of any language they are symbols associated with real-world or imaginary entities. These entities are the *referents* of nominals: they are what is communicated whenever a nominal or nominal phrase is used. In short, we may define nominals as *referring expressions*.

Nominals are basically of two types, corresponding to the traditional word-class distinctions of nouns and pronouns. Nouns constitute that class of nominals which bear a constant relationship to their referents. The natural world, as well as human creations, the social and cultural worlds, present a vast array of entities which may be expressed by nominals. Each language group, according to its interests, its ecological niche, its social and cultural forms, selects from this range and codes a subset of that range in its inventory of nouns. But the set of nouns is still vast. Therefore, it is absolutely necessary for communication that nouns bear a constant relationship to their referents. It simply would not do for *dog* to refer to our canine friends in one conversation, but in the next to our feline ones. Thus, a noun like *chair* always refers to an object from the class of possible chairs; while a proper noun like *Wewak* or *Harry* refers to a unique individual in the real world or in ongoing discourse.

Pronouns are quite different from nouns in this respect. They are often defined as 'taking the place of a noun'. But by this definition it is immediately clear that they cannot bear a constant relationship to their referents. In any language, a pronoun can stand in for any number of nouns. For example, *it* in English can stand in for *Wewak, wind, chair* and *love*. In contrast to the one-to-one constant relationship of nouns to their referents, pronouns exhibit a shifting many-to-one relationship. In one context, *it* may refer to Wewak, in another to the wind, in still another to love.

The shifting referents of *I* and *you* are even more obvious. When John is speaking to Peter, *I* is used to refer to John, and *you* to Peter; but when Peter is speaking to John *I* refers to Peter, and *you* to John. Pronouns, then, are shifting referring expressions in contrast to nouns, which are constant referring expressions.

4.2 Pronominal systems

Pronouns in all languages are characterized by belonging to a small, closed set. Nouns, on the other hand, belong to a very large and open set. Languages adopt new nouns with ease, but new pronouns normally only with great difficulty. Pronoun systems form a tightly integrated whole, constructed on the basis of a few distinctions. Because pronouns function as shifting referring expressions within the context of ongoing speech, it is from the participants and contents of acts of speaking that the basic building blocks of pronoun systems are drawn. The most fundamental element in any act of speaking is the speaker himself, because without the speaker there is no speech. Then follows the addressee, because he is generally the goal of speaking. People normally speak to communicate to one another. Thus, the most basic pronouns are those corresponding to the speaker and addressee, *I* and *you*, in that order.

The so-called 'third person' pronouns, *he*, *she*, *it*, present a somewhat different picture. These do not refer to participants in the speech act, but instead refer to participants in the context, in the text of the speech act. They are the 'true' pronouns, standing in for nouns previously established. In a text, *it* may refer to Wewak, the wind, love or a chair, depending on which of these entities was established previously in the discourse or in the environment of the ongoing speech act. In a sense, the third person is a non-person, as it does not correspond to a participant in the speech act. The Arab grammarians characterized it as 'the one who is absent'. This semantic value of the third person is often iconically realized in languages by its null morphological form, i.e. a zero morpheme. Although of shifting reference, third person pronouns are much closer in function to nouns than are first and second person pronouns, and, as we shall see, often participate in grammatical and semantic distinctions with the class of nouns, while the first and second person pronouns often do not.

While languages like French and English (in earlier usage) have plural pronouns corresponding to each person in the singular:

SG	PL	SG	PL
I	*we*	*je*	*nous*
thou	*you*	*tu*	*vous*
he, she, it	*they*	*il, elle*	*ils, elles*

this neat parallelism conceals an important semantic difference. When nouns are plural, they refer to more than one token of the entity referred to by the noun; *chairs* refers to more than one member of the class of chairs. For nouns, the plural is just a multiple of the singular. Third person and second person pronouns are parallel in this respect: *they* refers to multiple instances of the same entity, while *you* (PL) refers to an addressee consisting of more than one member. But first person pronouns are quite different. Most speech acts have a single speaker, so *we* is not equivalent to multiple *I*, but rather consists of *I* and not-*I* components. Many languages make this distinction between *we* and *you* (PL), *they* explicit. The not-*I* component can contain the addressee (the 'inclusive *we*'), or not (the 'exclusive *we*'). So, many languages have two plural pronouns corresponding to *I*, in contrast to the second and third person pronouns, as in Tok Pisin:

	SG	DL	PL	
		yumitupela	*yumi*	INCLUSIVE
1	*mi*	*mitupela*	*mipela*	EXCLUSIVE
2	*yu*	*yutupela*	*yupela*	
3	*em*	*emtupela*	*ol*	

-pela is a marker of nonsingularity that occurs with most nonsingular pronouns. The dual, indicating two tokens of the referent, is expressed by the numeral *tu* 'two', occurring after the pronoun base and before *pela*. Thus, the second person pronoun is *yu*, the plural *yu-pela* and the dual, *yu-tu-pela*. When we come to consider the first person pronoun, we find that the singular *mi* corresponds to two pronouns in the nonsingular numbers. One, the exclusive, is formed parallel to *yu*: singular *mi*, plural *mi-pela*, dual *mi-tu-pela*. This is as expected because the singular form *mi* is, of course, exclusive, not including the addressee. The exclusive form, then, follows the general pattern of the second and third persons. The inclusive forms are also transparently formed in Tok Pisin. The inclusive consists of the speaker plus the (possibly multiple) addressee. The inclusive forms are exactly that: *mi* + *yu* equals *yu-mi* inclusive plural and *yu-mi-tu-pela* inclusive dual.

Papuan languages are especially interesting in their pronoun systems because many of them exhibit restricted, abbreviated systems not commonly found elsewhere, and which become intelligible when seen in the light of the principles outlined above. And, further, Papuan languages very commonly make different distinctions in pronominal systems in different parts of the grammar; one may find a common six-member pronoun set like the earlier English or modern French for the independent pronouns, but fewer distinctions in the set of verbal prefixes which express the person and number of direct objects. For example, the system for the independent pronouns of Lower Grand Valley Dani (Bromley 1981) is identical to that of archaic English.

	SG	PL
1	*an*	*nit*
2	*hat*	*hit*
3	*at*	*it*

Applying a preliminary morphological analysis, we note correlation of *a* with singular and *i* with plural, and *n* with first person, *h* with second person and ∅ with third person. The prefixes which mark the object of the verb and the possessor of nouns are composed of similar morphological bits in the same pattern of distinctions:

	SG	PL	
1	*n-*	*nin-*	< *n-* 1 + *in-* PL
2	*h-*	*hin-*	< *h-* 2 + *in-* PL
3	∅	*in-*	< ∅ 3 + *in-* PL

But the suffixes which mark the subject in combination with certain modal distinctions are different from the above two systems not only in form, but also in the number of distinctions made. Some of the subject suffix sets display neutralization and extensions of person/number categories. The most basic of the subject suffix series occurs in the realis mode and consists of the same person/number distinctions as the above systems (*h* = realis mode):

	SG	PL	
'I hit him'	*wat-h-i*	*wat-h-u*	'we hit him'
'you (SG) hit him'	*wat-h-in*	*wat-h-ip*	'you (PL) hit him'
'he hits him'	*wat-h-e*	*wat-h-a*	'they hit him'

But the hortative/imperative mode exhibits neutralization of the number distinction in the third person, resulting in a five-way contrast:

	SG	PL	
'let me hit him'	*wasik*	*wasu*	'let's hit him'
'hit him' (to one)	*wasin*	*waʔni*	'hit him' (to two or more)
	waʔnek		'let him/them hit him'

That the number distinction should be neutralized preferentially in the third person is explicable in view of its non-participation in the immediate speech act. As it is less directly relevant in the immediate situation, the number contrast in this category is also less important than in the other two persons. Further, as mentioned previously, third person pronouns are those directly associated with nouns, and, as there is no inflection for number on Dani nouns, it is no surprise to find this distinction neutralized in these subject suffixes as well.

The hypothetical mode shows a further conflation of categories in which the second plural is identical to the third person (*l* = hypothetical mode):

	SG	PL	
'I almost hit him'	*waʔ-l-e*	*waʔ-l-o*	'we almost hit him'
'you (SG) almost hit him'	*waʔ-l-en*		
		waʔ-l-ep	'you (PL)/he/they almost hit him'

Note that it is the second person plural form which has been extended to cover the third person (compare this series with that of the realis mode above: front vowel + *p* is always second person plural). This extension is understandable in that the second person plural refers to a diffuse body of passive participants in the speech act, opposed to the active speaker and his group. It is the diffuseness and passivity of the second plural that associates it with the absent non-participants of the third person. Note that this would not apply to a second singular pronoun, which refers to a distinct individual who is the central goal of the speaker's act of talking, and which in no sense could be considered diffuse.

Finally, in the future potential mode there is no contrast for person, only number:

> *wasikin* 'I/you (SG)/he will hit him'
> *wasukun* 'we/you (PL)/they will hit him'

Note that the forms used to express the number distinction are those of the first person, the vowels *i* versus *u* (compare the realis mode system above). In other words, all distinctions of person are collapsed in favour of the first person, leaving the forms only able to signal a number distinction. This reflects the favoured status of first person pronouns, referring to the central participant of the speech act, the speaker. A puzzling fact about the above forms is that it is person which is neutralized, not number, suggesting that number is the most basic category. This, as we shall see below, is directly contradicted by the pronominal systems of other Papuan languages.

Dani is typical of Papuan languages in exhibiting both the skewing and abbreviation of pronominal systems, as well as their variation in different grammatical categories. I will henceforth only be concerned with the systems of independent personal pronouns, but the abbreviation characteristic of pronominal suffixes in certain Dani verbal categories is also found in the independent pronoun systems of other Papuan languages.

The simplest pronominal systems attested for any Papuan language are those of certain languages of the Chimbu family, such as Golin (Bunn 1974) and Salt-Yui (Irwin 1974). (Laycock (1977b) mentions a language of Irian Jaya, Morwap, which he claims has an even simpler pronominal system, consisting of first person opposed to everything else; but, as he himself admits, for various reasons these data are not of high reliability, and we will ignore this case here, pending further investigation.) To take Golin as an example, it has only two true pronouns: *na*, first person, undifferentiated for number, hence 'I/we', and *i*, second person, again indistinct for number, hence 'you'. There are no true third person pronouns: they are formed by adding *inin* 'self' to the word for man and woman: *yalini* 'he' < *yal* 'man' + *ini*, and *abalini* 'she' < *abal* 'woman' + *ini*. Number may be overtly expressed with these 'pronoun' forms with generic terms and the pluralizing word *kobe* – *na ibal kobe*, I/ we people PL, 'we'; *i ibal kobe*, you people PL, 'you (PL)'; *ibal kobe*, people PL, 'they' – or with the numeral 'two' to indicate the dual (*yasu* < *yal* 'man' + *su* 'two') – *na yasu* 'we (two)', *i yasu* 'you (two)', and *yasu* 'they (two)'. The non-distinctness of number for pronouns is thoroughgoing in Golin, as the bound pronominal affixes for both verbs and nouns also exhibit no contrast in number. The only exception to this concerns the first person, as there is a specialized first person singular subject suffix. However, this is infrequently used, and alternates with a general first person subject suffix, undistinguished for number (Bunn 1974: 26). It should be noted that the special treatment of the first person pronoun is again in keeping with its most central status.

Kuman, another Chimbu language, has grammaticized a distinction in number, but only in first person pronouns (Piau 1985):

	SG	PL
1	*na*	*no*
2	*ene*
3	*ye*

Interestingly, in its subject suffix series, Kuman makes a richer set of distinctions, distinguishing three numbers and three persons, but collapsing the second and third persons in the nonsingular (Piau 1985), a pattern reminiscent of the Dani hypothetical mode discussed earlier:

	SG	DL	PL
1	*-i*	*-bugl*	*-mun*
2	*-n*	*-bit*	*-iw*
3	*-uw*		

The Kuman situation, in which more distinctions are made in the bound pronoun forms than in the independent ones, seems to be rare among Papuan languages.

While Kuman represents an elaboration of the Golin system by adding number as distinctive, other Papuan languages elaborate by additional person categories. Some languages of Irian Jaya have pronoun systems consisting of three persons, but have no number distinctions, as in Manem (Voorhoeve 1975a): *ga* first person, *sa* second person and *aŋk* third person. Plurality can be overtly indicated by preposing the particle *kiŋ*. Nimboran (Anceaux 1965) is similar to Manem, but adds an inclusive category, which by definition is nonsingular, but which is not distinguished for number, as it may denote dual (you and I) or plural (you and us). The Nimboran system is then:

1	INCL	*io* 'you and I, you and us'
	EXCL	*ŋo* 'I, we'
2		*ko* 'you'
3		*no* 'he, they'

With Kuman we found a language in which number was distinctive in the first person, but not in the second and third persons. The next stage, in which number is distinctive in the first and second persons, but not in the third, is exhibited by Asmat (Voorhoeve 1965):

	SG	PL
1	*no*	*na*
2	*o*	*ca*
3	*a*	

This, of course, is also the system of Dani pronominal suffixes in the hortative/ imperative mode. From the Asmat system, by extending the number distinction to the third person, we can derive the familiar six pronoun system, composed of three persons, each with a singular and plural form, exemplified by the Dani independent pronoun system above.

Many Papuan languages have additional number distinctions, notably a dual. The acquisition of a dual follows the pattern established for plural: a dual distinction first appears in the first person, as in Kalam (Pawley 1966):

	SG	DL	PL
1	*yad*	*ct*	*cn*
2	*nad*	*nt*	*nb*
3	*nwk*		*ky*

Wiru (Kerr 1966):

	SG	DL	PL
1	*no*	*tota*	*toto*
2	*ne*	*kita*	*kiwi*
3	*one*		

Wiru exhibits the typical highlands conflation of second and third persons in the nonsingular, in this case in the dual and plural, while in Kalam it is restricted to the dual only. Many Papuan languages have dual members for all three persons, resulting in the familiar nine-term system, as in Alamblak (Bruce 1984):

	SG	DL	PL
1	*nan*	*nën*	*nëm*
2	*nin*	*nifɨn*	*nikëm*
3	*rër*	*rëf*	*rëm*

And a few Papuan languages add a paucal, or sometimes a trial, in addition to a plural and dual. Yimas and Chambri of the Lower Sepik family exhibit this system, as does the Kiwai (Ray 1933) pronoun system below:

	SG	DL	TRIAL	PL
1	*mo*	*nimoto*	*nimoibi*	*nimo*
2	*ro*	*nigoto*	*nigoibi*	*nigo*
3	*nou*	*neito*	*neibi*	*nei*

in which the dual and trial forms are derived from the plural by adding *-to* and *-ibi* respectively. A further interesting fact about Kiwai is that, while it has trial forms of the pronouns, it lacks a basic numeral for 'three', which is expressed by combining 'one' and 'two'.

An intriguing feature of many Papuan languages is the often transparent morphological association between the first and second persons, most commonly between the first person nonsingular and second singular. For example, in Suki, of the Fly River area, the two are identical in form (Voorhoeve 1970b):

	SG	PL
1	*ne*	*e*
2	*e*	*de*
3	*u*	*i*

This conflation is only attested in languages without an exclusive/inclusive distinction in first nonsingular categories. This suggests that the motivation for this conflation may be the presence of the addressee, corresponding to the second singular, in a statistically large number of uses of the undifferentiated first nonsingular, those corresponding semantically to the inclusive. A conflation motivated by the inclusive grouping can be explained by its higher salience than the exclusive (see Silverstein 1976); presumably a grouping of the primary speech-act participants, speaker and addressee, would be regarded as more important by the speaker than a grouping of himself and some non-participants.

Many languages of the central highlands of Papua New Guinea exhibit this grouping of second singular and first nonsingular in the subject suffixes on the verb, although this grouping may not occur in the personal pronouns. Consider Awa (Loving 1973b; Loving and McKaughan 1973), in which the personal pronoun system is:

	SG	PL
1	ne	ite
2	are	
3	we	se

with conflation of first and second nonsingular, while the subject suffixes are:

	SG	DL	PL
1	$-ga \sim -\Omega$		$-na \sim na\Omega$
2	$-na \sim na\Omega$	$-ya \sim -ya\Omega$	$-wa \sim -\Omega$
3	$-de \sim -\Omega$		

in which there is conflation of all persons in the dual, the second and third plural, and the second singular and first plural. Note the differences between the independent pronouns and subject suffixes. While the independent pronouns conflate the first and second persons in the plural, the subject suffixes conflate the second and third persons, the more general highlands feature. The subject suffixes have a distinct dual category, which the independent pronoun system lacks. Finally, the independent pronouns betray no similarity between the second singular and first plural, which are identical in the subject suffixes.

Some highlands languages stop short of absolute conflation between the second singular and first plural, but there remains a transparent morphological relationship between them. In Fore (Scott 1978), the personal pronouns form a familiar nine-term system:

	SG	DL	PL
1	náe	tasíge	táe
2	káe	tisíge	tíge
3	áe	isíge	íge

whereas the subject suffixes exhibit the conflation pattern typical of highlands languages:

	SG	DL	PL
1	*-u*	*-us*	*-uN*
2	*-a:N*		
		-a:s	*-a:*
3	*-i*		

Here we find the usual conflation of the second and third persons in the nonsingular. Further, there is a transparent morphological relationship between the second singular and first plural; the first plural is constructed by combining the first and second singular forms: *-u + -aN > -uN*. This formation of the first plural is widespread in highlands languages related to Fore.

The explanation offered above for the regular morphological relationship between the second singular and first plural in Papuan languages concerned the pivotal status of the second singular. As very many – as well as the most salient – of the uses of the first plural (the inclusive meaning) contain the second singular as a central member, a morphological formation based on this premise, as in Fore above, seems quite natural. Yimas pronouns present a different picture. Consider the Yimas first and second person pronouns:

	SG	DL	PAUCAL	PL
1	*ama*	*kapa*	*paŋkɨt*	*ipa*
2	*mi*	*kapwa*	*paŋkɨt*	*ipwa*

In Yimas there is a transparent morphological derivation in the non-singular numbers of the second person pronouns from those of the first person. In the most marked number, the paucal, the first person pronoun functions as the second person as well; but in the dual and plural, the second person is derived from the first by an infix *-w-*. A similiar situation occurs in languages related to Yimas, such as Chambri. It is possible, although not a convincing explanation, that this relationship arises from the fact that both first and second persons refer to the participants in the immediate speech act, and hence a morphological resemblance between them may not be too far-fetched. As the speaker naturally enough regards himself and his group as the more central, the morphological derivation will proceed from the first person as the base form. This contradicts the highlands patterns, in which the second singular serves as the base form for the first plural, but no other explanation seems forthcoming for the curious Yimas system.

4.3 **Demonstratives**

Closely correlated with pronominal systems are demonstratives. Both belong to the class of deictic expressions, those words of shifting reference which refer to the participants, setting and time of an ongoing discourse. Having already discussed pronouns, which refer to the participants of the speech act, I will now concern myself with demonstratives, which specify the spatial orientation of the speech act, locating objects with regard to the spatial positioning of the speech act and its participants (the location of the speech act in time is the function of tense, which I shall take up in the next chapter, on verbs). Demonstrative systems may be built up on two differing, but not exclusive, principles. Taking the three-way person distinction of the pronouns as basic, a language may have a three-way contrastive system of demonstratives: one for the location of the speaker, one for the location of the addressee, and one for locatives corresponding to neither of these, the 'other' location. Or a language may choose as a starting point the actual spatial position of the speech act, regarding the position of speaker as basic for this reckoning, and then indicate the location of objects removed from this central point. The minimal number of terms in such a system is two: 'this/here' for the speaker's location and 'that/there' for all other locations.

Korafe (Farr and Whitehead 1981) is an example of a language of the first type. This language has three demonstrative roots: *e* 'this/here' (the speaker's location), *a* 'that/there' (the addressee's location) and *o* 'that/there' (locations other than that of speaker or addressee). In this language an interesting secondary function of the demonstratives is to express the degree of the emotional involvement of the speaker in his utterance. The neutral form is the *a* demonstrative for the addressee's location. This is usual as a straightforward, matter-of-fact way of speaking, presumably speaking to interest the addressee, but without strong involvement of the speaker. The 'other' demonstrative *o* is used when the speaker wishes to dissociate, to *distance*, himself from what he is reporting; while the 'speaker's' demonstrative *e* is used when the speaker wishes to assert a *close* emotional involvement with his utterance. This is a fascinating iconic use of spatial terms to express internal psychological states.

The Korafe three-term demonstrative system is somewhat uncommon among Papuan languages (in contrast to Austronesian languages, in which it is heavily predominant). Rather more usual are demonstrative systems based on the second principle of construction, measuring distance from the position of the speaker. As mentioned above, the most basic system of this type is a two-term one, and this is reasonably common among Papuan languages, of which we can take Alamblak

(Bruce 1984) as an example. Alamblak has a demonstrative base *ɨnd-*, to which are added *-ar* 'near' to indicate speaker's location or *-ur* 'far' to indicate locations other than speaker. To these forms are then suffixed number and gender morphemes:

ɨnd-ar-r	DEM-near-M	'this (M)'
ɨnd-ur-t	DEM-far-F	'that (F)'
ɨnd-ar-m	DEM-near-PL	'these'
ɨnd-ur-m	DEM-far-PL	'those'
ɨnd-ar-kor-t	DEM-near-at-F	'this place (F), here'

A much more elaborate system of this type is exemplified by Nasioi (Hurd 1977). In this language there is again a generalized demonstrative base $a \sim e$, to which can be added a general nominalizer *-ung* ~ *-un* (*a-ung* 'this') or a case suffix: *a-aʔ*DEM-LOC 'here', *e-eʔ* DEM-INSTR 'like this'. To indicate distances removed from the central position of the speaker, suffixes indicating direction – inland, seaward, up, down, etc. – and relative distances are then added:

> *a-un-toong*
> DEM-NOM-down, north
> 'that down there or to the north'

> *a-un-toon-ko*
> DEM-NOM-down, north-far, moving from speaker
> 'that far down there, descending from us northward'

> *a-un-toom-peto*
> DEM-NOM-down, north-near, moving toward speaker
> 'that down there, closer, ascending toward us from the north'

> *a-(a)ʔ-daang*
> DEM-LOC-inland
> 'there inland from us'

> *e-eʔ-dan-to*
> DEM-INSTR-seaward-far
> 'by going seaward far from us'

A system combining the features of Korafe and Nasioi seems to be found in Fore (Scott 1978). This language has a demonstrative for the speaker's and addressee's positions, but for locations corresponding to neither, there are seven distinct demonstrative forms, indicating relative distance and vertical relationship to speaker, up versus down:

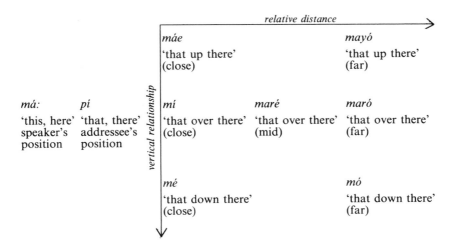

4.4 Gender and nominal classification systems

Gender or noun classification is a widespread feature of many Papuan language groups, especially those of the Sepik basin and adjoining lowland areas of Irian Jaya. The presence of gender or noun classification systems in these languages is an important typological fact, as such systems may play a central function in the grammatical or discourse structures of the languages. I mentioned in the first section of this chapter that the set of nouns in any language is always a very large, open set, probably containing more items than any other word-class. This is certainly true of Papuan languages; in all languages I know, the set of nouns is much larger than that of verbs, the next largest word-class. Many languages impose an internal order on this large, unwieldy set of words by means of systems of gender or noun classification.

One might inquire as to why the set of nouns is always so large. The answer is readily apparent: they provide an inventory of the entities in the world (or imagination) of interest to the speakers of the language. They provide enough descriptions of the world to enable the speaker effectively to express himself and the addressee to determine relatively easily what entities the speaker is actually talking about, i.e. the referent of the nouns used. Consequently, it is essential that the referents of nouns be relatively stable across contexts. To describe a river, one must use a noun 'river', whether one is travelling on it or photographing it. Given that the number of such items in any culture's experience is very large, the set of nouns is correspondingly large.

Classification systems allow a language to impose order within this set of nouns. Nouns are assigned to different groups, usually on the basis of given semantic features and properties of their referent. Typical semantic features used in noun classification systems are animacy, sex or shape. Nouns referring to animate beings may constitute a class opposed to those for inanimates; males may be contrasted with females; or long objects with round ones. An important difference between gender or noun classification systems of the New Guinea type and the classifier systems typical of southeast Asian languages is that in a noun class system a noun is usually uniquely assigned to a single class, whereas in a classifier system, a given noun may co-occur with more than one classifier, with different semantic features highlighted in each case (Dixon 1982; Becker 1975).

Exceptions to these rules among noun classifying languages often allow the language to economize on the number of noun roots, using the same noun root with different class markers to denote different referents from opposing classes. For example, in the Marind language of Irian Jaya (Drabbe 1955), there is a root *anVm* 'person', where *V* stands for different possible vowels for contrastive classes. If a male human is to be referred to, then *e*, the class marker for male humans, is found: *anem* 'man'. If a female human, then *u*, the class marker for female humans, is used: *anum* 'woman'. If the referent is plural, rather than singular, the plural marker *i* is employed: *anim* 'people', e.g. *Marind-anim* 'the Marind tribe'.

From the Marind example it should be apparent that one of the functions of noun classes is the more precise delimitation of nominal referring expressions. By applying *e* versus *u* versus *i* to the undifferentiated base *anVm* 'person', one may delineate clearly the intended referent: 'man' versus 'woman' versus 'people'. In Papuan languages the delimitation of possible referents of nominals is unquestionably the major function of the overt noun classification systems. In ongoing discourse in Papuan languages, the function of these systems is heavily anaphoric: to trace the referents of nominals through the discourse and to indicate, at least in part, whether two nominals have the same referent or not. That it is this anaphoric function of classification which is most basic, rather than the semantic grouping of nouns, is amply demonstrated by the presence, in two unrelated Papuan language families, the Torricelli and Lower Sepik families, of classification determined by the phonological shape of the noun, by its final consonant or syllable. As this classification is completely arbitrary semantically, it shows that semantic grouping cannot be the central role of classification. Further, as these languages have extensive concord, both within the phrase and within the governing verb, as well as very heavy ellipsis of nominal arguments, it is clearly the referential tracking function which is most important here: it is the noun class markers which allow tracking of participants through the discourse.

Considering what was said earlier concerning the constant conventional relationship between nouns and their referents as opposed to the shifting ones of pronouns, it would seem reasonable that classification of nominals would be manifest first in the pronouns and only secondarily (if at all) in the nouns. Because of the small set of pronouns and their anaphoric function, the range of possible referents for pronouns is enormous – the entire set of nouns and noun phrases. Of course, within a given speech act, the problem is less dismaying, as first person pronouns must contain the present speaker as referent and second person pronouns must contain the addressee. But the hapless pronoun of the 'other', the third person pronoun, finds no such support. Even within a given discourse, its potential range is quite large, and may be by no means adequately circumscribed. Hence, it is here that a noun classification system will appear, if in any place in the language. English is an example of a language of this type, in that the gender or noun classification system (the gender distinction) is only manifested in the third person singular: *he, she, it.* English is further typical of noun classifying languages in that the distinction is reduced or neutralized completely in the nonsingular numbers: *they.* Yessan–Mayo (Foreman 1974) exhibits the simplest classifying system found in a Papuan language, and is parallel to English:

	SG	DL	PL
1	*an*	*nis*	*nim*
2	*ni*	*kep*	*kem*
3M	*ri*	*rip*	*rim*
F	*ti*		

Like English, Yessan–Mayo has a gender distinction in the singular, but not in the nonsingular numbers. Unlike English, Yessan–Mayo has no neuter category, and so inanimate nouns, although unmarked for gender, are conventionally assigned to a gender class and select the appropriate pronoun: *liyp* 'moon' and *aka* 'house' with the feminine *ti*, and *yabel* 'sun', *me* 'tree' and *ok* 'water' with the masculine *ri*.

Iatmul, Abelam and other languages of the Ndu family extend the gender distinction to the second person singular. Note the Iatmul pronoun system (Staalsen n.d. a):

	SG	DL	PL
1	*wɨn*	*an*	*nɨn*
2M	*mɨn*		*nkwɨk*
F	*nyɨn*	*mpɨk*	
3M	*ntɨ*		*ntɨy*
F	*lɨ*		

And in Ngala, another Ndu language, the gender distinction is extended to the first person singular as well (Laycock 1965):

	SG	DL	PL
1M	w⁺in		
1F	ny⁺in	әyn	nan
2M	m⁺in		
2F	y⁺in	b⁺in	gw⁺in
3M	k⁺ir		
3F	y⁺in	(k⁺)b⁺ir	rәr

Note that the feminine pronouns for second and third singular are homophonous.

Although gender distinctions in the pronominal system are the most basic type of nominal classification system, many languages extend the classification to nouns. For such languages, agreement in class of modifiers with their head noun, and very often of verbs with their subjects or objects, is a common diagnostic feature. Alamblak of the Sepik Hill family (Bruce 1984) is a good example of a language with classification applied to nouns. It possesses a set of suffixes which specify the person, number and gender of the noun or noun phrase. Again, the gender distinction is only present in the singular:

	SG	DL	PL
1	-a	-në	-ném
2	∅	-f⁺in	-kë(m)
3M	-r		
F	-t	-f	-m

Examples of the use of the suffixes are *yima-m*, person-3PL; 'people' and *yima-ném* person-1PL, 'we people'.

Gender in Alamblak differs from gender in French in that many nouns can take either gender suffix, normally with a semantic difference. Nouns denoting human and higher animate beings (like pigs) always select on the basis of natural sex: *yima-r*, person-3SG M, 'man' and *yima-t*, person-3SG F, 'woman'. But nouns denoting lower animate beings and nouns for which sex is irrelevant usually select one gender as the unmarked choice, again largely on a semantic basis. Masculine gender (-*r*) refers to tall or long, slender or narrow objects, while feminine gender (-*t*) is used for typically short, squat or wide objects. The biological basis of this classification is immediately apparent. The following inanimate nouns are masculine because of their long, narrow shape: arrows, spears, string bags, tall slender trees; while the following nouns of different shape are feminine: houses, chairs, fighting shields, round squat trees. Longish, thin animals like fish, crocodiles, pythons or birds are masculine, while other animals are feminine: turtles, frogs, insects and death adders (short squat snakes, usually found in a coiled position).

Many of these nouns which are assigned a gender according to their shape may also occur with the opposite gender when the referent of the noun is atypical as to size or, if the referent is animate, when the sex is highlighted. Thus, *kuñ-* 'house' is normally feminine due to its squat shape, but it may occur with the masculine suffix if it denotes an unusually long house. Similarly, *nërwi-* 'slit drum' is also usually feminine, but may occur with the masculine marker if unusually slender. This implies that it was incorrectly made and its timbre is off. On the other hand *bariy-* 'hornbill' with the feminine instead of the usual masculine suffix indicates that the femaleness of the bird is in focus. Alamblak does have some seemingly arbitrary assignments like *doh-t* 'canoe', which is feminine in spite of its long, arrowlike shape, but some of these arbitrary assignments distinguish between homophonous roots: *ku-t* 'lime gourd' (feminine, but not short, or squat) versus *ku-r* 'molar' (masculine, but not long and narrow).

Gender in Mianmin of the Ok family (Smith and Weston 1974b) functions somewhat like that of Alamblak. Nouns occur with a suffix which specifies gender and number:

	SG	PL
M	*-e*	*-i*
F	*-o*	

With animate nouns the gender suffixes express natural sex: *naka-e*, man-M, 'man', *unang-o* woman-F, 'woman', but with inanimate nouns they express size or quantity. Masculine gender indicates singularity or small size or quantity: *men-e*, string bag-M, 'a string bag', *imen-e*, taro-M, 'small/one taro'. Feminine gender indicates plurality or large size or quantity (inanimate nouns may not occur with the plural suffix *-i*; this is restricted to animate nouns only): *men-o*, string bag-F, 'string bags', *imen-o*, taro-F, 'large taro/quantity of taro'. The roundness and squatness associated with feminine in Alamblak also seems to play a role in Mianmin gender assignment. For example, turtles and crabs are invariably feminine, as is the large, squat, flightless bird, the cassowary. Other birds, narrow and relatively long, are masculine, as in Alamblak, unless their plumage allows identification of their sex.

Mianmin differs from Alamblak in that it exhibits concord for gender between the head noun in a nominal phrase and its associated adjuncts. Alamblak merely adds the person/number/gender suffix to the final element of the nominal phrase. With Mianmin adjectives the gender suffix is optional; it may simply be attached to the final word of the phrase, as in Alamblak:

> *til-(e) nama-(e) sum-e*
> dog-M white-M big-M
> 'big white dog'

Concord between a postposition and its head noun is also possible:

> *tlum-e e lim-e lebaa*
> bridge-M its-M on-M across
> 'across the bridge'
>
> *tebol-o o lim-o wit*
> table-F its-F on-F up
> 'up on the table'

One of the most interesting gender systems found in any Papuan language is that of Marind, of southern Irian Jaya (Drabbe 1955), mentioned briefly above. Marind has a four-way classification of nouns. Gender in Marind is indicated by the final vowel of the stem, and stems often undergo ablaut to indicate gender: *anVm* 'person': *anem* 'man', *anum* 'woman', *anim* 'people'. The first class in Marind consists of male humans: its characteristic vowel is *e*. The second class contains female humans, as well as animals. It is indicated by the vowel *u*. Human nouns of both classes one and two have plural forms indicated by *i*. Thus, for humans and higher animates, we find the system:

	SG	PL
M human	*e*	
F humans/animals	*u*	*i*

Inanimate nouns are divided between classes three and four. These nouns do not have plural forms. Class three consists mainly of plants and trees: it is characterized mainly by *e*, *a* or *o*. Class four is a remnant class including clothing and decorations, some plants and trees, body parts and other diverse objects. It is characterized by *i*. Note the following ablaut patterns deriving nouns of different classes from the same root: *namek* 'brother' (CL 1), *namuk* 'sister' (CL 2), *namik* 'siblings' (PL, CL 1/2), *mbokraved* 'adolescent boy' (CL 1)', *mbokravid* 'adolescent boys' (PL), *vu* 'mother' (CL 2), *vi-sav* 'mothers, aunts' (PL), *namakud* 'animal' (CL 2), *namakad* 'thing(s)' (CL 3), *namakid* 'animals' (PL, CL 2). Exceptions and irregularities abound in the nouns referring to humans; for discussion see Drabbe 1955: 19–20.

Marind requires that adjectives qualifying nouns agree in class with their head nouns. Concord is indicated by ablaut of the final vowel of the adjective of the stem. The characteristic vowels again are: Class 1, *e*, Class 2, *u*, Class 3, *a*, Class 4 and plural of Classes 1 and 2, *i*. Consider the following examples with *akVk* 'light':

e-pe   anem e-pe   akek   ka
CL 1-the man CL 1-the light-CL 1 COP
'the man is light'

u-pe   anum   u-pe   akuk   ka
CL 2-the woman CL 2-the light-CL 2 COP
'the woman is light'

i-pe   anim   i-pe   akik   ka
PL-the people PL-the light-PL COP
'the people are light'

u-pe   ŋgat u-pe   akuk   ka
CL 2-the dog CL 2-the light-CL 2 COP
'the dog is light'

i-pe   ŋgat i-pe   akik   ka
PL-the dog PL-the light-PL COP
'the dogs are light'

e-pe   de   e-pe   akak   ka
CL 3-the wood CL 3-the light-CL 3 COP
'the wood is light'

i-pe   behaw i-pe   akik   ka
CL 4-the pole   CL 4-the light-CL 4 COP
'the pole is light'

For further examples of the ablaut in Marind adjectives and a list of typical adjectives, see Drabbe 1955: 22–3.

The most extensive system of nominal classification in Papuan languages is found in Nasioi and perhaps other Papuan languages of southern Bougainville. The system of Nasioi (Hurd 1977) parallels in certain respects the numeral classifier systems of southeast Asia. Nasioi presents a set of well over a hundred suffixes which are added to nouns, adjectives, numerals and even derived nominalized verbs to classify the referent of the head words. The classifiers number over 100, and are very specific semantically, such as *-ruta* 'eye', *-vo* 'mother and children', *-vari* 'tree', *-va* 'house', *-neʔ* 'paper, leaf, feather', *-raampu* 'tens of sago shingles' (see Hurd 1977: 162–7 for a comprehensive list). These classify nouns much like the well known numeral classifiers of southeast Asian languages (compare Becker's (1975) example of Burmese with the following):

nto-na-ruʔ
water-DER-fluid unit
'drop, container, lake of water'

nto-na-ri
water-DER-stream
'stream, river of water'

pooroʔ-koo-na-ruta
pig-PART-DER-eye
'pig's eye'

pooroʔ-koo-na-kang
pig-PART-DER-family
'family of pigs'

pooroʔ-koo-∅-naare
pig-PART-DER-talk
'complaint about a pig'

ke-vin-ta
two-vine-DL
'two vines, ropes'

kare-mii-ri
four-hills-PL
'four hills, mountains, ridges'

kare-vari-ru
four-tree-PL
'four trees'

Like Marind, Nasioi exhibits concord of all adjuncts with the head noun:

*nto-na-***ruʔ**	*bee-***ruʔ**-pi	*a-***ruʔ**-daang
water-DER-fluid unit	three-fluid unit-PL	this fluid unit-inland
'those three lakes inland there'		

In this pattern of concord, Nasioi differs from the typical numeral classifying languages of southeast Asia, which usually have only one occurrence of the classifier in the NP, and is rather more like the multiple classifying languages with adjectival concord found in New Guinea. The classification system of this language must be recognized as an intermediate type, not corresponding neatly either to the numerical classification systems typified by southeast Asian languages, nor to the more usual noun class/gender languages of New Guinea, but showing features of both.

The most unusual noun-class systems in New Guinea are found in two different language groups of the Sepik region: the Torricelli and Lower Sepik families. In these languages, the assignment of the bulk of noun-stems to their corresponding class is on the basis of their phonological stem. As far as is known, this feature is unique among the languages of the world. Fortune's (1942) grammar of Arapesh discusses the intricate system of nominal classification in this Torricelli language in considerable detail. A more recent study of the same topic in this language is Nekitel (1979). Grammars of other Torricelli languages which treat the nominal classification systems exist for Monumbo (Vormann and Scharfenberger 1914) and Olo (McGregor and McGregor 1982). Here I will illustrate this type of noun-class system with Yimas of the Lower Sepik family.

Yimas has around a dozen distinct noun-classes. All nouns obligatorily indicate both class and number (singular, dual and plural), and in some classes 'portmanteau morphemes' indicating both categories are found. All modifiers of a noun must agree with the head noun in number and class:

> *ama-na-ŋki-i*   *triŋk-i*   *mamakɨ-ŋk-i*
> 1SG-POSS-CL VI-PL tooth CL VI-PL bad-CL VI-PL
> *k-ramnaw-t*   *k-ia-k*
> CL VI-three-PL   CL VI-PL-this
> 'these three bad teeth of mine'

The concord affixes in Yimas are divided into two types, basically the adjectival set and the verbal set. Both types for class VI are illustrated above. The adjectival set are suffixes, and generally of the same phonological form as the final consonant or consonant cluster of the stem for the vast bulk of inanimate nouns whose class membership is determined phonologically. In the above example *triŋk* 'tooth' is a class VI noun, signalled by the stem ending in *-ŋk*. The possessive and adjective modifiers must agree in class with *triŋk*, and so they are suffixed with the adjectival suffix for class VI *-ŋk* and the plural morpheme *-i*. The other two modifiers occur with a different morpheme, the prefix *k-*. This is the verbal agreement marker for class VI. Yimas verbs agree in class and number with their central nominal participants, subject, object and indirect object. The verbal agreement markers are always prefixes, corresponding to the final consonant and sometimes to the preceding vowel of the noun stem. The class markers are followed by prefixes indicating number:

> *triŋk-i*   *k-ia-mpu-tupul*
> tooth CL VI-PL   CL VI-PL-3PL-hit
> 'they hit my teeth'

tanɨmp-ɨl   *p-ɨla-mpu-tupul*
bone CL VII-DL   CL VII-DL-3PL-hit
'they hit my two bones'

In the example on the previous page, the numeral and the demonstrative occur with the verbal concord prefix *k-*, indicating agreement with the class VI head noun *trɨŋk* 'tooth'. The numerals 'two' and 'three' and the demonstratives are nominal modifiers which consistently take the verbal agreement prefixes, rather than the adjectival suffixes. The numerals 'one' and 'four', on the other hand, occur with the adjectival suffixes, not the verbal prefixes.

Of the dozen Yimas noun-classes, four are semantic in basis, while the other eight are phonologically determined. The semantically based classes correspond to one for male humans, another for female humans, a third for higher animals like pigs, dogs, cassowaries and crocodiles, and the fourth for plants and plant products with an important function in the culture. This system can be represented diagrammatically as:

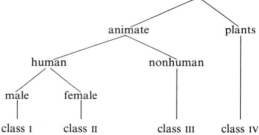

Classes I, II and III are morphologically similar in many respects, and seem to have developed from a single animate class in an earlier stage of the language. Classes I and II are identical in their verbal prefix forms: *na-* singular, *impa-* dual and *(m)pu-* plural, while class III is only distinguished by having a different form *tɨma-* for the dual verbal prefix. With regard to the nominal forms and the adjectival suffixes, classes I and III are the most similar, the only significant difference being the plural morphemes on the nouns themselves: *-um* for class I and *-wi* for class III. Class II is quite different in the nominal stem forms and adjectival suffixes. The system for classes I, II and III can be set out as follows:

	Class I	Class II	Class III
	Human males	Human females	Animals
SG noun	∅	*-maŋ*	∅
adj	*-n*	*-nmaŋ*	*-n*
verb	*na-*	*na-*	*na-*
DL noun	*-rɨm*	*-mprum*	*-rɨm*

adj	*-rɨm*	*-nprum*	*-rɨm*
verb	*impa-*	*impa-*	*tɨma-*
PL noun	*-um*	*-mput*	*-wi*
adj	*-um*	*-nput*	*-um*
verb	*pu-*	*pu-*	*pu-*

The adjectival suffixes for class II are clearly derived from adding the nominal markings for class II to the singular adjective concord for class I, with reduction of the resulting nasal cluster in the dual and plural: *-n + -mprum > -nprum, -n + -mput > -nput*.

Class IV, that of plants, is completely different in morphology from classes I to III. The morphological pattern of this class is the same as for those whose membership is determined phonologically. In all but one of these classes the dual is formed by suffixing *-il ∼ -ul* (rounded if the vowel of the previous syllable was /u/) to the class markers, and this applies to class IV as well. As the singular class marker for class IV is *-um*, the dual is *-umul*. The plural is rather irregular. The *-m* is dropped and the plural is signalled by *-ɲi*. So, 'tree species' singular *kwarum*, dual *kwarumul*, plural *kwaruɲi*. The adjectival suffixes correspond to the nominal endings except in the plural, for which the suffix is *-ra*. Another general feature of the inanimate phonologically based classes is that the verbal prefixes are derived from the shape of the final one or two segments of the nominal stem. If the stem ends in a consonant cluster, the verbal prefix is simply the final consonant. If the stem ends in a VC sequence, then the verbal prefix is simply the metathesis of this: CV-. As the marker of this class is *-um*, the singular verbal prefix is, as expected, *mu-*. The dual is regularly formed: *mu-ul-a-*, but the plural is, as with the noun and adjective endings, irregular: *∅-i-a*, with no overt class marker. In Yimas, the plural adjective *-ra* and the verbal prefix *∅-i-a* always correspond.

The number of inanimate phonologically based classes in Yimas is somewhat arbitrarily determined; but I will select as the criterion the existence of a distinct series of adjectival suffixes. By this criterion there are seven distinct phonologically based classes for inanimate nouns, falling into two subgroups. One group, class V, by far the largest in the language, contains all nouns ending in *-p, -t, -k, -m, -n, -ŋ, -r*, or *-l*. This class is similar morphologically in many ways to classes I to III, and they seem in large part to be specialization of this class V. The singular and dual of class V are identical to class III, but the plural is quite different. Class V nouns occur with a number of allomorphs of the plural morpheme: *-t, -ra* and *-i*. The adjective suffix for plural is invariably *-ra* and the corresponding verbal prefis is *∅-i-a*.

The other subgroup of inanimate classes contains the other six classes. They all share a great deal in their morphological formation, and by and large follow the rules outlined for class IV above. The dual is formed from the singular by a suffix *-il* ~ *-ul*, and the verbal prefixes derive from the final segment(s) of the nominal stem. The singular and dual are regularly formed in all but one of these classes, but the plurals are rather more idiosyncratic.

Class VI nouns are indicated by a stem final cluster *-ŋk*, and class VII by *-mp*. Classes VIII and IX are vocalic final: *-i* and *-aw* respectively. Finally, classes X and XI are indicated by final segments *-u* + velar, and differ in the corresponding plural markers: *-i* versus *-at*. Table 1 summarizes the system for classes IV–XI. A few of each of the classes are presented:

class IV: *tɨnum* 'sago palm', *irɨpum* 'coconut palm', *pɨlum* 'plant species', *maŋkum* 'vein'

class V: *tɨkɨt* 'chair', *numpuk* 'mountain', *wakɨn* 'snake', *yan* 'tree', *awak* 'star'

class VI: *kaŋk* 'shell', *trɨŋk* 'tooth', *pamuŋk* 'leg', *krayŋk* 'frog'

class VII: *impramp* 'basket', *nampurɨmp* 'wing', *tampaymp* 'hanger', *tanɨmp* 'bone'

class VIII: *awi* 'axe', *awtmayŋi* 'sugar cane', *nɨŋay* 'breast'

class IX: *trukwaw* 'knee', *ŋarwaw* 'penis', *yaw* 'road', *maywaw* 'side of abdomen'

class X: *antuk* 'mouth', *awruk* 'bandicoot', *naŋkupuk* 'meat'

class XI: *awŋk* 'egg', *mpunawŋk* 'elbow', *paynawŋk* 'scrotum', *kawŋk* 'wall'

It is clear from this small inventory that there is no semantic basis for the classification, which is determined on phonological grounds.

The noun classification systems of the Torricelli and Lower Sepik languages, here exemplified in some detail by Yimas, are among the most complex in the world and represent an extreme development in New Guinea. Nominal classification is a widespread feature in New Guinea, but in a language like Yimas it is all-pervasive, and much of the grammar revolves around the presence of such an elaborate system. Yimas discourse is highly elliptical, and the concordial system – especially with respect to verbs – is fundamental in the tracking of referents in discourse. This will be discussed in some detail in Chapter 6.

Thus far, I have been concerned with Papuan languages which display overt nominal classification in some portion of their nominal systems, either pronouns or nouns; but there are many other Papuan languages which possess a rather different, covert nominal classification system, in which nouns are placed into groups according to the different verb-roots with which they express the concept of existence. This was first analysed in detail in Lang 1975, which discusses the classificatory verb system in Enga. Enga has seven different verb-roots used with different classes of nouns. Thus, 'there are men' is expressed in Enga as 'the man

Table 1 *Inflections of Yimas nominal classes IV–XI*

		Class IV	Class V	Class VI	Class VII	Class VIII	Class IX	Class X	Class XI
SG	noun	-um	-p,t,k,m,n,ŋ,r,l	-ŋk	-mp	-i	-aw	-uk	-uŋk
	adj	-um	-n	-ŋk	-mp	-i	-aw	-uŋk	-uŋk
	verb	mu-	na-	k-	p-	i-	wa-	ku-	ku-
DL	noun	-um-ul	-rɨm	-ŋk-ɨl	-mp-ɨl	-i-l	-u-l	-uk-ul	-uŋk-ul
	adj	-um-ul	-rɨm	-ŋk-ɨl	-mp-ɨl	-i-l	-u-l	-uŋk-ul	-uŋk-ul
	verb	mu-ul-a-	tima-	k-ɨl-a-	p-ɨl-a-	i-l-a-	wɨ-l-a-	ku-l-a-	ku-l-a-
PL	noun	-ɲi	-t,-ra,-i	-ŋk-i	-mp-at	-mpɨt	-ut	-at	-uŋkwi
	adj	-ra	-ra	-ŋk-i	-ra	-ra	-ut	-ra	-uŋkwi
	verb	φ-i-a-	φ-i-a-	k-i-a-	φ-i-a-	φ-i-a-	ul-a-	φ-i-a-	ku-i-a-

stands', while 'there are women' is 'the woman sits'. This active, erect, longish classification for man, as opposed to the passive round, squat classification for woman is widespread in New Guinea (compare, for example, the Alamblak gender system discussed above), and has obvious biological foundations. The seven Enga classificatory verbs and their associated nominal classes are set out below (Lang 1975):

> *katengé* 'stand' for referents judged to be tall, large, strong, powerful, standing or supporting. Typical nouns: *akáli* 'men'; *ándá* 'house', *itá* 'tree'.
>
> *pentengé* 'sit' for referents judged to be small, squat, horizontal and weak. Typical nouns: *énda* 'woman', *saá* 'possum', *peté* 'pond'.
>
> *lyingí* 'hang' for referents hanging or protruding out of another object. Typical nouns: *ambúlyá* 'wasp, bee', *líti* 'mushroom', *dii* 'fruit, seed, flower'.
>
> *palengé* 'lie inside' for referents internal or subterranean. Typical nouns: *imú* 'worm', *móna* 'heart', *mapú* 'sweet potato'.
>
> *epengé* 'come' for referents which are intermittent, capable of growth, or liquid or gas. Typical nouns: *aiyúu* 'rain', *iti* 'fur, feathers', *taiyóko* 'blood'.
>
> *singe* 'lie' for referents which are orifices, locations, or crawling or aquatic. Typical nouns: *yuú* 'ground, land', *wapáká* 'eels', *néngekaita* 'mouth'.
>
> *mandenge* 'carry' for referents of sexual reproduction. Typical nouns: *pongó* 'penis', *kambáke* 'vagina', *ipi* 'testicles'.

This system of classification by verbs is similar to the gender system of Alamblak, in that a given noun may shift its class affiliation if its typical semantic features are altered in certain ways. Thus *itá* 'tree' usually collocates with *katengé* 'stand' because of its typical tall, erect position: *itá dúpa kate-ngé*, tree the stand-HABIT, 'there are trees'. If the tree is cut down, it no longer 'stands', but now 'lies': *itá poká-pae sí-nge*, tree cut-STATE lie-HABIT, 'there are (felled) trees'. Further, when the felled tree is cut into logs and organized in a wood pile, it 'lies inside': *itá tamó-pae pale-ngé*, tree rotten-STATE lie inside-HABIT, 'there is rotten wood'. These data demonstrate that the verbal classification is not a rigid formal system like gender in French or German, but rather a productive meaning-bearing system which highlights certain semantic features of an object relevant to our perceptual and physical interaction with it.

Waris (Brown 1981) has a classificatory verb system for existentials very similar to that of Enga, but has a further complication. It also employs classificatory prefixes with verbs to specify salient semantic features of their object noun:

> *wonda   ka-m mwan-vra-ho-o*
> net bag I-DAT CLASF-get-BEN-IMP
> 'give me a net bag'

> *nenas   ka-m li-ra-ho-o*
> pineapple I-DAT CLASF-get-BEN-IMP
> 'give me a pineapple'

Mwan- is the classifier for soft pliable objects like net bags, skirts, bark mats, while *li-* denotes oblong fruit objects like pineapples, ears of corn or pandanus fruits. Other classifiers in Waris include:

vela-	objects found inside a container
put-	spherical objects, typically fruit
ninge-	food cooked and distributed in leaf wrappers
vet-	food removed from fire ready to eat, without wrapper
lé-	leaf-like objects with soft or no stem
pola-	leaf-like objects with hard stem
ih-	grainy materials
tuvv-	pieces cut from longer lengths
kov-	lengths of vine

These prefixes are always added to verbs to express the relevant semantic features of their object nouns. As Seiler (1983) has pointed out, these classificatory verbal prefixes probably derive from earlier compounds of two verbs (see Chapter 5), in which the first verb has been re-analysed as one of these prefixes. Note that a number of the classificatory prefixes are closely related in form and meaning to an independent verb:

lev-	'cut off oblong fruit'
velau-	'remove'
puetv-	'pick fruit'
ningev-	'tie up'
ihv-	'remove grainy material from container'
tuvvav-	'chop into lengths'
kovvav-	'cut off (as vine)'

Thus, a sentence like

> *nelus ka-m ninge-ra-ho-o*
> greens I-DAT CLASF-get-BEN-IMP
> 'give me some greens'

presumably at an earlier stage meant something like 'tie up and get me some greens', but as the first verb was somewhat redundant in the context of the object, and simply specified the typical way of manipulating the object in the culture, it gradually lost its meaning as an independent verb, and became merely a classificatory prefix.

4.5 **Case systems**

Gender systems in languages attend to the highlighting of selected semantic features of the referent of a given noun. They are important in providing cues for the correct identification of referents of nominals in ongoing discourse. Gender is a grammatical feature concerned with the nominal itself and its extra-linguistic relations. Case is fundamentally different. It expresses relations internal to the linguistic system, relations between the nominal and its governing verb or between it and another nominal. Ongoing discourse in any language is a description of a sequence of events, actions or states. Central to any utterance in a discourse are the verbs, which express the events, actions or states; but equally necessary are the nominals expressing participants experiencing the events or states or performing the actions. In addition, a given utterance may contain nominals expressing props or goals of the action as well as its spatial or temporal coordinates. It is the function of case to indicate these semantic relations that nominals bear to verbals: whether performing or undergoing an action, whether the starting point or the end point, or whether a secondary cause or instrument in accomplishing the action. Languages employ a number of different means to indicate these case relations. Consider the following English sentences:

> *Mary killed John*
> *John killed Mary*

It is immediately apparent to any speaker of English that these two sentences do not have the same meaning. In the first example, it is Mary who does the killing and John who is killed, but in the second sentence, the opposite is true. For English, word-order plays a crucial role in expressing case relations. With a simple active verb, the nominal immediately before the verb functions as the performer of the action and that immediately after it as the undergoer. English has a secondary means of indicating case for other types of semantic relations:

> *Mary rented a flat **from** John*
> *John rented a flat **to** Mary*

In these examples English uses the prepositions *from* and *to* to indicate the starting and ending points respectively of a transaction. In English, the use of prepositions to indicate case relations is very common:

> *John died **from** malaria **in** the hospital*
> *John bought sago **for** Mary **in** the market **with** his salary **on** Friday*

The use of word order and prepositions/postpositions is common as a means of expressing case relations among the languages of the world, including Papuan ones.

Yessan–Mayo (Foreman 1974), Iatmul (Staalsen 1972) and Fore (Scott 1978) all use word-order to a certain extent, and postpositions are a feature of many Papuan languages. But Papuan postpositions contrast with English prepositions in that they generally express rather concrete locational notions like *above, under, beside, inside, along* rather than the more abstract semantic relations of instrument or beneficiary expressed by *with* or *for*. Instead of postpositions for these, Papuan languages use bound case affixes, along with many other languages of the world, notably the classical Indo-European languages like Greek, Sanskrit and Latin. Consider the following examples from Kewa (Franklin 1971):

> *ada-**para**   pá-lua*
> house-LOC go-1SG FUT
> 'I will go home'

> *ní-**ná** méáá-ria*
> I-BEN get-3SG PAST
> 'he got it for me'

> *ní paalá-**mé** ómá-lo*
> I fright-CAUSE die-1SG PRES
> 'I am afraid'

> *áá-**mé**   mena maapú-**para** tá-a*
> man-ERG pig   garden-LOC hit-3SG PAST
> 'the man hit the pig in the garden'

Spatial concepts expressed in English simply by prepositions like *along, inside* or *underneath* are expressed in Kewa by postpositions suffixed with an appropriate case marker: *ru-para*, inside-LOC, 'inside' or *rolo-para*, under-LOC, 'underneath', as, for example, in *ada ru-para*, house inside-LOC, 'inside the house'. The situation in Kewa is typical for Papuan languages. The more concrete spatial notions are expressed by postpositions, usually in combination with bound case affixes, but the more basic case relations are expressed directly, by whatever formal means the language employs.

In addition to word-order constraints and bound case affixes to nominals, there is a third means available for expressing case relations: the presence of affixes to the governing verb agreeing in person and number, and often in gender, with a nominal of a particular case relation. This method of indicating case relations is extremely widespread in Papuan languages, and I will illustrate this method with Yimas, a language for which this is the primary means for signalling case relations. Yimas has a single bound nominal case suffix, *-in ~ -nan*, which marks locational or instrumental nominals, while the other, more basic, case relations are indicated by verbal affixes in concord for person, number and gender with their corresponding nominal. The case relations signalled in this way are the performer of the action or the actor, the undergoer of the action, event, or state, the recipient of an act of transfer like giving, and the beneficiary of an action. Consider the following examples:

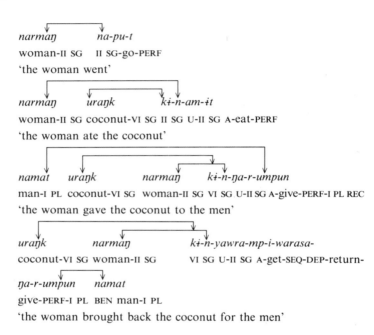

narmaŋ   *na-pu-t*

woman-II SG   II SG-go-PERF

'the woman went'

narmaŋ   *uraŋk*   *kɨ-n-am-ɨt*

woman-II SG coconut-VI SG II SG U-II SG A-eat-PERF

'the woman ate the coconut'

namat   *uraŋk*   *narmaŋ*   *kɨ-n-ŋa-r-umpun*

man-I PL coconut-VI SG   woman-II SG VI SG U-II SG A-give-PERF-I PL REC

'the woman gave the coconut to the men'

uraŋk   *narmaŋ*   *kɨ-n-yawra-mp-i-warasa-*

coconut-VI SG woman-II SG   VI SG U-II SG A-get-SEQ-DEP-return-

ŋa-r-umpun   *namat*

give-PERF-I PL BEN man-I PL

'the woman brought back the coconut for the men'

The above examples are perfectly grammatical sentences with the nominals omitted, with just the affixed verbs. When the nominals are present, they may occur in any order, word-order not being significant for case relations in Yimas.

Generally, it is the position of the affix in the verbal complex which signals the particular case relation, although for certain person and number combinations there are distinct forms for the performer versus the undergoer of the action: *ka-* is the first person singular form for the actor, while *ŋa-* is that for the undergoer. The first or outermost prefix to the verb is normally that for the undergoer of the action, while that closest to the verb stem(s) is that of the actor. The second example with two nominals associated with the verb *am-* 'eat' illustrates this. For sentences containing three nominal arguments, adding a beneficiary or recipient to the already present actor and undergoer (as with sentences involving *ŋa-* 'give'), an additional agreement suffix occurs, as in the third and fourth examples above.

While, on the whole, this is an efficient means of signalling case relations, it is not entirely without problems. For example, if two nominals governed by the same verb are associated with verbal affixes of the same morphological form, it is not possible to determine unambiguously the case relations:

> *narmaŋ*   *namarawt*   *na-n-tupul*
> woman-II SG man-I SG   I/II SG U-I/II SG A-hit
> 'the woman hit the man' or
> 'the man hit the woman'

While *narmaŋ* 'woman' and *namarawt* 'man' belong to two different classes, as determined by their adjectival and possessive concord suffixes, they nonetheless have identical verbal affixes. Consequently, there is no way in the above sentence to determine which nominal is actor and which is undergoer. In ongoing discourse this is less of a problem, because the language does possess means to signal whether an actor participant changes from one clause to the next; but in isolation such sentences remain ambiguous. It is conceivable that word-order could be invoked here, so that the actor must precede the undergoer in such cases, and this does seem to be the solution in other languages with similar verbal means for indicating case relations, as in Lakhota (Van Valin 1977), but it does not seem to be the case for Yimas. All languages have situations where their case signalling devices break down and ambiguity results, and this type of situation exemplified by Yimas is quite typical for languages with verbal systems for case relations.

I have dwelt at some length on a verb-based system for signalling case relations because, to a greater or lesser extent, this is typical of Papuan languages generally. The vast majority of Papuan languages use verbal affixation for at least one type of case relation, and very many use it for more than one. Papuan languages also usually supplement the verbal signalling of case relations with constraints on word-order and nominal case marking, and a number of languages use all three. The typical Papuan case marking system may be summarized as the use of verbal affixes, often in combination with word-order and/or nominal case affixes, for the central participants, actor and undergoer, and the use of nominal case markers for nominals functioning as adjuncts to the action or specifying its location. Thus, typically in Papuan languages, locative or instrumental nominals occur with suffixed case markers. From this point of view, one can regard Yimas as a model Papuan language (albeit an extreme one). The central participants, actor and undergoer, as well as the recipient and beneficiary, are indicated purely by verbal affixes, there being no word-order constraints or bound nominal case marking of any kind for these case relations. The instrumental adjunct nominals and all locational-type nominals are signalled by the single case suffix *-in ~ -nan*, and for these there are no corresponding verbal affixes or word-order constraints. This is the Papuan case marking schema boiled down to its essence: verbal affixation for the core participants and nominal case for the peripheral ones. This is not to say that nominal case suffixes are never used for core participants – they certainly are in some languages – nor that there may be cases of adjuncts or locational nominals being signalled by verbal affixes, as is occasionally found in Amerindian and Bantu languages; but these are only superficial embellishments on the basic principle enunciated above.

I will define the core participants or case relations (those likely to be expressed by verbal affixation) as the performer of an action or actor and the corresponding undergoer. The peripheral relations are those associated with adjuncts of the action, such as instruments, or those associated with its locational or temporal coordinates. Between these two rather clearcut categories there is an indistinct middle ground: the typically animate, intended goal of an action, i.e. its beneficiary or the recipient of verbs like 'give'. I will refer to these as dative nominals, adopting the usual name for the corresponding case in Indo-European languages.

Papuan languages split on this point into a number of groups. Some behave like Yimas, in which the dative nominals are assimilated to the class of core relations and are indicated by verbal affixation. For another group of languages, datives are assimilated to the class of peripheral relations and are suffixed with nominal case markers, as in these Iatmul examples (Staalsen 1972; n.d. a):

> *ntɨw ŋkəy-mpa waalə vɨ-ntɨ*
> man house-LOC dog see-3SG M
> 'the man saw the dog in the house'

> *ntɨw ampɨwntɨy-mpayə-ntɨ*
> man Ambunti-LOC come-3SG M
> 'the man came from Ambunti'

> *ntɨw kwɨla-mpa vɨyə-ntɨ*
> man axe-INSTR hit-3SG M
> 'the man hit (it) with an axe'

> *ntɨw waalə-nkətyɨ-ntɨ*
> man dog-ALL go-3SG M
> 'the man went to the dog'

> *ntɨw waalə wɨ-ŋkət kwɨy-ntɨ*
> man dog I-ALL give-3SG M
> 'the man gave me the dog'

Core relations in Iatmul are indicated by the absence of nominal case marking and, in the case of the actor, by a verb affix agreeing in person, number and gender. Peripheral relations are signalled by one of two case suffixes: *-(ŋk)ət*, an allative suffix indicating place toward which an action is directed, and a 'general' case suffix *-mpa*, covering instruments, locations and the place from which an action proceeds, the ablative. For Iatmul, the dative nominals (the recipient and beneficiary) are treated simply as allatives, suffixed with that case affix, and hence must be regarded as peripheral nominals for this language.

Yet a third possibility is exemplified by those Papuan languages in which a beneficiary may appear either as a core or as a peripheral nominal. In all such attested cases, there is no simple dative case corresponding to both recipients and beneficiaries, but a distinct case for each; and the alternation applies only to beneficiary nominals, as recipients are unexceptionally core. Barai of the Koiarian family (Olson 1981) illustrates this pattern well:

> *fu na kan-ie*
> he I strike-1SG
> 'he struck me'

> *bu iro fu-one a vaj-a*
> they yam he-POSS you give-2SG
> 'they gave you his yams'

> *na fu-efuo ire kira-ke*
> I he-BEN food prepare-FUT
> 'I will prepare food for him'

> *na a ire kira-j-a*
> I you food prepare-BEN-2SG
> 'I am preparing food for you'

In the first example the verb is associated with an actor and undergoer. Both nominals are suffixless, indicating their core status, and this is further demonstrated for the undergoer by the fact that it is also indicated by a verbal suffix agreeing in person and number. For the second example, with the verb 'give', the recipient nominal is unquestionably core as well, as it is unaffixed and is in agreement with the corresponding verbal suffix. The final two examples demonstrate the alternation for beneficiary nominals between core and peripheral status. In the former example, the beneficiary is peripheral: it occurs with the nominal case suffix *-efuo* and is not in agreement with a verbal suffix. But in the latter sentence, it is core, demonstrated by its being unaffixed and the corresponding verbal suffix agreeing in person and number.

The Barai pattern is closely related to, and presumably a historical development from, the treatment of beneficiaries in Fore, Hua, Dani and other languages of the highlands (see Whitehead 1981). In these languages a beneficiary may again appear either as core or peripheral, but when core, it always occurs in combination with a compounded verb structure, containing either 'give' or 'put', as in these Hua examples (Haiman 1980):

> *dgai-siʔ zuʔ   kie*
> I-BEN   house build 3sG DECL
> 'he built a house for me'

> *zu   ki-na   d-te*
> house build-3sG 1sG-put 3sG DECL
> 'he built me a house'

The first sentence contains a peripheral beneficiary suffixed with the benefactive case marker *-siʔ*, while the second involves a core beneficiary, occurring as the undergoer prefix to the verb *-to* 'put'. Such compounded verb structures for core beneficiary nominals are very widespread (see, for example, the earlier Yimas examples), and quite probably the sources, by re-analysis of the compounded verbs 'give' or 'put', of the benefactive verb suffixes, as in Barai above or Waris (Brown 1981).

Having established the division between the core and peripheral case relations, and discussed the middle-ground dative nominals, I wish now to develop an (admittedly sketchy) typology of case-marking in Papuan languages. As the core and peripheral case relations generally behave very differently in this regard, I will treat them in turn, beginning with the peripheral ones. As defined above, the peripheral case relations are those associated with the adjuncts or props of the action, such as secondary causes of the action or manipulated objects used as instruments, as well as those of the locational or temporal coordinates of the action. These locational case relations can be rather complex, comprising the place at which an action occurs, its place of origin or its place of destination, as well as the surface or interior of the location. I will here recognize five basic case relations of the peripheral type: instrumental (INSTR), the relation of an object manipulated by the actor used as a secondary cause in bringing about a change of state in the undergoer, as in *John cut the tree **with an axe***; causal (CAUSE), the relation of an uncontrolled, unmanipulated, but also nonvolitional entity bringing about a change of state or experience in the undergoer, as in *I'm shivering **from the cold***; locative (LOC), the relation of the place at which the action occurs, as in *I saw him **at the store***; ablative (ABL), the relation of the place or entity from which the action proceeds, as in *light emanates **from the sun***;

allative (ALL), the relation of the place or entity toward which an action proceeds, as in *I walked **to the house***. Semantically, the allative (ALL), and the sometimes core, sometimes peripheral, dative relation of recipient (REC) are related as the end point toward which the action is directed, and this is reflected in the English preposition: *I walked to the house* (ALL) and *I gave the book to Mary* (REC). Generally Papuan languages contrast with English in not recognizing the relationship between allatives and recipients and treat them quite differently morphologically. Only for that minority of languages in which recipients are invariably treated as peripheral is there any relationship between them and the allative, and for such languages, generally the allative case marker is used in both cases, as in the Iatmul examples above. In most Papuan languages, allative and recipient nominals are distinct.

The simplest case-marking system for peripheral case relations in any Papuan language is that of Yimas: all peripheral nominals are case-marked identically, with the suffix *-in ~ -nan*. From the undifferentiated system of Yimas, binary systems develop in three ways. One system, only attested by Iatmul (Staalsen n.d. a), contrasts an allative with all others. The Iatmul allative covers the recipient nominal, and this may contain the underlying motivation for such a system: the intended end point of the action opposed to everything else. The second binary system is more common, and is the basis of the more developed peripheral case systems of many highlands languages. In this type, represented by Dani (Bromley 1981), a distinct case-form for the locative and allative is opposed to a single case inflection for the instrumental, causal and ablative relations. The grouping of these three is semantically comprehensible, albeit in an inexplicit way, in that they all express something from which the action proceeds, either the place (ablative) or the involuntary causing force (causal) or the manipulated object used to cause the change in state (instrumental). For a number of languages with this grouping, however, causal is not included because it is viewed as a core argument, an involuntary actor, and I will treat this in Chapter 5 in discussing the behaviour of different verb-classes with core participants. Fore is a language lacking a peripheral causal case, but in other respects its case system is simply an elaboration of that of Dani. Fore has a case marker *-ti* which is used for both allative and locative functions and two more specific locative suffixes, *-taʔ* and *-piN*, indicating exterior and interior position respectively. The ablative and instrumental case suffixes are transparently derived from the allative and locative case endings by suffixing *-sa* to them: thus, *-ti + sa*, *-piN + sa* or *-taʔ + sa* for ablative and *-taʔ + sa* for instrumental. Fore parallels Dani in exhibiting a conflated category of allative/locative and one of ablative/instrumental. The situation is more complicated than for Dani in that the conflation of cases is not complete, but nonetheless, the same basic system is present. Such an opposition of ablative/instrumental versus locative/allative seems to be basic in many highlands languages, as, for example, Hua (Haiman 1980).

The third binary system is found in Kewa (Franklin 1971) and other languages of the Engan family. In Kewa the instrumental and causal cases are opposed to the ablative, locative and allative. This grouping is semantically transparent: causes – either involuntary forces or manipulated objects – versus locations – places in which an action occurs, or from which it proceeds, or toward which it is directed. Thus there is an important typological contrast in highlands languages concerning the status of the ablative. The Engan languages group it with the other locational cases, the locative and allative, whereas others, like Dani or Fore, group it with the causal cases, specifically the instrumental. I summarize the case systems discussed thus far as follows:

	Yimas	Iatmul	Dani	Fore	Kewa
INSTR				$-ta?+sa$	$-mé$
CAUSE			$-nen$		
ABL	$-in \sim -nan$	$-mpa$		$-ta? \sim ti \sim piN+sa$	
LOC			$-ma$	$-ti, -ta?, -piN$	$-para$
ALL		$-(\eta k)\partial t$		$-ti$	

I have been unable to locate a single example of a ternary system among Papuan languages. If such a system occurs, I would expect it to be characterized by the emergence of a further distinction among the locational cases, either a distinct ablative or an allative. An *a priori* plausible, but nonetheless hypothetical, ternary system would be one in which the allative emerges as distinct from the locative, but the ablative, instrumental and causal remain conflated. I would expect to find this in New Guinea (it is the bridge from the binary systems to the following quaternary system), but an example has not yet come to light.

A quaternary system is found in Alamblak (Bruce 1984), which has separate case forms for instrumental, locative and allative, but conflates the causal and ablative:

INSTR	$-e$
CAUSE	
ABL	$-pn\ddot{e}$
LOC	$-n$
ALL	$-ko$

Other attested quaternary systems arise by default: they are basically quinary systems, but lack a peripheral causal case. As noted above, this has been treated as a kind of actor and hence functions as a core case relation. Such systems are widespread and include Kâte (Pilhofer 1933) and Selepet (McElhanon 1972) of the Finisterre–Huon group and Kunimaipa (Geary 1977):

	Kâte	Selepet	Kunimaipa
INSTR	-zi	-ŋe	-nanga
ABL	-o-nek	-ɔn-gebɔ	-hananga
LOC	-o	-ɔn	-ha
ALL	o-pek	-ɔn-gen	-ti

The Kâte and Selepet ablative and allative case suffixes are clearly derived by using the locative form as the base; specific ablative or allative suffixes are added to the locative suffix.

Quinary case systems in which all cases have distinct forms are as yet unattested among Papuan languages, and are quite rare elsewhere in the world. English, for example, like Alamblak, is a quaternary system: INSTR *with*, CAUSE, ABL *from*, LOC *at* and ALL *to*. It is conceivable that a quinary system may turn up in a Papuan language, but its absence is by no means surprising.

Turning now to the realization of the core case relations, I repeat my earlier contention that they are primarily signalled by concordial verbal affixes. Papuan languages which lack verbal affixes for at least one core case relation are extremely rare. I know of only two, Yessan–Mayo (Foreman 1974) and Podopa (Anderson and Wade 1981); there are probably others, but they clearly constitute a very small minority. Languages without verbal concordial affixes rely on other means for signalling case relations: Podopa, by nominal case-marking and Yessan–Mayo, by nominal case-marking and word-order constraints. Yessan–Mayo has an obligatory word-order of actor–undergoer–verb:

> *an toma mati-ye*
> I talk hear-NR PAST
> 'I heard the talk'

> *an ti-ni aki-ye*
> I she-DAT fear-NR PAST
> 'I was afraid of her'

Animate undergoers are suffixed with the dative case marker *-ni*, while inanimates are not. With verbs involving three arguments, like 'give', the order is actor–recipient–undergoer–verb; but there is some leeway here, in that the recipient and undergoer may shift positions. Because of the difference in animacy between them, there is little likelihood of ambiguity arising here, and further, the animate recipient takes the dative case marker *-ni*, which the inanimate undergoer lacks:

> *an ri-ni awes nuwa-ti*
> I he-DAT food give-FUT
> 'I will give him food'

The same pattern applies to beneficiary nominals:

> *an ri-ni   por wuri pi-ti*
> I   he-DAT pig one shoot-FUT
> 'I will shoot a pig for him'

I have glossed -*ni* as dative because its use on recipient and beneficiary nominals seems to be basic. It is a very common development in languages for a dative case-marker to generalize to animate undergoers, presumably through the shared semantic component of animacy. Languages as disparate as Spanish, Bikol (Mintz 1971) and Hindi, as well as other Papuan languages of the Sepik basin, such as Autuw (Feldman 1983) and Waris (Brown 1981), all exemplify this development. The generalization of the dative case to animate undergoers also has a more systematic basis, as it is exactly such nominals which condition ambiguity in the clause: generally, only animate undergoers are potential actors. The -*ni* case marker always disambiguates such clauses by indicating which of the animate nominals is the undergoer. Theoretically, this should make the Yessan–Mayo word-order constraints superfluous, but this does not seem to be the case; outside of marked word-orders like topicalizations, the actor must precede the undergoer.

For languages with only one core relation marked on the verb, word-order and nominal marking again normally play a case-signalling role, as the case indication in the verb is not sufficient for distinguishing actor from undergoer. Papuan languages with agreement for a single core argument of a transitive verb fall into two groups: on one hand is the majority grouping, exemplified by Iatmul (Staalsen n.d. a), Vanimo (Ross 1980), Kewa (Franklin 1971) and many others, in which it is the actor which is indicated by the verbal affix; on the other hand is the single language Barai, in which it is the undergoer which is marked on the verb. Iatmul (Staalsen n.d. a) has verbal agreement for the single case argument of an intransitive verb:

> *ntïw yɨ-ntï*
> man go-3SG M
> 'the man went'

> *takwə kɨya-lɨ*
> woman die-3SG F
> 'the woman died'

and the actor of a transitive verb:

> *ntïw takwə vɨ-ntï*
> man woman see-3SG M
> 'the man saw the woman'

takwə   ntɨw   vɨ-lɨ
woman man see-3SG F
'the woman saw the man'

Note that exactly the same verbal suffixes indicate the single core argument of intransitive verbs and the actor of the transitive verb. For basic clauses with transitive verbs the actor must precede the undergoer, even though the gender difference in the above examples is sufficient to distinguish which nominal is actor. This constraint is necessary in cases in which both nominals are of the same gender:

ntɨw   nyan   vɨ-ntɨ
man child see-3SG M
'the man saw the child'
*'the child saw the man'

If we adopt Dixon's (1979) notation and symbolize the argument of the intransitive verb by s and the actor and undergoer arguments of the transitive verb by A and U respectively, then the Iatmul verbal case-marking system may be schematized as follows:

Iatmul   U

i.e. the verbal prefixes group s and A together against this U. This is referred to as a nominative–accusative case-marking system, or accusative for short. In such systems a nominative case, the formal grouping of A and s, is opposed to the accusative, the marking of the U. For Iatmul, the verbal suffixes mark the nominative, and the lack of verbal agreement, plus the lack of a nominal case suffix typical of the peripheral cases, indicates the accusative.

Barai (Olson 1981) also case-marks its core arguments according to an accusative pattern, but the details differ somewhat. Consider these Barai examples:

e   ije   ruo
man the come
'the man came'

e   ije   barone
man the die
'the man died'

e   ije   ame   kan-ia
man the child hit-3PL U
'the man hit some children'
*'the men hit a child'

> *e   ije   ame   kan-i*
> man the child hit-3SG U
> 'the man hit a child'

Barai parallels Yessan–Mayo and Iatmul in requiring the actor to precede the undergoer, and this word-order constraint functions to distinguish the two when they are of the same person and number. When actor and undergoer differ in this feature, Barai verbal affixation, as with Iatmul, is sufficient to specify their functions. The argument of intransitive verbs, the s argument, has no corresponding verbal affix, as seen in the first two examples. This also applies to the actor of transitive verbs. The U, the undergoer of transitive verbs, is signalled by a verbal suffix, as in the last two examples. -*ia* signals a third plural undergoer, so the third sentence must involve a plural undergoer, not a plural actor. A third singular undergoer would be expressed by the corresponding third singular suffix -*i*, as in the final example. Barai, like Iatmul, is a language with a nominative–accusative case marking schema, but differs from Iatmul in that it is the U which is indicated by a verbal suffix, not the A and s. The A and s are grouped together in not being indicated by a verbal affix. Barai case-marking can be schematized as follows:

Barai U

A very great number of Papuan languages, probably the majority, indicate both the actor and the undergoer of transitive verbs by verbal affixes. Fore (Scott 1978) is a fairly typical example of this type of language:

> *wa   kana-i-e*
> man come-3SG S-DECL
> 'the man comes'

> *wa   mási a-ka-i-e*
> man boy 3SG U-see-3SG A-DECL
> 'the man sees the boy'

> *wa   na-ka-i-e*
> man 1SG U-see-3SG A-DECL
> 'the man sees me'

Fore again demonstrates an accusative case-marking pattern for the core cases. The s and A cases are grouped together and expressed by a set of verbal suffixes, while the U is indicated by a verbal prefix, diagrammed as:

Fore   U

The Fore pattern, in which S and A are indicated by suffixes and U by prefixes, is very common in Papuan languages and attested in a number of different Papuan groups. This points up a significant generalization about the verbal morphology of Papuan languages: if verbal affixes for both core cases are present, U usually precedes A in linear order in the verb. This Fore pattern, U–V–A, and another common pattern, V–U–A, account for the great majority of Papuan languages with double verbal affixation, although all six possibilities are found:

(1) U–V–A Fore and many other languages of the Eastern Highlands of Papuan New Guinea; Dani, Ekagi and other languages of highland Irian Jaya; Baruya, Kapau and other Angan languages; Daga; Nabak; Usan.

(2) V–U–A Nasioi, Asmat, Nimboran, Siroi, Waskia, Arafundi

(3) U–A–V Yimas (partially).

(4) A–V–U Au, Olo and Kamasau of the Torricelli family. This order seems to be diagnostic of this genetic grouping, as it is not attested elsewhere. This is probably closely correlated with the unusual clausal word-order of A–V–U, also common within this grouping and not outside of it.

(5) V–A–U Sentani, Alamblak, Manambu. This is the most common of the actor-first affix orders, but still a minority pattern.

(6) A–U–V Marind, Yimas (partially).

Fore, Barai and Iatmul all case-mark their core cases according to a nominative–accusative pattern, grouping the S and A in one case (nominative), opposed to another case (accusative) for the U. This is the overwhelmingly common verbal case-marking schema for Papuan languages. Only a handful of languages show any other pattern, but two other possibilities are available, and are attested elsewhere in the world. One possibility, exemplified by Yimas in certain person and number combinations, as well as Anggor (Litteral 1980) and Yele (Henderson and Henderson 1979), is to treat all three differently:

Yimas, Anggor

as illustrated by these Yimas examples:

> *ama-wa-t*
> 1SG S-go-PERF
> 'I went'

na-ka-timayk-it
3SG U-1SG A-show-PERF
'I showed him'

na-ŋa-timayk-it
3SG A-1SG U-show-PERF
'he showed me'

For the first person singular, *ama-* is the s form, *ka-* the A form, and *ŋa-* the U prefix. This three-way differentiation is restricted to certain person and number combinations; for others, there are fewer distinctions. For example, *pu-* is the third plural prefix for s, A and U.

Still a third possibility is to treat the s and U together as one case opposed to the A, as in this diagram:

A

This is the ergative–absolutive, or ergative for short, case-marking schema. In such a system the A is treated morphologically in one way (the ergative case), and the s and U in another (the absolutive). This system is not attested among Papuan languages as an arrangement of the verbal case-marking for core relations. Papuan languages either treat s, A and U all distinctly in their verbal affixation (very rare) or case-mark accusatively, grouping s and A in one affix series, opposed to a different affix series or other formal treatment for U (almost universal). Verbal case-marking according to an ergative schema does occur in other parts of the world, notably North America (see, for example, Silverstein 1976 on Chinook) and the Caucasus, but is unattested in New Guinea. And this is in spite of the fact that nominal case-marking along an ergative pattern, to which I will now turn, is rather common.

Ergative case-marking on nominals is common in languages of the highlands areas of both Papua New Guinea and Irian Jaya, and has resulted from the spread of a peripheral case-marker to the actor, a core relation, in order to meet certain grammatical needs. This development is perhaps most transparent in Dani (Bromley 1981). Dani, like other highlands languages, has verbal case-marking for both A and U on an accusative pattern; compare these with Fore discussed earlier:

ap   nik-k-e
man eat-REAL-3SG A
'the man ate'

ap   n-(w)at-h-e
man 1SG U-hit-REAL-3SG A
'the man hit me'

> *ap* *∅-wat-h-i*
> man 3SG U-hit-REAL-1SG A
> 'I hit the man'

The s and A cases are indicated by verbal suffixes, but the U by a verbal prefix, a clear example of an accusative schema. Like all languages with verbal case-marking, Dani suffers from the problem of potential confusion between actor and undergoer when they are both animate, a problem compounded for Dani because, unlike Yimas, it has no gender distinctions for nominals. One solution to this dilemma, exemplified by Iatmul above, is to require a rigid word-order for actor and undergoer; a second, found in Yessan–Mayo, is to case-mark animate undergoers; and a third, present in Dani, is to case-mark the actor. Case-marking the actor of a transitive verb results in an ergative case-marking schema: the marked A is opposed to the unmarked s and U. The formal marker for the ergative is the peripheral case-marker for the ablative, causal and instrumental. The extension of the instrumental and causal case to the actor is not surprising: both are causes of the event, either primary or secondary, and identity between the ergative and instrumental case markers is a common feature of languages, including other Papuan languages such as Enga (Lang 1973), Kewa (Franklin 1971), Kâte (Pilhofer 1933) and Selepet (McElhanon 1972). All of these languages exemplify this extension of a peripheral case-marker to a core case.

The ergative case-marker is primarily used in Dani to disambiguate the case relations of the two core nominals by indicating which is actor. If there is no possible ambiguity, the ergative case-marking is largely absent:

> *ap*   *wekki*   *wat-n-an-h-e*
> man charcoal hit-1SG U-put-REAL-3SG A
> 'the man smeared charcoal on me'

If there is potential ambiguity and, especially, if the actor is the more unlikely of the two animate nominals, then the ergative marker is used:

> *wam-en* *∅-na-sikh-e*
> pig-ERG 3SG U-eat-RM PAST-3SG A
> 'the pig ate him'

Without the ergative marker this sentence would likely mean 'he ate the pig'.

> *ap*   *palu-nen*   *∅-na-sikh-e*
> man python-ERG 3SG U-eat-RM PAST-3SG A
> 'the python ate the man'

Again, without the ergative case-marker this sentence would mean 'the man ate the python'. The ergative case-marker is further demanded in these sentences because it is extremely unusual for pigs or pythons to eat people, and the presence on a nominal of an ergative case-marker is to some extent an indication of its unexpected functioning as an actor.

This disambiguating function of ergative case-marking is basic for many highlands languages (noted, for example, for Hua by Haiman (1980)), and the Dani system probably represents the model from which most ergative highlands languages developed. But some highlands languages of the Engan and neighbouring groups have another, although related, function for the ergative marker. In these languages, rather than simply identifying the actor, the ergative marker expresses the actor's control, i.e. that the actor is a volitional, independently acting performer. This is illustrated most interestingly by Podopa (Anderson and Wade 1981). For Podopa, the actor of most transitive verbs (and of some intransitive verbs as well) may occur with or without the ergative case suffix, but with a semantic difference. The ergative suffix indicates that the actor is acting independently, is self-motivated, and exerts his personal control over the situation; while its lack indicates that the actor is performing according to his set social obligations, not according to his own independent will, and does not assert his personal control over the situation. With verbs denoting the gathering, preparation and exchange of food, the ergative case is considered socially inappropriate. It would highlight the actor's personal and independent role in the activities associated with food, and would mark him, or the speaker, as boastful or stingy. As all activities associated with food are governed by strict social conventions, the absence of the ergative case is the normal and socially appropriate usage. For verbs expressing commands or requests, the ergative case is used if the actor's social position is such that it is appropriate for him to address commands or requests to the addressee. The ergative asserts his right to do so. If the actor does not have this right, then the ergative suffix should not be used. Other types of verbs obey similar rules of appropriate usage.

Podopa combines both rationales for the use of the ergative case: disambiguation and the expression of control. When the actor and undergoer agree in animacy, the ergative case-marker must be used with the actor for disambiguation. When they differ in animacy, the ergative marker may be present or absent. If present, it expresses the assertion of the actor's control in the social senses discussed above, while its absence indicates that no such independent control is being claimed. Such a pattern is probably not unusual in highlands languages; it is clear from a perusal of Haiman's (1980) grammar of Hua that similar principles operate there.

An ergative system with a difference is found in Waris (Brown 1981). This language has followed the pattern noted for Yessan–Mayo of extending the dative case-marker to animate undergoers for disambiguation:

> *di   ka-va ye-m   dembre-hun-v*
> money I-TP   you-DAT put PL U-PL REC-PRES
> 'I give the money to you'
>
> *ye-m   ka-va helvakomandha-v*
> you-DAT I-TP   kill-PRES
> 'I kill you (intentionally)'

Waris diverges from Yessan–Mayo in that the dative case-marker is extended to still other types of undergoers: those which do not undergo a definite and complete change of state occur with the dative marker, those which *do* undergo a definite change of state do not have the dative marker:

no change in state	change in state
ti-m he-the-v	*ti he-v*
tree-DAT chop-INT-PRES	tree chop-PRES
'chop on a tree'	'chop down a tree'
meya-m hevra-v	*meya powal-v*
table-DAT hit-PRES	table split-PRES
'bang on a table'	'split a table'
tup-m vend-v	*wong vend-v*
door-DAT hit-PRES	drum hit-PRES
'knock on a door'	'pound a drum' (it resounds)

The spread of peripheral case-markers to undergoers to indicate partial affect is widely attested cross-linguistically, although I know of no other examples among Papuan languages. Note the contrast between the presence or absence of the peripheral nominal marker *on* in the above English glosses. A possible explanation of this development is that, as peripheral nominals are less central or less involved in the action than core nominals, the core relation, the undergoer, when marked by a peripheral case-marker, is reasonably interpreted as being less involved or less affected by the action.

The really important, and fascinating, fact about Waris is that the dative marker is also extended to s nominals, when associated with intransitive verbs expressing *uncontrolled* changes of states:

> *he-m   daha-v*
> he-DAT die-PRES
> 'he is dying'

ka-m takola-na
I-DAT slip and fall-PAST
'I slipped and fell'

obat-ra   ka-m-ba kanandha-na
medicine-CAUSE I-DAT-TP recover-PAST
'I recovered because of the medicine'

Waris must be regarded as a partially ergative language because certain types of s and u nominals occur with the dative case-marker, according to the principles presented, but A nominals never do. It differs from the Dani and Podopa types discussed above, because for Waris it is the s and u nominals (the absolutive) which are marked, not the A (ergative). It also contrasts with Podopa in that it is *uncontrolled* s nominals which are marked, not the controlled ones. The sharp contrast between Dani and Podopa, on the one hand, and Waris, on the other, arises from the different peripheral case-markers which have been generalized to core relations. For Dani and Podopa, the ablative/instrumental case-marker has been generalized. It is semantically a more active notion, associated with the place/entity of origin and causal means of the action and is plausibly associated with the performer of the action, the actor and, indirectly, with the notion of control. But for Waris it is the dative case-marker which has been generalized. This is semantically a more passive notion, essentially denoting uninitiating, receptive participants or places or entities toward which the actor directs the action. In that they are non-initiating, they are non-controlling, and plausibly associated with the undergoers of transitive actions and the non-initiating, non-controlling s nominals of intransitive changes of state. The differences can be summarized as:

Dani, Podopa: ABL/INSTR→ERG (A[+control])
Waris: DAT→ABS (U, S[−control])

These developments highlight a point made earlier, but worth reiterating here, that nominal case-marking on core nominals in Papuan languages is a secondary affair. The basic Papuan case system is verbal marking on an accusative pattern for the core relations, S, A and U, and nominal case-marking for peripheral nominals. When nominal case-marking is found on core nominals it is from generalization of a peripheral case-marker, as demonstrated by the above three languages.

5

Verbs

5.1 Properties of verbs

In the previous chapter I described nouns as providing an inventory of the objects of interest in the world (or imagination) of the speakers of a language. They do this by providing a convenient system of names for this set of significant entities. Verbs contrast with nouns in that they are the word-class associated with actions, events or states. Whereas objects exist in their own right, this is not true of events or states. Events as stated only occur by virtue of some object or objects undergoing or performing them. Thus, we may consider the set of verbs in a language as a script outlining the various modes by which objects may interact. Developing this metaphor still further, we may view a language as a play, with the nouns constituting the cast of characters, and the verbs, the lines, the means of interaction of the characters in the different scenes.

Let me consider a concrete example here, the difference between the English words *rock* and *hit*. *Rock* is a noun and refers, as nouns prototypically do, to an object in the world, in this case a hard, solid mineral object of the natural world. As rocks are concrete objects they are freely apprehensible by our senses: we can see them, touch them and, if they are small enough, manipulate them with our hands. Further, they are susceptible to changes in state: they can be moved, broken, crushed or thrown. Finally, the boundaries of what is a rock or what is not are fairly sharp, both from the surrounding space and from other objects. As we can manipulate a rock, we can determine its boundaries in space, and by noting the features of this object bound in space in this way, we are able to sort rocks from trees or mothers. Given all these properties of the objects called rocks and human perceptual and cognitive mechanisms, it seems warranted to hypothesize that a noun corresponding to *rock* is rather a predetermined category in the vocabularies of all languages. This would not exclude further nouns in a language to refer to types of rocks such as *boulder*, *pebble* and *stone*. These may or may not be found, but all languages would have the core term *rock*.

Now let me contrast the English verb *hit*. This English word denotes an action, prototypically that of a human lifting a hand, moving it through space toward some object, and bringing it into contact forcefully with the surface of that object. Note that actions are not apprehensible to our senses in the same way as objects: we cannot manipulate an action, in fact we cannot even really see an action. All we can see of an act of hitting are the participants engaged in it, the person raising his hand, moving it through space, coming into contact with a surface of an object, and then withdrawing from it. Obviously, there is no actual unitary action of hitting to be seen, but rather some participants engaged in a series of actions which we interpret as a single act and describe with the label *hit*. Closely correlated with this property of actions is the fact that, unlike objects, they do not have discrete boundaries which separate them from other actions. Consider the actions described by the following additional English verbs of contact: *touch, grab, scratch, slap*. All four of these share many of the features of *hit*, but also contrast in some. *Touch* contrasts with *hit* in that for *touch* the contact is not forceful. *Grab* contrasts with *hit* in that the hand does not withdraw from the object contacted, but rather closes itself around it. *Scratch* adds the component that after coming into contact with the object the hand drags along the surface of the object, resulting in some damage to its surface. Finally, *slap* contrasts with *hit* in that slapping necessarily implies contact with an object with the flat palm surface of the hand, while *hit* has no such requirement; in fact, one need not contact the object with the hand at all in hitting: contact by an object held by the hand such as a cane is sufficient. It is important to note that the actions described by these five verbs are not really all that different from each other: all require the basic actions of raising the hand, moving it through space and contacting the surface of an object. The boundaries distinguishing one from another are not sharp. If *touch* is distinguished from *hit* largely by the force of the contact, obviously there is no absolute boundary between touching and hitting. Contact between my upper arm and the hand of a 120 kg rugby player might be described by him as *touching* and by me as *hitting*.

This points up the central property of the set of verbs in a language. The description of a real-world event by a particular verb is basically an interpretation by the speaker, and, further, the interpretations available to him are none other than the set of verbs his language provides. This is a restatement of the earlier idea that the set of verbs is the speaker's script. Unlike the relationship between objects and the set of core nouns, which is largely predetermined by human perceptual and cognitive mechanisms, the set of verbs in a language and the real-world events denoted by them is far more arbitrary. This is not to say that there are no inherently highly central human acts which must be described in any human language. There certainly are. However, it seems not to be the case that every language must have a unique verb to describe that act, in the way every language has a noun *rock* to describe that real-world object. Eating is without question a central human act, and one might propose that all languages would have a verb to denote just this act. But Yimas and a number of other Papuan languages show such a statement to be false: the Yimas verb *am-* covers the range of English *eat*, *drink* and *smoke* (tobacco). The arbitrariness of the relation between events and the linguistic description of those events must always be borne in mind when trying to understand the essential features of the verbal systems of Papuan languages.

5.2 Verbal semantics in Papuan languages

In section 4.1, I made the observation that the set of nouns in a language is always much larger than the set of verbs. I proposed the explanation that nouns must provide a sufficiently detailed inventory of the objects of interest in the world of the speakers of the language. As the range of significant objects in the environment of any language community is very large indeed, the language must provide a reasonably finely grained classification of this environment for it to serve as an efficient means of communication.

There is in principle, however, no reason why verbs should follow this pattern. I have already pointed out that verbs like *hit* or *grab* do not describe a simple event, but a rather complex series of events. It would be logically quite possible to describe such actions as hitting in terms of the individual sub-actions, so that *hit* in such a language might be *hand raise-go-touch-push-remove* and *grab* might be *hand raise-go-touch-hold*. A language which followed this logic consistently would be able to get by with a much reduced inventory of verbs from the point of view of English, and this is, in fact, the pattern that a good number of Papuan languages exhibit.

Of all Papuan languages, the closely related Kalam and Kobon are the most remarkable in applying this idea in the most thoroughgoing fashion. I will consider Kalam here, described in Pawley (1966) and a number of unpublished papers by the same author. Kalam immediately strikes one as a language in which the speakers are excessively specific in their description of events. While an English speaker might say 'I fetched firewood', a Kalam speaker would express this (Pawley 1980) as:

> *yad am mon   pk   d   ap   ay-p-yn*
> I   go wood hit hold come put-PERF-1SG
> 'I went and chopped wood and got it and came and put it'

Note that the Kalam speaker breaks down the act of fetching firewood into its component acts, and expresses each one by a separate verb. Note that Kalam requires that the chopping of the wood be mentioned, which, although not a component of fetching, normally expressed in Kalam as *am d ap* 'go hold come', is a necessary prerequisite to fetching firewood. To leave out any of these verbs would result in the description seeming incomplete to a Kalam speaker.

Not only are the Kalam descriptions of events more specific than their English equivalents, they also seem more concrete as well. Consider the following example:

> *stoa ap-y   tap-skoy taw-y   d   am ñ-ng   g-p-yn*
> store come-ing present buy-ing hold go give-to do-PERF-1SG
> 'I have bought a present for [a friend]'

Note that Kalam requires the indication of the place of buying, the store. Also, it has no direct equivalent for the rather abstract preposition *for*. Rather, the meaning for *for* is broken down into its concrete sub-actions and each of these is expressed by a verb: *am ñ-* 'go give'. This is the treatment commonly meted out in Kalam to English prepositions:

> *ywt   d-y   pk-p-yn*
> stick take-ing hit-PERF-1SG
> 'I hit it *with* a stick'

> *yad Wŋnn md-p   am-jp-yn*
> I   Wŋnn exist-3SG go-PROG-1SG
> 'I'm going *to* Wŋnn's [place]'

So English *with* corresponds to the Kalam verb *d* 'hold' and *to, at* or other prepositions of location to *md*, 'exist, be located at'. This realization of English prepositions by verbs is very widespread among Papuan languages:

Yimas: *panmal   uraŋk   ki-n-ŋa-yara-ŋa-t*
               man-I SG coconut-V SG V SG-1SG A-1SG U-get-give-PERF
               'the man got a coconut *for* me'

Barai: *fu burede ije sime **abe** ufu*
(Olson 1981)   he bread   the knife take cut
               'he cut the bread with a knife'

Au: *hirak k-uwaai k-**eit***   *Yemnu*
(Scorza in press) he   3SG-sleep 3SG-be located at Yemnu
               'he slept at Yemnu'

Each of these three languages parallels the Kalam examples above: Yimas uses *-ŋa* 'give' for English *for*, Barai *abe* 'take' for *with*, and Au *-eit* 'be located at' for *at*.

This pervasive tendency of Kalam to describe in a sequence of component events what would be conceived as a single event in English and labelled by a single English verb is closely correlated with perhaps its most salient typological feature: the back'. In addition to this aspectual contrast, restricted to a subset of the verb stems, Marind also possesses two productive aspectual prefixes for extended and completive aspect, which may be added to any verb:

epa-no-kiparud	*menda-no-kiparud*
EXT-1SG A-tie	PERF-1SG A-tie
'I am tying'	'I have tied'

It is not difficult to imagine how a Marind-like system could develop into that of Telefol. With some phonological changes, a morphological re-analysis could occur, so that the former productive aspectual derivation becomes a morphophonemic difference in verb-stems. The aspectual affixes for completed and extended aspect would themselves become associated with one or the other verb-stem, resulting in a Telefol-type system.

A particularly rich and interesting inflectional system for aspect is found in Kiwai (Ray 1933). In addition to changes in the initial segment of verb-stems to show number, discussed in the previous section, Kiwai exhibits changes in the final segment of its verb-stems to indicate aspectual contrasts, much as in Telefol. Continuative stems for extended events must end in one of the following non-low vowels, *e, i, o, u*:

ogu	'come'	*obore*	'copulate'
arubo	'fly'	*omi*	'sit'
abodo	'sing'	*orou*	'lie prone'
aberumo	'beat'	*opuse*	'rot'
idibi	'build'	*aparo*	'breathe'

while punctiliar stems expressing momentary aspect always terminate in the low vowel *a* or the diphthong *ai*:

edea	'leave'	*asomai*	'peep'
iasusia	'win'	*atimai*	'close'
idumia	'wink'	*aurai*	'prick'
odoria	'rip'	*osiai*	'embrace'
opodia	'break'	*osome ai*	'kiss'

Many verbs have two verb-stem forms, one terminating in a non-low vowel for extended aspect, and the other terminating in a low vowel or diphthong for momentary aspect:

	Continuative			Punctiliar	
etebe	'keep bending'		*etebai*		'bend once'
orobi	'hold'		*orobai*		'catch hold of'
ateri	'walk with back to one another'		*ateriai*		'pass on road'
esei	'hate'		*eseiai*		'put away'
aguro	'shake the head'		*agurai*		'nod'
adoro	'grow, chew'		*adorotai*		'bite off'

In addition Kiwai has several aspectual suffixes, which provide still more specific contrasts in aspect. There is a suffix *-ti*, which indicates several performances of an action, an iterative aspect:

ipesu-ti	'lose several things one at a time'
asesu-ti	'cut pieces from something over and over again'
ragiwu-ti	'give separately to several individuals'
opogu-ti	'continue knocking at one door'
adi-ti	'repeatedly set fire to the same thing'

There is also a suffix *-diro*, indicating continuous performance of an action:

omudo-diro	'go on dragging'	*orou-diro*	'remain lying down'
orobi-diro	'hold for a long time'	*omi-diro*	'stay'
ogirio-diro	'crawl for a long time'	*ovioro-diro*	'remain elevated'

Finally, there is a suffix *-wado*, expressing a frequent or regular performance of an action:

oriodorai-wado	'go astern frequently'
iaeedai-wado	'pull the bowstring many times'
owogurumi-wado	'dip something often'
idiai-wado	'come up from below often'

A second category of verbal inflection belonging to the class of inner operators is that of directionals/elevationals, illustrated in the following Yimas examples:

na-wi-impu-pu-t
3SG s-up-go by water-away-PERF
'he went upriver (away from speaker/village)'

na-il-ŋka-pra-t
3SG s-down-go by land-toward-PERF
'he came downhill (toward speaker/village)'

> *na-na-il-am-ɨn*
> 3SG S-EXT-down-eat-PRES
> 'he is eating down below'

As these examples indicate, the directional/elevational prefixes (*wi-* 'up' and *il-* 'down') have two functions; to indicate direction of motion, as in the first two examples, and to indicate the spatial position of the actor of a verb with respect to the position of the interlocutors of the speech act, as in the last example. Verbs expressing motion must additionally be specified for the direction of the motion with respect to the speaker or village. This is accomplished by the suffixes *-pu* 'motion away from village/speaker' and *-pra* 'motion toward village/speaker', related to the verbs 'go' and 'come' respectively.

Directionals/elevationals are realized morphologically in two ways: either as affixes, exemplified by the Yimas examples above, or by independent verb-stems in a verb serialization structure. In this manner they parallel aspectual morphemes. An example of a language in which directionals/elevationals are expressed through serialized verb-stems is Dani (Bromley 1981):

> *pi   a-k-a*   *ki   a-k-a*
> descend come-REAL-3SG A   enter come-REAL-3SG A
> 'he came down'   'he came in'

As is Barai (Olson 1981):

> *ajia   va*   *aru   ro*
> ascend go   enter come
> 'go up (away from speaker)'   'come in (towards speaker)'

Barai contrasts with Dani and parallels Yimas in that the direction towards or away from the speaker must always be specified by a separate verb-stem. In Dani this only applies to the direction towards the speaker. The directional/elevational verb-stems stand by themselves to indicate motion away from speaker: *pi*, descend, 'go down', *ki*, enter, 'go in'.

The number of distinctions made in the affixal systems for directionals/ elevationals varies widely in Papuan languages. The simplest systems, found in Kewa (Franklin 1971) and Yessan–Mayo (Foreman 1974), contrast downward motion with upward (examples from Yessan–Mayo):

> *ni   mati eys-ruw-ti*
> you bag hang-up-FUT
> 'you will hang up the bag'

> *ni   mati ras-kwun-ti*
> you bag put-down-FUT
> 'you will put down the bag'

Yimas is of intermediate complexity in this feature. In addition to 'up' and 'down', shown in the examples above, the distinctions *ma-* 'inward motion' and *tu-* 'outward motion' are made:

> *na-ma-impu-pu-t*
> 3SG S-in-go by water-away-PERF
> 'he went inside a river passage (away from speaker/village)'

> *na-tu-ŋka-pra-t*
> 3SG S-out-go by land-toward-PERF
> 'he came out of the bush (toward speaker/village)'

Alamblak, geographically contiguous but genetically unrelated to Yimas, has two sets of directional/elevational affixes. A suffixal set locates the position of an event with respect to that of the speaker, along the dimensions of up (*ko*), down (*-we ~ -he*) or same level (*-i(t)o*):

> *dbëhnay-r-ko*   *yifi-r-we*
> sick-3SG M-up   go-3SG M-down
> 'he was sick up there'   'he went down there'

The prefixal set has a richer set of distinctions. They are used with motion verbs to indicate sloping motion up or down, motion straight down, or motion on a level plane. Motion along a level plane and motion sloping up are further distinguished for direction away from or towards speaker. This may all be summarized as:

	Level	Sloping up	Sloping down	Straight down
towards speaker	*yari(m)-*	*yua-*	*mi-*, *yhë(m)-*	*wa-*
away from speaker	*ri(m)-*	*u-*	*më-*	

> *mi-brñi-r*   *wa-fayk-r-t*
> slope down-move away-3SG M A   straight down-get-3SG M A-3SG F U
> 'he went down'   'he got it down below'

In serial verb constructions, a single directional/elevational prefix applies to all verb-stems:

> *wa-rim-ak-ni-n-m*
> IMP-level away-get-go-2SG A-3PL U
> 'get them and go away (from me)'

If both a prefix and a suffix occur, the first verb is modified by the prefix and the second by the suffix:

> *wa-yarim-ak-ni-n-m-ko*
> IMP-level toward-get-go-2SG A-3PL U-up
> 'get them toward me and go up there'

The most complex systems of directionals/elevationals attested among Papuan languages are those found in the Nimboran group of languages, from which I will discuss Kemtuk (Wilden 1976) (for Nimboran proper, see Anceaux 1965). As is common, the primary distinction is between direction towards speaker and away from the speaker, but within this grand division, there is a further distinction between same level as or different level from the speaker and, if the latter, motion up or motion down. This system can be summarized in the following chart:

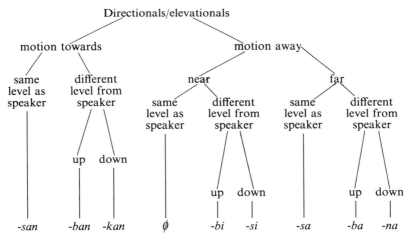

Some further recurring partials can be isolated here: *s-* indicates same level, but *-b* clearly signifies different level, motion up; *-a* signifies motion away from speaker to a position far away, while *-i* signifies motion away from speaker to a position near. Finally, *-an* signifies motion towards speaker. Some examples of the uses of these suffixes follow:

> *genam mea iti-ban-d-u*
> I   FUT give-up toward-FUT-I
> 'I will get it and give it to you up there'

> *genam mea iti-si-l-u*
> I   FUT give-down near away-FUT-I
> 'I will give it to you down there near here'

genam mea iti-sa-l-u
I   FUT give-level far away-FUT-I
'I will give it to you away way over there'

Such complex systems, while especially prominent in the Nimboran group of languages, seem to be an areal feature. Anggor (Litteral 1972), an unrelated language belonging to the Senagi family across the border in Papua New Guinea, illustrates a similar level of complexity in directionals/elevationals, and it seems likely that such systems will be found to be widespread as other languages of the area become better known. See also Cowan's (1965) grammar of Sentani, a language adjoining the Nimboran group.

The final types of inner operators to be considered are those for modality. Modality is an inflectional category relating to the intention of the actor and his potential or actual performance of the action. It expresses different kinds of semantic relations between the actor and his action: whether he needs to perform it, or desires to, or simply is able to. Note that these relations all relate to the will of the actor, his intentions toward the action. Extending the notion of modality beyond its traditional use, I will consider the nature of the actual performance of the action also under this category of modality: whether the actor tried to perform the action or whether he succeeded in bringing about an event by manipulating another participant who in fact performed it (i.e. a causative relation).

Like the other inner operators, aspect and directionals/elevationals, modality may be realized morphologically in two ways, by bound morphemes or serialized verb constructions. For example, the conative modality (the actor *tries* to perform the action) is almost universally signalled in Papuan languages with a serial verb construction involving the verb stem 'see':

Yimas: *na-mpɨ-kwalca-tay-ntut*
             3SG U-3DL A-arise-see-RM PAST
             'they both tried to wake him up'

Asmat: *yitim-por*
(Drabbe 1959a) arise-see
             'try to awaken somebody'

Hua: *ke   hu-ko-mana*
(Haiman 1980) talk do I-see-OTHER INCONSEQUENTIAL
             'I tried to talk (but to no avail)'

Barai: *akoe   ga*
(Olson 1975) throw see
             'try throwing it'

Ekagi: *maki-dou*
(Doble 1962)   put-see
                 'try on'

Other modality distinctions exhibit much greater cross-linguistic variation. Here I will only be concerned with two other types of modality, causatives and desideratives.

Causative constructions are those expressing the idea that the actor brings about a change of state in some object, often through coercing or otherwise persuading some secondary actor to perform it. Examples in English abound: *John enlarged the room, John made Sam clean his room* or *John got Sam to clean his room.* In the first example, John does something to the room which results in its being enlarged, while in the latter two John does something to Sam which results in his cleaning his own room. All are causative constructions; in all cases John brings about a change of state in the room, but in the latter two examples he accomplishes this through the intermediary actor Sam, whom John persuades to act in this way. Note that the causative relation is realized morphologically in the first example by a verbal affix *en-*, but in the latter two cases by the verb-stems *make* and *get*.

Papuan languages show the same morphological differences exemplified for English. In some Papuan languages the causatives may be indicated by a bound affix:

Asmat: *sa-m*   *os-om*
(Drabbe 1959a):   dry-CAUS   go away-CAUS
                             'make dry'   'make someone go away'

Kewa: *ma-piraa-ru*
(Franklin 1971)   CAUS-sit-1SG PAST
                             'I caused someone to sit down'

Moni: *ma-bitiya*   *ma-undiya*
(Larson and Larson 1958)   CAUS-shut   CAUS-sleep
                             'put out'   'put to sleep'

Enga: *akáli dokó-mé énda   dóko kuma-sá-py-á*
(Lang 1973)   man the-ERG woman the   die-CAUS-NR PAST-3SG
                             'the man killed the woman'

Other languages use verb-stems in a manner similar to English *make* or *get* causative constructions. The most common verb stem used is 'say':

Yimas: *na-ka-tɨmi-wapal*
              3SG U-1SG A-say-climb
              'I caused him to climb up'

Barai:	*na k-ia* *e* *ije va-e*
(Olson 1981)	I say-3PL U person the go-PAST
	'I caused them to go'

Enga:	*akáli dokó-mé énda dóko Wápaka pe-ná l-é-á*
(Lang 1973)	man the-ERG woman the Wabag go-3SG say-IM PAST 3SG
	'the man caused the woman to go to Wabag'

If we compare the last example from Enga in the two sets above, we find that Enga has both a morphological causative with *-sa* and a syntactic causative with *lá-* 'say'. The *-sa* form is restricted to certain intransitive verb-stems, making them transitive, and prohibits the presence of a secondary actor. The *lá-* construction is more productive and always allows a secondary actor.

This situation is common among Papuan languages. Kiwai (Ray 1933) also has both types of causatives, a verbal prefix *ow-* (*iw-* for nonsingular) and an independent verb-stem *owai-* (*iwai-* for nonsingular) 'make, cause'. This latter is plausibly derived from *ow-*, the causative prefix, plus *-ai*, the verb-stem terminator for momentary aspect:

ow-ogu	*iw-asio*
CAUS-go	CAUS-go across
'bring one thing'	'carry many things across'

nou imeime wade-go g-iwai
he   all   good-VB 3SG PAST-cause (NSG)
'he made them all well'

Both types of constructions are used with intransitive verbs to make them transitive, but with different semantic types. The prefix is normally used with motion or transfer verbs, while the verb-stem is found with stative verbs, roughly parallel to the class of English adjectives.

Yimas has three different types of causative constructions. There is a morphological causative with the suffix *-(a)sa*, restricted to a smallish set of stative verb-stems:

yan   na-ka-kumprak-asa-t
tree-V SG V SG U-1SG A-broken-CAUSE-PERF
'I broke the tree'

In addition, there are causative constructions formed with serialized verbs with two different verb-stems, *tal-* 'hold, get' and *timi-* 'say':

na-ka-tal-kwalca-t
3SG U-1SG A-hold-arise-PERF
'I woke him up'

> *yan   na-mpu-timi-wapal*
> tree-v SG V SG U-3PL A-say-climb
> 'they made him climb the tree'

The two verbs are used under different semantic conditions. *Tal-* 'hold' is used when the causation is accomplished by physical manipulation of an object (hence the use of 'hold'). Consequently, it tends to be used with verbs of motion, indicating that the motion was initiated by some manipulation of the causing actor. *Timi-* 'say' is much more productive. It can be used with any verb-stem to indicate that the action was performed by someone under the direction of a causing actor. Such causation is prototypically performed verbally; hence the use of 'say' in these constructions.

Alamblak (Bruce 1984) also has three different types of causative constructions; but, in this language, two of the constructions involve bound morphemes. There is a basic causative construction involving verb serialization with either *kak-* 'get' or *hay-* 'give':

> *hinu-t doh-t   hay-ni-më-t-t*
> flood-F canoe-F give-go-RM PAST-3SG F A-3SG F U
> 'the flood took the canoe away'

This is the least constrained of the causative constructions, merely requiring close proximity of the participants. The first of the morphological causatives involves the prefix *ha-*:

> *ha-fkne-më-r-m*
> CAUSE-enter-RM PAST-3SG M-3PL U
> 'he caused them to enter (by entering with them)'

In addition to close proximity, this construction applies the further constraint that the participants act together, ensuring virtual simultaneity between their actions. The most constrained construction involves the prefix *ka-*:

> *ka-fkne-më-r-m*
> CAUS-enter-RM PAST-3SG M-3PL U
> 'he caused them to enter (by physically taking them)'

Besides the close proximity of participants and their simultaneity of action, this construction requires that the participants be in physical contact, and that the causing actor physically manipulate an essentially passive undergoer. A basic generalization about Alamblak causatives correlates the morphological bonding of the causative morpheme with more restrictive semantic constraints on the construction. The serial construction has the fewest constraints; the prefix *ka-* has the most. This principle seems to be operating in the grammar of many of the world's languages (for a survey, see the articles in Shibatani 1976).

Desiderative constructions indicate a desire on the part of the actor to perform an action (X *wants* to). Although English uses the same verb *want* in the two constructions *John wants to leave* and *John wants Mary to leave*, this actually disguises certain fundamental semantic differences between them. Note that in the first case it is John who leaves, but in the second it is Mary. The verb *want* in both examples is linked to John; hence the constructions state something about John's wishes. In the first example, John has certain desires, and the result of these intentions is that he would leave. In the second case, however, John also has certain wishes, but the aim of these is not his leaving, but Mary's. In the second case, Mary's wishes are as much at issue as John's. Hence, if his intentions are to be realized, he must *communicate* them to Mary, resulting in her departure; this is not necessary in the first example, because the goal of his intentions is simply his own action.

While the English structure is keyed to John's will, so that the two constructions are seen as similar, Papuan languages take the opposite tack, noting that an act of communication is essential in the second case, but not in the first. Therefore, generally in Papuan languages these two constructions will look very different. Consider these Yimas examples:

> *ama tupuk am-ɨŋ*
> I   sago eat-IRR
> 'I want to eat sago'

> *tupuk am-tu-mpwi   pia-ka-i-c-umpun*
> sago eat-INF-words words-1SG A-say-PERF-3PL DAT
> 'I want (told) them to eat sago'

The first Yimas example corresponds to the first English case, in which the performer of the intended action and the intender are the same – in other words, situations in which no act of communication is necessary. The verb is simply suffixed with the irrealis suffix *-ŋ ~ -k*. The suffix usually signals a future action which is generally expected to occur. It marks the verb of purposive clauses:

> *tupuk am-ɨŋ   ama-wa-t*
> sago eat-PURP 1SG S-go-PERF
> 'I went (in order) to eat sago'

When used as the main tense inflection on an independent verb, as in the first desiderative construction above, the suffix indicates a future action, expected and, by extension, wanted by the speaker to occur.

The second Yimas example corresponds to the second English case, in which the performer of the action and the intender are not the same, a situation in which communication between the intender and the performer of the action is necessary.

Note that the Yimas construction involves a complement of that prototypical communicative verb 'say'. There is a main verb 'say' in the form 'I say words to them', and a complement structure 'words to eat sago' in apposition to this main verb. The suffix -*mpwi* on the complement identifies it as one involving speech. If it were a complement of action, the suffix would be -*nti*, if of desire, -*wampuŋ*. Clearly, the Yimas construction attends primarily to the overt act of communication involved in getting wishes accomplished, and this may be seen as a manifestation of the tendency mentioned at the beginning of the chapter for Papuan languages to be explicit in their verbal descriptions.

Enga (Lang 1973) has desiderative constructions somewhat similar to Yimas. When the actor and intender are the same, the verb 'feel' occurs with a complement of desire:

> *nambá Wápaka pá-a-nya   mási-ly-o*
> I   Wabag   go-INF-POSS feel-PRESS-1SG
> 'I want to go to Wabag'

However, when the intender and actor are different, the verb 'say' must introduce the complement:

> *émba Wápaka pú-p-í   láká lá-o   mási-ly-o*
> you   Wabag   go-PAST-2SG that say-SIM feel-PRES-1SG
> 'I want you to go to Wabag'

In competition with the first desiderative construction involving a coreferential intender and actor, Enga also possesses a construction involving 'say'. This construction is restricted to first person actors, and the desire indicated is very strong:

> *nambá Wápaka pú-p-ú   láká lá-o   mási-ly-o*
> I   Wabag   go-PAST-1SG that say-SIM feel-PRES-1SG
> 'I want to go to Wabag very badly'

This use of 'say' in desiderative constructions is pervasive in Papuan languages, probably correlated with the explicitness of expression remarked on above. Many Papuan languages parallel Enga in using 'say' in constructions in which the intender and actor are the same, as well as those in which they differ:

Iatmul: *klə-vat   wə-ntɨ*
(Staalsen 1972) get-PURP say-3SG M
                 'he wanted to get'

Hua:	*do-gu-e*	*hi-e*
(Haiman 1980)	eat-FUT-OTHER DECL	say 3SG-OTHER DECL
	'he wants to eat'	

Selepet:	*ari-we*	*s-m*	*o-an*
(McElhanon 1975)	go-1SG FUT	say-SA	do-1SG IM PAST
	'I want to go'		

Kâte:	*ra-pe*	*mu-rɔ*	*e-n-are-kak*
(McElhanon 1975)	go-1SG IMP	say-SA	do-1SG U-give-3SG A PAST
	'I want to go'		

Note that, in contrast to Selepet, the Kâte construction is an impersonal one, with the intender indicated as an undergoer.

5.5 Outer operators: tense, status, illocutionary force, evidentials

In the previous section I established tense as an outer operator in contrast to the inner operator aspect. Outer operators modify the entire sentence, situating it in time and indicating what kind of act the speaker is trying to accomplish by uttering it. Of the four types of outer operators, tense is undoubtedly the best known. It locates the event described by the utterance in time with respect to the time of the utterance. The simplest tense system is that exemplified by Japanese, Yidiny (Dixon 1977) or possibly English, in which events prior to the time of speaking (past) are contrasted with those simultaneous with or posterior to it (non-past). No known Papuan language has such a simple system.

Contrasting with tense, but related to it and often interacting with it, is the category of status. Status expresses the actuality of the event, whether it has been realized or not. The basic distinction here is a binary one, realis versus irrealis, but few languages express it in just this way. Many languages, English included, make a number of distinctions along the continuum from real to unreal; for example:

$$\text{real} \Leftarrow \text{necessary} - \text{likely} - \text{possible} \Rightarrow \text{unreal}$$

In English these distinctions are realized by different modal auxiliaries: *it must rain, it will rain* or *it may rain*.

All future events, events occurring after the time of the utterance, are *unreal* events at the time of the utterance, and hence the description of these in many languages will fall under the category of status rather than tense. Strictly speaking, if we look at the time continuum stretching out on either side of the moment of speaking, the continuum may first be bifurcated by status, treating all events after the moment of speaking as unreal, and all events before or simultaneous with it as real. Tense would then only properly apply to the real span of the temporal continuum, dividing it minimally into events before the moment of utterance (past) and those overlapping with it (present). The following diagram illustrates this point:

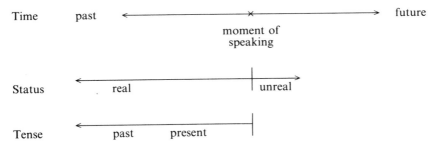

Or, to represent this in terms of a tree, status is the hierarchically dominant category:

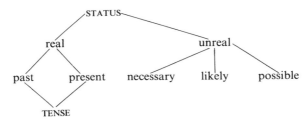

Having established these two separate categories and defined the relations between them, it must be pointed out that in many languages there is much interaction between these categories. This is not surprising, because the two combine to divide up the whole temporal continuum so that any event may be located on it with respect to the moment of speaking. Although there are two semantic categories here which, as we shall see, many languages keep sharply different morphologically, it is easy to see how they could be realized in some languages by a single morphological category, which I shall call *tense, conceding to traditional usage. This *tense is a morphological category in such languages, a hybrid of the semantic categories, status and tense (the asterisk is to differentiate the morphological category from the semantic one).

*Tense is a familiar category in European languages. The three-way *tense distinction in Latin between past, present and future exemplifies this. The future *tense in Latin is semantically a status category, but because the morphological formations of all three *tenses are the same, it is best to treat it as a single inflectional category. (Interestingly, the future in Latin comes from an earlier subjunctive mood (Palmer 1954), the inflection prototypically associated with unreal status.)

*Tense systems in Papuan languages are generally more elaborate than in European languages. In almost all cases more than one past tense is distinguished, indicating the removal in time of the past event from the moment of speaking.

Marind (Drabbe 1955) has four *tenses: a remote past, for events before yesterday; a near past, for events through yesterday; a present; and a future. Yessan–Mayo (Foreman 1974) also has the four-*tense system of Marind, but the remote past covers all events before today, and the near past, events of today. Enga (Lang 1973) and Alamblak (Bruce 1984) add an additional *tense distinction in the past. Besides a present and a future, there are three past *tenses: the immediate past, for events earlier today; the near past, for events of yesterday; and the remote past, for events before yesterday. Yimas makes yet a further distinction in the past. It has a specific past *tense for the recent past, covering from two days to roughly five days before today. The remote past then refers to all times up to five days before today.

Many Papuan languages also have more than one future *tense. Remembering that future is often, strictly speaking, a status distinction, rather than a tense, the question arises whether *tense is the best cover term for this inflectional category. The answer to this depends on whether the distinctions in the future actually reflect distinctions in status, as well as on the overall morphological picture. Consider, for example, Fore (Scott 1978) and Yimas. Fore has five *tense distinctions: a near past, for past events from yesterday to a week back; a remote past, for events before that; a present; a definite future, for events which are expected to occur; and a dubitative future, for events whose occurrence is quite doubtful. All distinctions are mutually exclusive, and the morphemes involved occur in the same suffixal position. Note that the semantic categorizations of the two futures are clearly status distinctions. Rather than marking how far removed in the future the events are from the present moment of speaking (tense), they indicate how likely the events are to occur – their reality along a dimension from real to unreal (status). The Fore future tense then has a secondary categorization for status. The Fore *tense system may be schematized as:

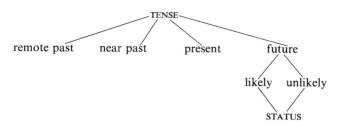

As tense is clearly the senior partner in the system, it is justifiable to call the inflectional category *tense.

Now consider Yimas. In addition to its four past *tenses and a present, it has two futures: a near future, for events to occur tomorrow, and a remote future, for events after tomorrow. All of these are indicated by mutually exclusive morphemes in a suffixal position. Note that the distinctions in the future are semantically those of tense: they indicate the interval of time between the present moment of speaking and the future event, not its likelihood of occurrence. All of these are clearly tense suffixes but, interestingly, all can be replaced by a single irrealis suffix for status, removing the event from the temporal continuum. The irrealis suffix indicates either that the occurrence of the event in the future cannot be fixed or that it occurred in the legendary past, so that again it is beyond real time. The Yimas system can be schematized as:

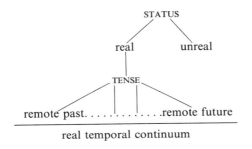

Although status is the senior partner here, the great majority of distinctions are those of tense, so the system should best be labelled one of *tense. To buttress this claim, I should point out that in addition to this set of *tense suffixes, Yimas also has an independent set of clear *status* prefixes, involving a four-way contrast: real events; likely events; potential but unlikely events; and unreal events. These are clear status markers in the language, and occur independently of the *tense suffixes, interacting with them in complex ways:

> *tawra   kakanan ana-wa-n*
> money without POT 3SG-go-PRES
> 'without money, it is possible, but unlikely, he will go'

> *tawra   kantɨkɨn ka-n-wa-n*
> money with   LIKELY-3SG-go-PRES
> 'with money, he is likely to go'

These examples are in the present tense and indicate the likelihood or unlikelihood of a close-at-hand future event from the vantage point of the present time. The potential prefix is used with past tense suffixes to indicate contrafactuals:

> *mɨ-rɨm ampɨ-ya-ntuk-ump-ɨn*   *antɨ-ka-wa-ntut*
> they-DL POT 3DL-come-RM PAST-SEQ-OBL POT-1SG-go-RM PAST
> 'if they had come, I would have gone'

This could be paraphrased as 'in the remote past it was possible, but unlikely, that those two would come and, as a result, that I would go; but these unlikely events did not in fact happen'. This use for potential events which did not in fact happen is normal with markers of past tense and perfective aspect:

> *anti-ka-tumuk-ut*
> POT-1SG-fall-PERF
> 'I almost fell down'

It is probably a safe generalization that most Papuan languages are tense-dominated in that, of the two outer operators, tense and status, tense is the more prominent inflectional category. But this is by no means true of all these languages: in Hua (Haiman 1980), for instance, tense plays no role. In addition to inflection for illocutionary force, verbs take suffixes to indicate status. There is a three-way distinction: real ($\emptyset$), likely (*-gu*) and possible (*-su*). The likely suffix corresponds to predictions, and the possible suffix to wishes. A verb with no status suffix indicates a real event, which is either past or present tense: *hu-e*, do 1-OTHER DECL, 'I did' or 'I do', as tense is not a relevant category for the Hua verb. A similar situation is found in Kuman (Piau 1985), Golin (Bunn 1974) and Siane (Haiman 1980); such systems are probably an areal feature of the languages between Goroka and Mt Hagen in the central highlands of Papua New Guinea, tense-dominant languages being found on either side of this area.

Angaataha (Huisman 1973) has both status and tense inflections in the verb, but status is clearly the more important. Verbs are characterized first as denoting real and unreal events, and those for real events are then specified for tense. Unlike Yimas, there are no separate future tenses; future is always expressed by the irrealis. The following schema represents the Angaataha system:

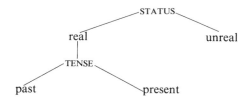

The primacy of status over tense is further demonstrated by the variety of verb forms. There are verb-forms which are inflected for both tense and status, those inflected for neither, and those inflected for status but not for tense. There are no verb-forms inflected for tense but not for status; so the Angaataha system cannot be reduced to a three-way *tense distinction of past, present and future, because such an analysis would offer no explanation of why certain verb-forms can be inflected for future but not for past or present. In the view presented here, in which future belongs to status and present and past to tense, this is perfectly explicable, for they are distinct inflectional categories.

As a final case of a status-dominant language, consider Dani (Bromley 1981). This language has three status distinctions: real, likely and possible:

real: *wat-h-i*
             kill-REAL-1SG A
             'I killed him'

likely: *was-∅-ik*
             kill-LIKELY-1SG A
             'I will kill him'

possible: *waʔ-l-e*
             kill-POT-1SG A
             'I may kill him'

Both the real and likely status categories have optional tense inflections; a remote past is found in the real category, and a near and remote future in the likely:

remote past: *wat-h-ik-i*
                     kill-REAL-RM PAST-1SG A
                     'I killed him long ago'

near future: *was -∅-ikin*
                     kill-LIKELY-SG NR FUT
                     'a singular someone will kill him'

                     (Plural actor in near future is expressed by *-ukun*.)

remote future: *wat-∅-hvp*
                     kill-LIKELY-RM FUT
                     'someone will kill him in the distant future'

The Dani system is then summarized as:

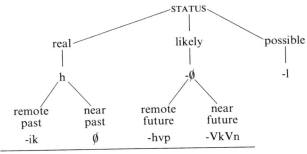

In many languages there is a close correlation between status and illocutionary force. For example, in Latin the subjunctive is not only the inflectional category associated with unreal status, but also functions to express illocutionary acts associated with as yet unrealized events, such as exhortations, wishes, prohibitions or commands. Dani parallels Latin in this respect. The inflection for likely status is the normal indication for hortative or imperative illocutionary acts, depending on the person of the actor:

was-∅-ik	*was-∅-in*	*waʔ-∅-nek*
kill-LIKELY-1SG A	kill-LIKELY-2SG A	kill-LIKELY-3
'let me kill him'	'kill him'	'let him/them kill him'

In other languages there are distinct inflections for illocutionary force. In Alamblak (Bruce 1984) there are prefixes for both imperatives and hortatives, which are not related to the unreal suffix:

nuat wa-ya-n-t	*nuat a-ya-nëm-t*
sago IMP-eat-2SG A-3SG F U	sago HORT-eat-1PL A-3SG F U
'eat the sago!'	'let's eat the sago'

Iatmul (Staalsen 1972) has a prefix for imperatives and a suffix for wishes:

a-yɨ-mɨla	*yɨ-kaa-ntɨ*
IMP-go-2SG M	go-WISH-3SG M
'go!'	'would that he would go'

The languages of the central highlands of Papua New Guinea are especially rich in affixes for illocutionary force. In Fore (Scott 1978) and Hua (Haiman 1980) all verbs must be explicitly marked for illocutionary force, there being no unmarked declarative forms as in the three languages already mentioned. The illocutionary force suffixes are obligatory and are always the outermost suffixes. In Fore there are three distinct verbal suffixes which indicate illocutionary force:

tum-en-e	*tum-is-in-o*
descend-2SG A-DECL	descend-INTENT-2SG A-Q
'you descend'	'will you be descending?'

tum-o
descend-SG IMP
'descend!'

while for Hua the illocutionary force suffixes are portmanteau with a partial specification of the person/number of the actor, as discussed in section 5.3:

vo-e   *do-ve*
lie 1-OTHER DECL   eat 1-OTHER Q
'I lie/lay down'   'did I eat?'

mi-o
give-PL IMP
'give!'

Hua has a somewhat richer inventory of illocutionary force suffixes than Fore, including, besides these three, an emphatic declarative, an exclamatory, an expectant etc. In its overall system it parallels more the Chimbu languages to its west than its more closely related sister, Fore.

The final set of outer operator morphemes I will consider are evidentials. These mark the truthfulness of a proposition expressed by the utterance, generally in terms of the way the speaker has ascertained this. Did he see it with his eyes? Is it hearsay etc? These are only found in declarative speech acts, indicating the speaker's basis for making his assertion. To my knowledge, evidentials are restricted in Papuan languages to the Engan family and languages geographically contiguous to it in the Southern Highlands Province. It is clearly an areal feature. The simplest system of evidentials is that attested by Kewa (Franklin 1971): was the action seen by the speaker or not?

ira-a-ha   *ira-a-ya*
cook-3SG NR PAST-SEEN   cook-3SG NR PAST-UNSEEN
'he cooked it (I saw it)'   'he cooked it' (hearsay)

Fasu (Loeweke and May 1980) has a much richer array of evidentials, including: seen by the eyes; not seen by the eyes, but heard with the ears; neither heard nor seen, but deduced from evidence; hearsay from a known source; hearsay from an unknown source; and mere supposition:

a-pe-re   *pe-ra-rakae*
SE-come-EN   come-CUST-HEARD
'[I see] it coming'   '[I hear] it coming'

pe-sa-reapo   *pe-sa-pakae*
come-PAST-DEDUCED   come-PAST-HEARSAY UNKNOWN
'[I've concluded] it's coming' '[I've heard] it's coming'

pe-sa-ripo   *pe-sa-pi*
come-PAST-HEARSAY KNOWN   come-PAST-SUPPOSE
'[I've heard] it's coming'   '[I think] it's coming'

Oksapmin (Lawrence 1983) makes a distinction in past tenses which seems to be very close to being an evidential distinction. The past tenses distinguish between events seen from the perspective of a participant as a performer of the event and events seen by an observer of the event:

> *su-yaa-∅*
> kill-PL IM PAST-ACTOR'S VIEW
> 'they have just killed it' (their viewpoint)
>
> *su-yaa-he*
> kill-PL IM PAST-OTHER'S VIEW
> 'they have just killed it' (someone else's viewpoint)

This viewpoint distinction seems closely related to the evidential category because one's participation in an event as active performer rather than passive observer is doubtless related to the salience the event holds and one's consequent commitment to its truthfulness. Viewpoint plays an important role in Oksapmin discourse by allowing the narrator to vary the perspective of the text to achieve different pragmatic or dramatic effects.

6

Syntax

6.1 The role of syntax

Syntax may be defined as the principles by which words are combined to produce meaningful utterances. Syntax may be used to produce meaningful sequences of words at a number of different levels of grammar. For example, the nominal phrases *old men and women* and *men and old women* do not refer to the same set of individuals, while the sentences *the man saw the woman* and *the woman saw the man* do not describe the same events. The order of words, the syntax of the constructions, determines the differences in meaning, and from this we may conclude that syntax plays a crucial role in the production of English utterances.

Many other languages, notably many Papuan languages, do not follow English in according such a central role to syntax. In Yimas, the order of words is generally quite irrelevant in determining meaning, this role being primarily performed by morphology. Consider the following examples:

> *payum   ŋaykum   yuwa-m*
> man-PL woman-PL good-M PL
> 'good men and women'

> *payum   ŋaykum   yuwa-nput*
> man-PL woman-PL good-F PL
> 'men and good women'

The order of words in these two examples is completely unconstrained; all conceivable combinations are acceptable. Any combination with the masculine plural adjective form *yuwa-m* will express 'good men and women', while any with the feminine plural will express 'men and good women'. In Yimas, word-order does not function to determine these meanings; it is solely a function of the morphology.

This is equally true for Yimas clauses:

> *payum   narmaŋ   na-mpu-tay*
> man-PL woman-SG 3SG U-3PL A-see
> 'the men saw the woman'

payum narmaŋ   pu-n-tay
man-PL woman-SG 3PL U-3SG A-see
'the woman saw the men'

Again the order of words here is irrelevant, although Yimas, like most Papuan languages, commonly puts the verb finally. Unlike English, the order of the nominals does not determine their roles as actor or undergoer; this too is performed morphologically in Yimas, not syntactically. The pattern of inflection of the verb determines the semantic functions of its associated nominals. In the first example the verbal prefixes indicate a plural actor and a singular undergoer. The associated plural noun *payum* 'men' must therefore be the actor, and the singular noun *narmaŋ* 'woman', the undergoer, resulting in 'the men saw the woman'. In the second example, the inflectional pattern is the opposite. The verbal prefixes indicate a singular actor and a plural undergoer; hence, the singular noun *narmaŋ* 'woman' must now be actor, and the plural noun *payum* 'men', undergoer, expressing the meaning 'the woman saw the men'. In both examples, the order of the nouns is unchanged; only the verbal affixation alters, thereby altering the meaning. As with the nominal phrases above, syntactic rules of word-order play no role here, the meaning of the utterance being completely expressed by the morphological structure.

The role accorded to syntax in the grammar of Papuan languages varies, but it generally plays a less important role in these languages than it does in English. Probably only a minority of Papuan languages behave in nominal phrases like Yimas; more commonly, the order of words in phrases does play some role in their interpretation. But with regard to clauses, the Yimas pattern does seem to be the general rule. In only a minority of Papuan languages does the word-order of nominals in clauses play a role in their interpretation.

6.2 Clause structure

As pointed out above, word-order is not generally significant for indicating semantic functions in Papuan languages. Many may be regarded as free word-order languages. Although the verb is usually positioned clause-finally, this rule is rigid only in some languages. In a great many Papuan languages, peripheral nominals such as locatives or temporals commonly occur after the verb. Yimas is even freer: the actor frequently occurs after the verb. The general impression of clause structure in Papuan languages in comparison to English is its overall looseness, and this no doubt results from the fact that syntax plays a much less central role.

Let me develop this argument further by a more detailed contrastive analysis of English and Yimas. As I have already pointed out, word-order in English is significant for semantic relations. The two sentences *the man saw the woman* and *the woman saw the man* differ in meaning. As the only structural difference between them is in word-order, clearly it is word-order that signals the meaning differences. In Yimas, word-order plays no such role. The sentence

> *payum narmaŋ na-mpu-tay*
> man-PL woman-SG 3SG U-3PL A-see
> 'the men saw the woman'

always has the same meaning regardless of the word-order. If we wish to express 'the woman saw the men', no change in the word-order is necessary. We would simply need to change the prefixation to the verb, as discussed above.

But differences do not stop there. In English we can pronominalize the nominals: *he saw the woman, the man saw her* or *he saw her*. But we cannot just drop the nominal arguments entirely and produce a grammatical sentence *saw*. But in Yimas we can do all of these things:

> *m-um narmaŋ na-mpu-tay*
> PRO-3PL woman 3SG U-3PL A-see
> 'they saw the woman'

> *m-um m-ɨn na-mpu-tay*
> PRO-3PL PRO-3SG 3SG U-3PL A-see
> 'they saw her'

> *na-mpu-tay*
> 3SG U-3PL A-see
> 'they saw her'

In other words, the verb on its own functions perfectly well as a sentence in Yimas, while this is certainly not true of English. For English, the syntactic position of subject must always be filled in an independent clause, and for many transitive verbs the object position must also be filled: **he assassinated, *he deprived, *he assaulted*. Syntactic rules in English not only determine the semantic functions of the nominals, they actually frame the sentence, producing a structure which makes a sentence possible and without which there can be no grammatical sentence in English. Syntactic rules for English specify that any English sentence must be minimally made up of a subject nominal and a verb, in that order. If the verb is transitive, it will be followed by an object nominal. So, for any transitive verb in English, a clause containing it must be formed according to the following informal rule:

> Sentence = Nominal + Verb + Nominal

From this syntactic structure millions of English sentences can be produced, differing only in the selections of verbs and nominals.

This syntactic superstructure is wholly irrelevant for Yimas. Here, a sentence consists minimally of a verb, with no necessary associated nominals. There are no syntactic rules necessary to produce a sentence in Yimas. A verb is produced by the morphological rules in the language. Hence, we find:

> *na-mpu-tay*
> 3SG U-3PL A-see
> 'they saw her'

If the clause is to contain associated nominals, they can be added, in any order, according to constraints that may be imposed by the verb. Peripheral nominals, like locatives or temporals, may be freely added:

> *num-un   na-mpu-tay*
> village-OBL 3SG U-3PL A-see
> 'they saw her in the village'

Core nominals, like actor and undergoer, are more restricted. They may be added subject to the proviso that their specifications for person, number and class agree with one of the verbal prefixes for core arguments. So:

> *narmaŋ   na-mpu-tay*
> woman-II SG 3SG U-3PL A-see
> 'they saw the woman'

is grammatical because *narmaŋ*, a class II singular noun, is in concord with the verbal prefix *na-* for singular nouns of classes I–III. But

> **krayŋ   na-mpu-tay*
> frog-VI SG 3SG U-3PL A-see
> 'they saw the frog'

is ungrammatical because the added core nominal *krayŋ* is a singular class VI noun, but the verb has no corresponding prefix for this number and class combination.

In Yimas, the core nominals are simply in apposition to the verb, which alone is obligatory to the clause. The core nominals are much like optional modifiers to the verb as the head of the clause, rather in the way that adjectives are optional modifiers of their head nouns. It is not surprising, then, that in the great majority of Yimas clauses the verb occurs without any associated nominals at all. The position of these optional nominals with respect to the verb is free, exactly as the position of Yimas adjectives with respect to their head nouns is also free. A consistent typological view of Yimas is now emerging. It is a language in which syntactic rules play no role in the organization of its phrases and clauses. Words are formed by the morphological rules of the language and then freely thrown together, subject only to the constraint that such collocations make sense semantically.

How different is English from this point of view. For English, syntax is central. Words cannot be thrown together freely. They must be combined according to the abstract syntactic principles of sentence formation. *The man saw the woman* is grammatical in English and obeys the syntactic rules of English. **Saw the woman the man* is not a grammatical English sentence because it violates these rules. The nominals are not in apposition to their verb in English, but they and the verb together constitute the irreducible core of the English clause. In contrast, the core of the Yimas clause is simply the verb.

This dominance of morphology over syntax as the basic organizing parameter of the grammar is true of Papuan languages as a whole. In Yimas, I pointed out that it is the verbal affixation which is pivotal in clause structure. Yimas lacks nominal case-marking for all core nominals. Other Papuan languages differ in this respect. Fore (Scott 1978) is an especially enlightening case. Like Yimas, it has verbal affixation for both actor and undergoer, and such an inflected verb can stand on its own as a complete sentence:

> *a-ka-i-e*
> 3SG U-see-3SG A-DECL
> 'he sees him'

The order of the nominals before the verb is free:

> *naebá yaga: naninta: a-mu-w-e*
> I   pig   food   3SG U-give-1SG A-DECL
>
> *yaga: náebá naninta: a-mu-w-e*
>
> *naninta: náebá yaga: a-mu-w-e*
>
> 'I gave the pig food'

All three sentences have the same meaning, regardless of the order of the nominals. Given the semantics of the nominals, there is of course only the one possible meaning: 'I' is the only possible actor, and 'the pig' the only possible recipient. The interpretation becomes more indeterminate when more than one nominal is a potential actor. Consider the following sentence:

> *wa   mási a-ka-i-e*
> man   boy   3SG U-see-3SG A-DECL
> 'the man saw the boy'

Both nominals are third singular, so the verbal affixation for third singular actor and undergoer are of no use in determining their semantic functions. This sentence can only mean 'the man saw the boy'; the alternative 'the boy saw the man' is in fact impossible for this sentence. The sentence is interpreted so that the actor precedes the undergoer. One might conclude that word-order plays a role in organizing Fore clauses when the actor and undergoer are of the same person, number and animacy – the situation in which the verbal morphology fails. This is not really true, as the following sentence demonstrates:

> *mási wá-má   a-ke-i-e*
> boy man-ERG 3SG U-see-3SG A-DECL
> 'the man sees the boy'

Here the undergoer precedes the actor, contradicting any possible syntactic rule for a prescribed actor–undergoer order. The morphology comes to the rescue, adding the ergative suffix *-ma* to the actor, again allowing the word-order of the nominals to be free. There is no syntactic principle involved here, merely an interpretive convention by the hearer that when all else fails, the first potential actor should be assumed to be the actor. That this is really just an interpretive convention and not a rigid syntactic rule is further demonstrated by the following sentence:

> *yaga: wá   a-egú-i-e*
> pig   man 3SG U-hit-3SG A-DECL
> 'the man hits the pig'

Although *yaga:* 'pig' precedes *wá* 'man', this sentence is still interpreted with *wa* 'man' as actor. Humans are higher on the animacy scale and are viewed as more likely than pigs to be actors. If a syntactic principle prescribing that actor must precede undergoer operated in Fore, then *yaga:* 'pig' would be interpreted as actor. But this is not possible. In order for it to function as actor, *yaga:* must be marked with the ergative case:

> *yaga:-wama wá   a-egú-i-e*
> pig-ERG   man 3SG U-hit-3SG A-DECL
> 'the pig attacks the man'

Again the morphology makes the interpretation convention superfluous. As the morphology now uniquely identifies semantic functions, word-order is free:

> *wa   yága:-wama a-egú-i-e*
> man pig-ERG   3SG U-hit-3SG A-DECL
> 'the pig attacks the man'

The strategies for Fore involved in determining the semantic functions of core nominals may be summarized as:

(1) verbal morphology; if that fails, then (2)
(2) nominal case marking; if that fails, then (3)
(3) animacy differences; if that fails, then (4)
(4) interpretation convention; first potential actor is actor, if everything else is equal

The Fore hierarchy of strategies clearly demonstrates the importance of morphology over syntax in this language. (1) and (2) are unquestionably morphological rules; (3) is a semantic interpretation convention. Only (4) could in any sense be considered a syntactic rule. But even that probably states it too strongly. It seems more profitable to view it also as simply a convention of semantic interpretation that, when there are no semantic grounds for choosing one nominal as actor over another, then one just takes the first one.

Not all Papuan languages behave like Yimas or Fore. Languages of a simpler morphological structure, like those of the middle Sepik area, rely more heavily on principles of word-order in determining the functions of nominals, probably as a counterbalance to the reduced role of morphology. In Iatmul (Staalsen 1972), the actor must precede the undergoer:

> *ntɨw nyan vɨ-ntɨ*
> man child see-3sg M
> 'the man saw the child'
> *'the child saw the man'

The verbal suffix *-ntɨ* for third singular masculine actor is insufficient to determine which nominal is actor, as both nominals have these features. The obligatory rule that actor precedes undergoer determines that *ntɨw* 'man' is the actor. Unlike Fore, in which this convention applies only when the morphology fails, this is a rigid syntactic rule for Iatmul. Even when the morphology is sufficient, the actor must precede the undergoer:

> *ntɨw takwə   vɨ-ntɨ*
> man woman see-3sg M
> 'the man saw the woman'

> **takwə   ntɨw vɨ-ntɨ*
> woman man see-3sg M

The *ntɨ* suffix in both examples clearly identifies *ntɨw* 'man' as actor in both examples, yet the second example in which it occurs after the undergoer is ungrammatical. This demonstrates that the principle that actor precedes undergoer is not simply an interpretive convention when all else fails, as in Fore, but has in Iatmul the status of a rigid syntactic rule.

Yessan–Mayo (Foreman 1974), spoken up-river from Iatmul, completely lacks verbal affixation for core nominals. It follows a common practice of languages of the Sepik by suffixing animate undergoers – the nominals potentially confused with actors – with the dative case, clearly identifying the actor by its lack of any nominal case-marking. This is the opposite choice from that of Fore, which marks the actor in such unclear circumstances with the ergative case, leaving the undergoer unmarked. Nonetheless, Yessan–Mayo applies the same rigid syntactic constraint as Iatmul: the actor must precede the undergoer:

> *an toma mati-ye*
> I   talk   hear-NR PAST
> 'I heard the talk'

> **toma   an mati-ye*
> talk   I   hear-NR PAST

> *an ti-ni   aki-ye*
> I   her-DAT fear-NR PAST
> 'I was afraid of her'

> **ti-ni   an aki-ye*
> her-DAT I   fear-NR PAST

With a ditransitive verb like 'give', associated with a dative recipient, there is a little more freedom. The dative nominal and the undergoer may occur in either order, but the actor must precede both:

> *an ri-ni   awes nuwa-ye*
> I   him-DAT food give-NR PAST
> *an awes ri-ni   nuwa-ye*
> I   food him-DAT give-NR PAST
> 'I gave him food'

Because of the dative case marking, no ambiguity is possible in any of the sentences, regardless of the word-order used. But Yessan–Mayo, like Iatmul, has made the convention that actor should precede undergoer a syntactic rule, resulting in the ungrammaticality of the above deviations from this rule.

Barai represents the next stage in the development of word-order as an independent principle in the organization of clause structure. Remember that for

Iatmul and Yessan–Mayo all clauses must have the same structure: the actor must precede the undergoer. In other words, the syntactic word-order principle is strictly linked to semantic functions and may not be stated independently of them. Compare this with English. For English all transitive clauses may have two syntactic realizations, an active and a passive: *the boy hit the ball* versus *the ball was hit by the boy*. In English the notion of subject is a purely syntactic one, independent of semantic functions. Both actor and undergoer roles can fill the subject position, according to the clause type.

Barai is one Papuan language similar in this respect to English, and it is the only Papuan language I know to exhibit this type of structure. Like Iatmul and Yessan–Mayo, the usual order of a Barai clause is actor–undergoer–verb (Olson 1981):

> *fu-ka   na kan-ie*
> he-really I   hit-1SG U
> 'he really hit me'

The *-ka* is a modal clitic assigned to the prominent nominal, as described in section 5.2. As *kan-* 'hit' is a controlled predicate, *-ka* occurs on the actor. If the actor is indefinite or inanimate, the word-order must be rearranged to undergoer–actor–verb, and the *-ka* clitic now occurs on the undergoer:

> *na-ka   ine   bij-ie*
> I-really stick poke-1SG U
> 'a stick really poked me'

Clearly, with controlled predicates, the *-ka* is associated with a position, i.e. the leftmost nominal. This is the most prominent nominal for such verbs. This nominal position is not tied to a particular semantic role, but both actor and undergoer can occupy it, depending on the types of nominals in the clause. The syntactic organization of a Barai clause is not directly tied to the semantic functions of actor and undergoer, like Iatmul, but is rather like English, in that the clause is organized around a prominent nominal position (Barai leftmost nominal, English subject). This notion is syntactic, not semantic, and for Barai, syntax must be recognized as an independent parameter in the organization of the clause. This is the only Papuan language I know for which this holds, whereas it is the norm for European languages.

6.3 Clause chaining

In this section I turn to what is probably the most distinctive feature of Papuan languages in general and, further, their most alien feature to speakers of the languages of Europe. The discourse of most Papuan languages is structured along radically different principles from that of English. All languages must have means by which clauses are put together to form sentences, and sentences to form texts. A text is not just a random assemblage of clauses and sentences. Such an assemblage would be meaningless, without coherence. A text is a coherent linking of clauses and sentences, and this coherence is achieved by rules of the language which state how clauses and sentences can be joined.

As I mentioned above, the system by which most Papuan languages achieve this at first strikes speakers of English as very alien. Consider the following sentence from Iatmul, constructed by joining a number of clauses together (Staalsen 1972):

> nkəy-ət   yɨ-kə   waalə klə-laa   yə-nt-əy-an
> house-ALL go-and dog   get-and then   come-3SG M-UNREAL-if
> ntɨ nkət   vɨ-kɨyə-wɨn
> 3SG M-ALL see-UNREAL-1SG
> 'If he comes after he has gone to the house and got the dog, I will see him'

The primary division in the sentence occurs after *yə-nt-əy-an* 'if he comes'. The first half includes *yə-nt-əy-an* and all the material preceding it; it corresponds to what would be identified as a subordinate conditional clause in English. The second half corresponds to a main clause and contains the fully inflected verb *vɨ-kɨyə-wɨn* 'I will see'. Note there are no overt conjunctions connecting the two clauses in Iatmul, such as English *if*. Rather, the verbal morphology serves this function.

But the subordinate conditional clause is itself complex, consisting of a number of subclauses. Preceding *yə-nt-əy-an* are two minimally inflected verbs *yɨ-kə* 'go and' and *klə-laa* 'get and then'. Again, there are no real conjunctions connecting these subclausal units. The verbal affixes *-kə* and *-laa* perform this role. Iatmul verbs are normally inflected for status and the person and number of their actor. But these verbs have no such affixation, only the 'linking' suffixes, *-kə* and *-laa*. These verbs take their specifications for status and the person and number of the actor from the closest following verb inflected for these features, in this case *yə-nt-əy-an*. They are dependent for these on this verb, and I will call them 'dependent verbs'. Many studies of Papuan languages call them 'medial verbs' because of their usual medial position in the sentence. English has something of these dependent verbs in structures like *Sitting down, John struck the fly.* The verb *sitting* has no inflection for tense or for person and number of actor. These are supplied by the fully inflected verb *struck*, upon which it is dependent. The suffix *-ing* on *sitting* is a linking suffix, indicating that the act of sitting and act of striking are simultaneous.

Contrasting with these minimally inflected dependent verbs are the fully inflected verbs *yə-nt-ay-an* and *vɨ-kɨyə-wɨn*. But these two verbs are not of equal syntactic status. *Vɨ-kɨyə-wɨn* is the main verb of the whole sentence, and it terminates the

sentence. Only it can be inflected for the outer operator, illocutionary force: *a-vɨ-*
mɨla, IMP-see-2SG M IMP, 'see (it)!' (*a-yə-mɨla-əy-an*, IMP-come-2SG M IMP-UNREAL-
if). *Vɨ-kɨya-wɨn* is a truly independent verb: it can stand on its own as a complete
sentence and is not linked overtly to any other sentence. *Yə-nt-əy-an* is rather
different. Although fully inflected for status and person and number of its actor, and
thus independent from the viewpoint of these features, it may not stand alone as a
complete sentence, and is overtly linked to the clause containing *vɨ-kɨya-wɨn* by the
suffix *-an* 'if'. It terminates a clause which is subordinated syntactically to the final
main clause. This is a subordinate clause/main clause relationship. The subordinate
clause is a conditional, and functions like an adverbial modifier to the main clause.
The subordinate clause functions like a part of the main clause, and this relation of a
part within the whole, or embeddedness, is how I will define subordination. Verbs of
such subordinate clauses, although fully specified in Iatmul for status and for person
and number of the actor, are necessarily linked to a main clause, and are therefore
not independent. I will refer to such verbs of subordinate clauses as 'subordinate-
dependent' and fully inflected verbs of main clauses as 'independent'. This assigns a
three-way typological distinction to the verbs of the Iatmul sentence above:

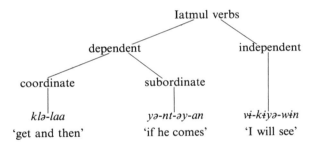

Note that I have now coined the term 'coordinate-dependent' for the dependent
or 'medial' verbs discussed above, which take their specification for status and for
person and number of the actor from a following fully inflected subordinate-
dependent or independent verb. By my definition of subordination, clauses
containing such verbs are not considered subordinate. They do not function as
arguments of some main clause. They do not function as embedded parts within a
whole, but are linked to a fully inflected verb in a linear string, much like beads on a
necklace. Because the linking of the clauses is at the same structural level, rather than
as part within whole, I regard such clauses as coordinate and verbs of such clauses as
'coordinate-dependent'. The remainder of this section will deal with coordinate-
dependent verbs, which for the purposes of this section I will abbreviate to
'dependent verbs'. Subordinate dependent verbs and subordinate clauses will be the
topic of section 6.4.

An important distinction that must be clearly established is between dependent verbs on the one hand, and serial or compound verbs on the other. Serial or compound verb structures are constructions in which verb-stems are juxtaposed to form a complex predicate, which then takes a single set of core and peripheral arguments to form one clause. Dependent verbs may each take their own set of core and peripheral arguments so that each dependent verb corresponds to its own clause. Contrast the following Yimas examples:

> marɨmp-ɨn ama-awŋkwi-sɨpaŋ-ɨt
> river-OBL   1SG s-down in water-bathe-PERF
> 'I bathed in the river'

> marɨmp-ɨn awŋkwi-mp-i   antɨ-nan   yampara-mp-i
> river-OBL   down in water-SEQ-DEP ground-OBL stand-SEQ-DEP
> ama-tɨpaŋ-ɨt
> 1SG s-bathe-PERF

'I went down into the river, stood on the ground and washed'

The first example is a serial verb construction. The verb-stems are juxtaposed to form a single complex predicate which is associated with a single core argument *ama-*, 1SG s, and peripheral argument *marɨmp-ɨn* 'in the river'. Grammatically, the serialized verbs form a single word with one set of core argument prefixes and one tense suffix.

The second example illustrates dependent verbs. Like Iatmul, dependent verbs in Yimas always take their actor and tense specifications from the independent verb, in this case *ama-sɨpaŋ-ɨt* 'I washed'. The dependent verbs have minimal inflection: suffixes -*mp*, to indicate that the relationship between the clauses is one of sequence, and -*i*, to mark the verbs as dependent. However, each of the dependent verbs is associated with its own peripheral arguments, *marɨmp-ɨn* 'into the river' and *antɨ-nan* 'on the ground', whereas in the serial verb construction the peripheral argument *marɨmp-ɨn* 'in the river' is associated with both verb-stems, with the complex predicate as a whole. This is the primary characteristic differentiating dependent verbs from serial verbs. Dependent verbs may select their own peripheral nominals, serial verbs may not. Dependent verbs form the centre of individual but dependently linked clauses; serial verbs form a single complex centre of one clause. This difference in structure is undoubtedly correlated with the fact that serial verb constructions quite often become lexicalized, the meaning of the whole not predictable from its parts. This results from the single clause structure of serial verb constructions; the complex predicate gradually becomes seen more as a simplex lexeme. This is rarely, if ever, true of dependent verbs. The chaining of dependent verbs is normally fully productive grammatically, with no ad hoc restrictions or idiosyncratic meanings. This follows from the fact that dependent verbs constitute whole clauses, which may be chained together to form sentences.

The constraints that languages apply to serial verb constructions show some variation. Minimally, for all languages, the verb-stems in a serial construction must share a single set of peripheral nominals. Yimas goes even further, requiring that all the verb-stems have a single set of core nominals:

> impa-mpu-yakal-irɨm-tay-ntut
> 3DL U-3PL A-EXT-stand-see-RM PAST
> 'they stood watching them two'

In the example the verbal affixes *mpu-*, 3PL A, and *impa-*, 3DL U, are associated with the complex predicate as a whole. This view is warranted because the prefixes cannot be plausibly associated with the closest verb stem *irɨm-* 'stand', as it is intransitive and the complex predicate is transitive. Further, the extended aspect inner operator *yakal-* must modify both verb-stems. Shared inner operators is another common feature of serial verb constructions in many languages. This never applies to dependent verbs, which may always independently select their inflections for inner operators.

Barai also opposes serial verb constructions to dependent verbs, but the constraints are less rigid than in Yimas. Again, peripheral nominals must be shared, but the verbs in some serial constructions may select their own independent set of core nominals:

> mufuo   fu fi fase isoe-ke
> late afternoon he sit letter write-UNREAL
> 'in the late afternoon, he will sit and write a letter'

In this example the verb *isoe* 'write' occurs with a core nominal *fase* 'letter', which bears no relationship to the other verb *fi* 'sit' in the serial construction. But the peripheral nominal *mufuo* 'late afternoon' must modify both verbs. If the peripheral nominal is to modify only one of the verbs, a construction with a dependent verb rather than a serialized structure must be used. The first verb will occur with an obligatory linking suffix *-na* 'and then':

> fu fi-na   mufuo   fase isoe-ke
> he sit-and then late afternoon letter write-UNREAL
> 'he will sit and in the late afternoon will write a letter'

Note that the dependent verb *fi-na* 'sit, and then' takes its unreal status specification from the final independent verb *isoe-ke* 'will write'.

I conclude that dependent verbs must be sharply distinguished from serial verbs. In addition to the systematic syntactic and semantic differences between them which were pointed out, there is also a very general morphological difference. Serialized verbs usually appear in their base stem forms and are juxtaposed with no connecting morphology. Dependent verbs, although stripped down inflectionally from independent verbs, usually have some overt morphology, at least a linking suffix.

The amount of semantic information encoded in the linking suffixes of dependent verbs varies quite widely. Normally, they encode differences of temporal relations between the clauses. The simplest temporal contrast, and the one which underlies all more complex ones, is between simultaneous and sequential actions. Within a Papuan context 'simultaneous' means that the period of duration of the two actions must overlap, either partially or fully. Sequential actions are those in which there is no temporal overlap. This is well illustrated by Kewa (Franklin 1971):

> *ní réko-a   ágaa lá-wa*
> I   stand-SEQ talk say-1SG NR PAST
> 'I stood up and spoke'

> *épo   lá-ri   épa-wa*
> whistle say-SIM come-1SG NR PAST
> 'I whistled while I came'

In the first example, the act of standing is completed before the act of speaking. There is no overlap between the events; this is a sequential relationship. The second example illustrates simultaneous events. The actor whistles during the time in which he is coming. The time extent of the two events overlaps; in this case the duration of whistling is contained completely within the ongoing act of coming.

Barai (Olson 1981) contrasts a simultaneous relation with three distinct types of sequential relations. Sequential relations distinguished are immediate sequence, in which the first action terminates and then is immediately followed by the second action; delayed sequence, in which the first action terminates, is followed by a time lapse with no relevant action, and is then followed by the second action; and span sequence, in which the first activity is prolonged over a period of time until the inception of another action. The Barai system can be schematized as follows:

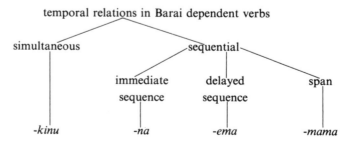

temporal relations in Barai dependent verbs

simultaneous		sequential	
	immediate sequence	delayed sequence	span
-kinu	*-na*	*-ema*	*-mama*

Examples of each type follow:

> *bu   ire   i-kinu   vua   kuae*
> they food eat-SIM talk say
> 'they were eating and talking'

> *bu   ire   i-na   vua   kuae*
> they food eat-IM SEQ talk say
> 'they ate and then told stories'

> *na nae-ema   suoke   una   rua-e*
> I   sleep-DEL SEQ morning again come-PAST
> 'I slept and then (after an interval) came back in the morning'

> *fu rua-mama ij-ia   keke*
> he come-SPAN that-LOC arrive
> 'he kept coming until he arrived there'

Iatmul (Staalsen 1972) exemplifies one of the most elaborate systems of contrasts in temporal relations. This language possesses seven different temporal relation suffixes for dependent verbs. As with the other systems, the primary distinction is between simultaneous and sequential. Temporal suffixes for simultaneous events distinguish between events which are in a causal relation from those which are not, i.e. the clause with the dependent verb constitutes the motivation for the action of the following verb. Simultaneous events in a causal relation are further distinguished according to whether the action of the dependent verb terminates during the event of the following verb, or is concurrent with it:

> *vɨ-kɨva   yə-wɨn*
> see-SIM NCAUS come-1SG
> 'I chanced to see it as I came'

> *vɨ-sɨmpla   yə-wɨn*
> see-SIM CAUS EXT come-1SG
> 'I saw it while coming (coming in order to see)'

> *vɨ-sɨmplalaa   yə-wɨn*
> see-SIM CAUS PERF come-1SG
> 'in the course of coming I saw it (as I intended to)'

-kɨva is the simple noncausal simultaneous, while *-sɨmpla* and *-sɨmplalaa* apply to causal simultaneous situations, distinguishing between continuing and terminating motivating events respectively. *-sɨmplalaa* is itself morphologically complex, made

up of -*simpla* plus the basic sequential temporal suffix -*laa*, to be discussed now.

Sequential relations are indicated by four different temporal suffixes, but the basic one is -*laa*, indicating simply that the action of the dependent clause terminates before that of the following begins:

> vɨ-*laa* yə-wɨn
> see-SEQ come-1SG
> 'having seen it, I came'

Nothing but a sequential time relation is expressed by this suffix. The other sequential suffixes are complex, made up of -*laa* plus another morpheme, which indicates whether the undergoer of the dependent verb is totally affected, partially affected or unaffected by the action:

> vɨ-*yəkɨy-laa*   yə-wɨn
> see-TOTAL AFFECT-SEQ come-1SG
> 'having seen all, I came'

> vɨ-*lampi-laa*   yə-wɨn
> see-PART UNAFFECT-SEQ come-1SG
> 'having seen none, I came'

> vɨ-*ləvɨy-laa*   yə-wɨn
> see-UNAFFECT-SEQ come-1SG
> 'having seen none, I came'

The Iatmul system of temporal suffixes for dependent verbs may be summarized as follows:

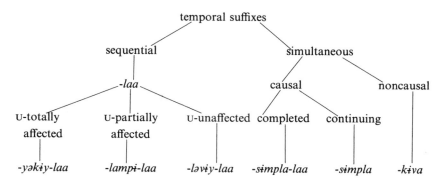

In all cases investigated so far, the dependent verbs have taken their actor specifications from the final independent verb; in other words, all dependent verbs must have had the same actor as the following independent verb. In many languages this is in fact a rigid constraint. In Iatmul, if two verbs joined together in a sentence have different actors, then two independent verbs must be used, joined by the conjunction *maa*, indicating a change in actor:

> *klə-ntɨ   maa   yə-ntɨ*
> get-3SG M DIFF A come-3SG M
> 'he₁ got it, and he₂ came'

in which the person getting and the person coming must be different individuals.

This constraint on the use of dependent verbs is not operative in many other Papuan languages. Rather, such languages have morphemes which indicate whether the actor of the dependent verb is the same as that of the following verb or different. This is the phenomenon known as 'switch reference' – is the referent of the actor of the dependent verb the same as or different from that of the following verb? In some languages, although temporal relations of simultaneity and sequence are indicated for dependent verbs with the same actor, this does not apply to dependent verbs with a different actor. Nasioi (Hurd and Hurd 1970) is one such language; consider the following examples:

> *kad-o-ma   nan-ant-in*
> talk-1SG-SIM SA go-1SG-IM PAST
> 'while talking, I went'

> *madatini nai-u-kotaaʔ   bo-in*
> medicine drink-3SG-SEQ SA die-3SG-IM PAST
> 'he drank medicine until he died'

> *aaʔ oʔno-di-ko   b-a-ud-in   pontoʔ-a-d-uʔnun*
> here be 1PL-PL-DA 3POSS-SG-child-male born-self-SG-RM PAST
> 'while we were here, his son was born'

> *daʔ po-ko   nan-amp-e-ain*
> you come-DA go-1PL-DL-FUT
> 'when you come, we (EXCL) two will go'

The first two examples involve the same actor for both verbs. In the first example, the actions are simultaneous and the dependent verb is suffixed with *-ma*, indicating a simultaneous temporal relation with the same actor. In the second example the actions are sequential: the man drinks medicine and then he dies. *-kotaaʔ* marks a dependent verb in a sequential temporal relation with the same actor. Further, it normally implies that the first action precipitates the second. The latter two examples both involve actions with different actors, and this is signalled by the suffix

-ko, for different actors. Although the first of these two sentences expresses a simultaneous relation between the actions, and the second a sequential relation, this is not indicated by the dependent verb. The dependent verb suffix simply indicates that the actors are different, the temporal relations being deduced from context.

Other languages contrast with Nasioi in combining the expression of temporal relationship with the indication of same versus different actor. Barai is a language of this type: simultaneous actions are distinguished from sequential actions for dependent verbs with both same and different actors:

> *bu   ire   i-kinu   vua kune*
> they food eat-SIM SA talk say
> 'they were eating and talking'

> *bu   ire   i-na   vua kuae*
> they food eat-SEQ SA talk say
> 'they ate and then told stories'

> *bu   ire   i-ko   no vua kuae*
> they food eat-SIM DA we talk say
> 'they were eating while we were talking'

> *bu   ire   i-mo   no vua kuae*
> they food eat-SEQ DA we talk say
> 'they ate and so we were talking'

-kinu and *-na* mark dependent verbs with the same actor as the following verb, indicating simultaneous or sequential temporal relations respectively. Different-actor dependent verbs occur with either *-ko* for simultaneous events or *-mo* for sequential events. *-mo* also commonly has the further implication of a causal relationship between the two events, as in the above example.

In all cases thus far the dependent verbs have had no specification for their own actors, taking this specification from a following independent verb fully inflected for the person and number of the actor, or from some overt pronoun in the next clause. Many Papuan languages allow this only in the case of same-actor dependent verbs. Different-actor dependent verbs must be specified by verbal affixation for the person and number of their actor, but by a different inflectional system from that for actors of independent verbs. Kewa (Franklin 1971) is one such language:

> *ní réke-no   ágaa lá-a*
> I stand-DA 1SG talk say-3SG NR PAST
> 'I stood up and he talked'

> *nipú réke-na*   *ágaa lá-ma*
> he   stand-DA 3SG talk   say-1PL NR PAST
> 'he stood up and we talked'

-no is the switch reference morpheme for first singular actors. It indicates that the actor of the dependent verb on which it is suffixed is first singular, but that the next verb will have a different actor. *-na* indicates third singular actor for the dependent verb and also signals that the referent of the actor of the next verb must be a different referent. Consider this example:

> *nipu réke-na*   *ágaa lá-a*
> he   stand-DA 3SG talk   say-3SG NR PAST
> 'he₁ stood up and he₂ talked'

Both the dependent and the independent verb have actors whose specifications are third singular. The presence of the switch-reference suffix *-na* on the dependent verb indicates that the actors may not have the same referents. Hence, one individual stood up and a different individual talked. Switch-reference systems along the lines of that of Kewa are quite common in New Guinea, being found as well in Chimbu languages, in Huon family languages and in some Madang area languages.

The most complex switch-reference systems are those found in the Gorokan and Kainantu language families. These languages employ an additional morpheme on the dependent verb, the 'anticipatory actor suffix', which signals the person and number of the actor of the following verb. I will first consider Fore (Scott 1978) of the Gorokan family. All dependent verbs in Fore must take an anticipatory actor suffix. Same-actor dependent verbs consist of a temporal suffix, either *-ma* for sequential or *-ʔte* for simultaneous actions, a dependency marking suffix *-ki* and an anticipatory actor morpheme, which, when occurring on a same-actor dependent verb, signals its own actor as well as that of the following verb:

> *máe-ma-ki-na*   *kana-i-e*
> get-SEQ-DEP-3SG A come-3SG A-DECL
> 'he gets it and comes'

> *máe-ʔte-ki-ʔta*   *kána-ʔku-un-e*
> get-SIM-DEP-1PL A come-FUT-1PL A-DECL
> 'we shall get it and come'

Different-actor dependent verbs differ in one crucial respect. They may not take the temporal suffixes *-ma* and *-ʔte*, but instead obligatorily occur with a suffix indicating the person and number of the actor, as well as expressing a three-way distinction of tense: present, past and future, normally agreeing with the tense specification of the final independent verb. It is the presence of these actor/tense suffixes on dependent verbs which signals a change in actor:

> *kana-a:-kí-tá*   *a-ka-us-e*
> come-3SG A PRES-DEP-1DL A 3SG U-see-1DL A-DECL
> 'he comes and we both see it'

> *kaná-uʔ-ki-na*   *a-ka-ʔtá-i-e*
> come-2SG A PAST-DEP-3SG A 3SG U-see-NR PAST-3SG A-DECL
> 'you came and he saw it'

> *kana-isí-ki-nisí*   *a-ka-ʔkubu-a:s-e*
> come-3DL A FUT-DEP-2DL A 3SG U-see-FUT-2DL A-DECL
> 'they two will come and you two will see it'

While independent verbs make a four-way distinction in tense – remote past, near past, present and future, and within future a binary status distinction of likely versus unlikely – dependent verbs only make a simple three-way tense distinction of past, present and future in these suffixes. The tense of the dependent verb is determined by that of the independent verb: past for remote and near past, present for present, and future for both likely and unlikely future. These suffixes also indicate the person and number of the actor of the dependent verb, and their presence further signals that there is a change of actor in the next verb. The anticipatory actor suffix on the dependent verb then indicates the person and number of the actor of the next verb. It is possible and quite common to have more than one change in actor in the same sentence:

> *kana-a:-ki-ni*   *ká-ká-i-ki-na*
> come-2SG A FUT-DEP-3PL A 2SG U-see-3PL A FUT-DEP-2SG A
> *ú-wai-mú-ʔkubu-a:n-e*
> say-3PL U-give-FUT-2SG A-DECL
> 'when you come and they see you, you will tell [it] to them'

This illustrates two different-actor dependent verbs followed by an independent verb. The actor switches from second singular to third plural and then back to second singular.

Hua (Haiman 1980) belongs to the same Gorokan family as Fore and has roughly the same structure, but is morphologically somewhat simpler. Same-actor dependent verbs are simply suffixed with the anticipatory actor suffix, indicating its actor as well as that of the next verb: *hu-ʔda*, do-1SG A, 'I did and I ...'. Different-actor dependent verbs require a switch-reference suffix, which parallels the Hua final verb suffixes discussed in section 5.3 in having three allomorphs, depending on the person and number of the actor:

-na 2SG, 1PL ~ *-ʔga* DL ~ *-ga* OTHER

These, plus the vowel alternations of the verb-stem, also discussed in section 5.3, indicate the person and number of the actor of the dependent verb:

	S	DL	PL
1	*hu-ga*	*hu-ʔga*	*hu-na*
2	*ha-na*		
		ha-ʔga	*ha-ga*
3	*hi-ga*		

The mere presence of the suffix *-na* ~ *-ʔga* ~ *-ga* signals a change in actor. The actor of the next verb is then indicated by the anticipatory actor suffix: *hu-ga-na*, do 1-DA OTHER-3SG A, 'I did and he . . .'.

The dependent verb-forms in the Kainantu family resemble rather more those of Fore than those of Hua, and this is readily explicable in view of the fact that the Fore area adjoins that of the Kainantu family. There is a good body of evidence in both the phonology and morphology of Fore to suggest diffusion from languages of the Kainantu family. Dependent verbs in Tairora (Vincent 1973) are inflected with an anticipatory actor suffix expressing the person and number of the actor, sometimes combined with an indication of tense:

> *ne-ro* *bi-ro*
> eat-3SG A go-3SG A PAST
> 'he ate and went'
>
> *ne-ro* *bi-reba*
> eat-3SG A go-3SG A FUT
> 'he will eat and go'
>
> *na-reba* *bi-reba*
> eat-3SG A FUT go-3SG A FUT
> 'he will go to eat'

-ro is the neutral form for third singular. When used on an independent verb, as in the first example, it signals a present or a near past tense. When used on a dependent verb, it indicates that the verb has the same actor as the following verb. In these cases the tense of the dependent verb is specified by that of the following independent verb: past in the first example and future in the second. Unlike Fore and Hua,

however, same-actor dependent verbs in Tairora may be specified for tense, as in the last example. In such cases, the tense morphemes function as relative tense indicators, specifying the time of the event of the dependent verb relative to that of the independent verb. Thus, in the final example above, the future tense on the dependent verb indicates an act of eating occurring *after* a future act of going, 'I will go and then I will eat' or 'I will go to eat'. A striking feature of Tairora dependent verbs is their minimal morphological differentiation from independent verbs, as opposed to the much sharper difference in form in Gorokan family languages like Hua or Fore. Note that the same form *ne-ro* could function as a dependent or independent verb, depending on its position in the sentence.

Dependent verbs with a different actor from the following verb require a suffix combining the indication of the person and number of the actor with expression of tense, and this is in turn followed by an anticipatory actor suffix:

> *na-iba-ro*   *bi-ro*
> eat-3SG A PAST-3SG A   go-3SG A PAST
> 'he₁ ate and he₂ left'

> *na-ira-ro*   *bi-reba*
> eat-3SG A FUT-3SG A   go-3SG A FUT
> 'he₁ will eat and he₂ will go'

If one compares these forms with the different-actor dependent verb-forms of Fore discussed above, it is immediately apparent that the only formal difference is the presence of the dependent verb suffix -*ki* in the Fore forms.

I have defined switch reference as the monitoring of the sameness or difference of the referents of the actors of two verbs. One question that this definition immediately presents is, what counts as sameness of reference? More specifically, what happens in cases when the actors differ in number, but the singular actor of one verb is included in the plural actor of the other? Reesink (1983) discusses this problem, and notes that, although there is a great deal of variation in the way Papuan languages handle it, there are some generalizations that may be offered. I will simply summarize here his observations. Both the person and the number categories of the actor nominals must be considered. Same-actor marking is most likely to be used in cases where the person specification remains the same, and only the number changes, such as:

> 'he shot a pig and they carried it'
> 'I shot a pig and we carried it'
> 'they shot a pig and he carried it'

When the person specification changes the pattern is more complicated. If the change is from a plural actor to a singular one, some languages may choose same actor marking. These are examples such as:

> 'you all shot a pig and he carried it'
> 'we shot a pig and you carried it'
> 'we shot a pig and he carried it'

In all three examples, the singular actor of the second verb is to be regarded as being included in the group of the plural actor of the first. Papuan languages vary most widely in their treatment of examples like these. Some languages like Kewa require these to be different-actor forms, while others like Usan allow either same or different actors. The crucial rule in all cases of free choice of same- versus different-actor marking is whether the speaker considers the shift in participants important enough to signal as different actor. Thus, if the exclusivity of the singular actor is at issue, i.e. its separateness from the group actor, then different-actor morphology will be used. Otherwise, same actor is the norm.

Different-actor marking is definitely favoured in changes from singular number to plural:

> 'he shot a pig and you carried it'
> 'he shot a pig and we carried it'
> 'you shot a pig and we carried it'

Again, in all these examples, the singular actor is included in the group of the plural one. These three examples are more likely to have different-actor morphology than the previous three, in spite of the fact that they only differ in the order of the number specifications of the actors, singular to plural versus plural to singular. But note the changes in the person specifications in the two sets. In the first three examples the transition is from a higher person specification to a lower, while in the latter three it is from a lower person to a higher. Many sources (e.g. Silverstein 1976, Dixon 1979) have established a topicality hierarchy of person of $1 > 2 > 3$. Clearly, the greater likelihood of different-actor morphology in the last set of examples is a reflection of a jump in topicality from a lower person to a higher one. This jump is a shift in participants important enough to register as different actor. Note that in all this discussion I am regarding different actor as the marked member of the opposition. This seems to be justified in terms of its behaviour as discussed here and below, as well as by the fact that different-actor dependent verbs are always more complicated morphologically than same-actor verbs. The form and function coincide in identifying different actor as the marked form.

Having discussed differences in the person and number specifications of the actors in relation to switch-reference marking, let me now consider differences in the semantic functions of the nominals monitored. Switch reference is defined as monitoring same versus different *actor*, and this definition is generally accurate; but there is one construction for which this generalization does not hold. In section 5.2 of the previous chapter I discussed the impersonal verbal constructions expressing uncontrolled states or events. In these constructions an inanimate cause nominal functions as the actor, while the undergoer is the animate participant experiencing the state or event:

Wahgi:

(Luzbetak 1954) *na peng to-nom*
I   head hit-3SG PRES
'I have a headache'

Usan:

(Reesink 1983) *wo toar   wâ-r-â*
he sickness 3SG U-hit-3SG A PRES
'he is sick'

When these uncontrolled constructions occur in clause chains, it is common in many Papuan languages for the dependent verb before the uncontrolled construction to take *same-actor* marking if the animate undergoer of the uncontrolled predicate and the actor of the earlier dependent verb are coreferential. This is presumably due to the animacy of the undergoer, which leads the switch-reference morphology to monitor it, rather than the inanimate causal actor. Examples follow:

Usan:

(Reesink 1983)

munon isig eng sarau aib eb-et migeri   wâ-r-â
man   old this work big do-SA exhaustion 3SG U-hit-3SG A
wegiba
cease 3SG FUT
'the old man, working hard and becoming exhausted, will cease'

Telefol:

(Healey 1966)

daám boóyó fákán-bi-nal-a-ta   daál
fence that   make-DEL SEQ-SA-3SG M A-then tiredness
tebe-bʔ-ee-b-u
happen-PERF-3SG U BEN-PAST-3SG F A
'he got tired of fencing'

> *tál-nal-a-ta*   *sook ang-ko-ól-u*
> come-SA-3SG M A-then rope wrap-finish-DA-3SG F A
> *kaán-sé*
> die-3SG M FAR PAST
> 'he came and committed suicide and died'

Kosena:

(Longacre 1972)

> *minkáká sipivi mal-é-Pa*   *Ókáva*
> then   jeep in put-SA-1SG A Okapa
> *moi-si-yúwá-Pa*   *vondéPa mi*
> up-1SG U-leave-3SG A PRES-1SG A Thursday that
> *maaváPá i-lá-um*
> here   go up-PAST-1SG A
> 'then I got a jeep, and it left me at Okapa, and on Thursday I came here'

Two salient points need to be made concerning these examples. Note that the dependent verb preceding the uncontrolled predicate is marked as same actor, monitoring the coreference between its actor and the undergoer of the uncontrolled predicate. But the uncontrolled predicate is invariably marked as different actor, even though its undergoer is coreferential with the actor of the next verb. The Kosena different-actor dependent verb has the same form as Fore, the verb being inflected with a suffix indicating tense and the person and number of its actor, followed by an anticipatory actor morpheme. Why the switch-reference system should behave differently when going from a coreferential actor to an undergoer from when it goes from a coreferential undergoer to an actor is not completely clear, but one explanation does suggest itself. The switch-reference system operates from left to right, as does the pattern of clause chaining generally. If the switch-reference system really is at base an *actor* monitoring system, as I have maintained, the following seems possible. The actor of a dependent verb is checked for coreference with the nominals of a following uncontrolled predicate. Because the inanimate actor of this verb is so low in topical status, it is ignored, and the undergoer is then monitored as coreferential with the actor of the previous verb. Hence, the dependent verb is marked with the same-actor morphology. However, when the turn of the uncontrolled predicate comes, its actor still remains the inanimate cause, and it is this nominal against which the nominals of the next verb are checked for coreference. As the animate actor of the next verb is not coreferential with the inanimate causal actor, the uncontrolled predicate is thereby marked as having a different actor.

The second point concerns the Kosena and the second Telefol example. Note that the predicates in the uncontrolled clauses do not express inherently uncontrolled bodily states or events, but rather are normally controlled events: 'wrap' and 'leave'. The actors of the verbs are inanimate objects, incapable of volition, so the resulting construction takes on exactly the same syntactic character as the impersonal constructions of inherently uncontrolled body states or events. This clearly demonstrates that it is the lack of control or volition which is the relevant parameter here, whether this resides in the predicate itself or in the choice of actor. Uncontrolling inanimate actors are simply actors of very low status, and are likely to be overlooked in favour of an animate undergoer when coreference with the actor of a previous verb is being monitored by the switch-reference system.

The final question to be considered about switch-reference systems concerns their behaviour in languages in which syntactic word-order constraints play an independent role in the organization of clause structure. Switch-reference systems monitor the reference of actor nominals, and the notion of actor is a semantic one, independent of syntactic structure. However, in the case of Barai (Olson 1981), the one clear case of a Papuan language in which syntax plays an independent role in clause structure, the switch-reference system is similarly syntactically based. For in Barai, instead of monitoring coreference of actors (a semantic notion), the switch-reference system actually monitors the coreference of nominals in a particular syntactic position, a transparent case of the syntactic basis of a switch-reference system. In the previous section I pointed out the prominence of the leftmost nominal position for Barai controlled predicates. It is the coreference of the nominals occupying these positions in chained clauses which is checked by the switch-reference morphology:

> *fu miane   sak-i-na   barone*
> he firestick bite-3sg u-same die
> 'a firestick bit him and he died'

> *miane   ije fu sak-i-mo   fu barone*
> firestick the he bite-3sg u-diff he die
> 'the firestick bit him and he died'

sak 'bite' is a controlled predicate, so it selects the leftmost position as the most salient. In the first example, the actor *miane* 'firestick' is indefinite, so it ranks lower than the animate undergoer *fu* 'he'. The animate undergoer then assumes the leftmost nominal position. In the second example, *miane* 'firestick' is definite, so it retains the leftmost position associated with actors of controlled predicates. In the first example, the undergoer nominal *fu* 'he' occupying the leftmost nominal position is coreferential with the single nominal argument of *barone* 'die', so the dependent verb *sak-i-na* registers 'same'; while in the second example, the actor *miane ije* 'the firestick' occupies the leftmost position, and it is not coreferential with the single nominal with *barone* 'die', so the verb *sak-i-mo* registers 'different'. Clearly what is same or different here is not the reference of actors, but that of the nominals occupying the leftmost position.

Consider these further examples:

> *na i   me-na   ine   bije-ie*
> I   work do-SAME stick poke-1SG U
> 'I was working and a stick poked me'

> *are   ije ine kano-mo   fu tuae*
> house the tree hit-DIFF it break
> 'a tree hit the house and it (the tree) broke'

In the first example *bij* is a controlled predicate with an inanimate actor *ine* 'stick' and an animate undergoer *na* 'I', here unexpressed. The undergoer outranks the actor, and would occupy the leftmost position. As the leftmost actor nominal in the first clause and the leftmost undergoer nominal in the second (i.e. *na* 'I') are coreferential, the dependent verb registers 'same'. In the second example, the actor *ine* 'tree' is indefinite, and outranked for leftmost position by the definite undergoer *are* 'house'. As this nominal and the single nominal of *tuae* 'break' are not coreferential, the dependent verb is marked as 'different'.

Finally, consider these two examples with uncontrolled predicates:

> *na visinam-ie-na   do   ije ised-ie*
> I sicken-1SG U-SAME water the displease-1SG U
> '[something] sickens me and the water displeases me'

> *kusare ije na tot-ie-mo   fu saere*
> flower the I escape memory-1SG U-DIFF it wither
> 'the flower escaped my memory and it withered'

In section 5.2 of the previous chapter I discussed the difference between controlled and uncontrolled predicates in Barai. While controlled predicates select the leftmost nominal position as their prominent position, uncontrolled predicates select the immediately preverbal position – the position of the undergoer – as prominent. In both cases it is the corresponding prominent position which is monitored by the switch-reference system. Because, with uncontrolled predicates, this position is always occupied by the undergoer (the undergoer, being animate, will never be outranked by an actor for this position), the switch-reference system in these cases essentially monitors coreference of undergoers. In the first example, the undergoer *na* 'I' of *visinam* 'sicken' is coreferential with the undergoer of *ised* 'displease', so the dependent verb indicates 'same'. In the second example, *na* 'I' is not coreferential with the single nominal of *saere* 'wither', and so the verb *tot-ie-mo* 'escape memory' registers 'different'. Note that the single argument of *saere* 'wither' is in fact coreferential with the actor – *kusare ije* 'the flower' – of *tot* 'escape memory', but the verb still registers 'different'. This clearly demonstrates that the switch-reference system of Barai can never be reduced to the same versus different actor of other languages, but that the semantics of verb-classes, as well as the syntactic position of nominals, is essential to its working.

Angaataha (Huisman 1973) of the Angan family presents a grammatical feature unique to Papuan languages, although further research may show it to be present in other languages of the same family. This may be termed a 'switch-location' system. Angaataha dependent verbs which are specified by the switch-reference system as same actor may be further specified as to whether the actor performs the action in the same place or in a different place. Different-actor dependent verbs are not inflected in this way. Same place is indicated by *-té* and different place by *-mé*:

> *áhewisa-té*   *émpîm-ô*
> put down-SAME PLACE sit down-1SG REAL
> 'I put him down and sat down (there)'

> *áhewisa-mé*   *nunté émpîm-ô*
> put down-DIFF PLACE go   sit down-1SG REAL
> 'I put him down, went and sat down (elsewhere)'

I have defined dependent verbs as those linked in a linear string to a following independent verb, much like beads on a necklace. The dependency of the verbs is in the nature of the specifications for the outer operators – status, tense and illocutionary force. The dependent verbs take their specification for these from the independent verb. In the simplest cases, dependent verbs may not be inflected for these operators at all, while independent verbs must be. The dependent verbs are covered by whatever might be the inflections of the independent verbs. It is important to note that this applies only to outer operators; dependent verbs may freely select from the set of inner operators – aspect, directionals and modality.

Papuan languages vary in the strictness of the constraints they apply to the inflection of dependent verbs for outer operators. Minimally, all languages require that dependent verbs may never be specified for illocutionary force. An inflection for illocutionary force is always diagnostic of independent verbs, and in some languages, like Fore (Scott 1978), it is the only outer operator which is prohibited for dependent verbs:

kana-a:-kí-tá   *a-ka-us-ó*
come-3SG A PRES-DEP-1DL A 3SG U-see-DL A-Q
'is he coming and we see it?'

The Fore independent verb suffix *-o* indicates a yes/no question. It may never occur on a dependent verb and its presence, or that of the declarative suffix *-e*, always indicates an independent verb. Note that the scope of the question marker is over both verbs, i.e. both verbs are yes/no questions. The dependent verb is dependent on the independent verb for its specification for illocutionary force.

Consider now the other outer operator in the Fore example, tense. The final verb has no overt specification for tense, which amounts to a zero morpheme for present tense. The dependent verb is inflected for tense, by the portmanteau suffix *-a:*, indicating a third person actor in the present tense. The presence of the suffix further signals switch reference: the actor of the next verb will be different. While the dependent verb is inflected for tense, the tense specification must agree with that of the independent verb. This is overwhelmingly the common situation, but in rare cases different-actor dependent verbs may be inflected with near or remote past tense suffixes to emphasize a prior completion of the action. The independent verb may be either present or near past tense, and the portmanteau morpheme for switch reference is usually present, but may be past:

kana-ʔtá-a:-kí-na   *wa-ʔta-i-e*
come-NR PAST-3SG A PRES-DEP-3SG A go-NR PAST-3SG A-DECL
'he$_1$ came and then he$_2$ went'

kana-nt-á:-kí-na   *wa-i-e*
come-RM PAST-3SG A PRES-DEP-3SG A go-3SG A-DECL
'he came and now he goes'

In the first example, the dependent and independent verb still agree in tense, the near past, although the portmanteau switch-reference morpheme registers present. In the second example, the dependent verb has a remote past tense morpheme, while the switch-reference morpheme is present. The independent verb is also present tense, with no overt tense suffix. In both examples, at least one of the tense suffixes on the dependent verb agrees with the independent verb. Further, the remote past tense morpheme often expresses in Fore a perfect aspect meaning, a completed action with continuing relevence. This is an inner operator meaning and seems the most plausible use for the morpheme above, as the remote past meaning is clearly not meant here. The actor has *just* come and is now going: he did not arrive a week ago and is now going. The primary tense of this example is present, as indicated by the final verb. In any case, the upshot of all this is that, although Fore verbs may be *inflected* for tense independently from the independent verb, it is by no means clear that they may actually be *specified* for tense independently. The tense marking of the independent verb is still primary and restricts the range of any tense marking on the dependent verb. A similar situation can be found in Suena (Wilson 1969b) of the Binandere family.

Fore and Suena (and Tairora (Vincent 1973), which behaves similarly) are unusual among Papuan languages. For most Papuan languages, dependent verbs may not even be inflected for tense, which is wholly specified by the independent verb:

Kewa:
(Franklin 1971)

> ní réko-a ágaa lá-wa
> I stand-SEQ SA talk say-1SG NR PAST
> 'I stood up and spoke'

Barai:
(Olson 1981)

> a Eroni-do fase isoe-mo fu rua-e
> you Eroni-POSS letter write-SEQ DA he come-PAST
> 'you wrote Eroni a letter and then he came'

In the Kewa and Barai examples, the tenseless dependent verb has the same tense reading as the independent verb.

The final outer operator to consider is status. The same constraints we observed for tense and illocutionary force also apply to this operator: all dependent verbs must have the same status specification as the independent verb. In Hua (Haiman 1980), same-actor dependent verbs may not even be inflected for status, but different-actor dependent verbs, while inflectable for status, must have the same status specification as the independent verb:

> fu-mo do-ro-na u-gi-e
> pig-TP eat-PERF-3SG A go-UNREAL 3SG-DECL OTHER
> 'he will eat the pork and go'

> mi-su-ga-na do-gi-e
> give-UNREAL-DA OTHER-3SG A eat-UNREAL 3SG-DECL OTHER
> 'I will give it to him and he will eat'

The suffix *-su* is the form for unreal status used on a dependent verb.

Barai (Olson 1981) also requires dependent verbs to agree in status specification with the independent verb. For example, the verbal suffix indicating delayed sequential events has two forms, depending on whether the independent verb is specified as real (i.e. past or present tense) or unreal:

> *na nae-ema   suoke   una   rua-e*
> I   sleep-DEL SEQ morning again come-PAST
> 'I slept and then I came back'

> *na va-ekiro   isuame   una   rua-ke*
> I   go-DEL SEQ tomorrow again come-UNREAL
> 'I will go and then will return tomorrow'

-ema is the form for dependent verbs expressing real events, and *-ekiro* for those for unreal events. Finally, consider Angaataha (Huisman 1973) of the Angan family. Both dependent and independent verbs have an obligatory inflection for status, involving a binary distinction of real and unreal, but both must carry the same specification:

> *tehoáa-t-os-one-hé   na-insée*
> make fire-1SG A-PERF-1 REAL-DA eat-3SG A-REAL
> 'after I made a fire, he ate'

> *tehoáa-t-os-ane-hé   nan-tá-isée*
> make fire-1SG A-PERF-1 UNREAL-DA eat-UNREAL-3SG A
> 'after I make a fire, he will eat'

The inflection for status on the dependent verb is only obligatory for different actor forms, as above. Same-actor dependent verbs, as in Hua, may not even be inflected for status:

> *tehoáa-t-até   kát-ô*
> make-fire-1SG A-SIM talk-1 REAL
> 'while I made a fire, I talked'

> *téhe-t-até   nan-t-ô*
> cook-1SG A-SIM eat-UNREAL-1
> 'I'll cook and eat'

To conclude this section, I must point out that the systems of clause chaining discussed here, while truly representative of Papuan languages, are by no means universal. In at least one area, the south central coast of New Guinea, in languages like Kiwai and Marind, clause chaining is not found. Interestingly, these languages also lack significant verb serialization – further evidence that these two grammatical constructions, although distinct, are related. In languages of this area, verbs are fully inflected forms, there being no distinction between dependent and independent verbs. Sentences are formed by linking fully inflected verbs in a coordinate structure:

Marind:

(Boelaars 1950)

> *ndam-o-ka-kiparud jah*   *ma-n-man*
> FUT-2SG-first-tie   and then FUT-1SG-come
> 'you tie first and then I will come'

Kiwai:

(Ray 1933)

> *irisina auto omidai tewo*   *g-itai*
> fish   away take-SG cooked fish IMP-broil
> 'take the fish and broil it'

All verbs in the two examples are independently inflected and could stand on their own as complete utterances. This is in contrast to dependent verbs in clause-chaining languages, which may never constitute complete utterances in themselves.

6.4 Subordination

All Papuan languages, either of the chaining type or otherwise, have subordinate clauses. In the Iatmul example at the beginning of the previous section, there is a form *ya-nt-əy-an*, come-3SG M-UNREAL-if, 'if he comes', which I termed a subordinate-dependent verb, abbreviated as 'subordinate verb'. Subordinate verbs are the predicates of clauses functioning in a syntactic relationship of subordination, the embedding of one clause into another. To investigate the morphological structure of subordinate verbs, compare this Iatmul form with (coordinate)-dependent and independent verbs:

> dependent: *klə-laa* get-SEQ 'get and then'
> subordinate: *ya-nt-əy-an* come-3SG M-UNREAL-if 'if he comes'
> independent: *wi-kiyə-win* see-UNREAL-1SG 'I will see [him]'

The dependent verb is morphologically the most divergent, as well as the simplest. A temporal suffix is added to the bare stem. No affixation is supplied for tense/status, or for person and number of the actor. The subordinate and independent verbs are more similar. Both are inflected for tense/status and for the person and number of the actor. They differ in that the subordinate verb necessarily has a subordinating suffix – in this case the conditional suffix *-an* – which marks the entire clause governed by this predicate as subordinate, as functioning as a unit within the main clause governed by the independent verb.

These features of Iatmul are more or less general for Papuan languages. Most Papuan languages have subordinate verb-forms which are similar to independent verbs, in that they may be independently inflected for tense/status, a feature we saw in the previous section to be generally denied to dependent verbs. For Hua (Haiman 1980) I demonstrated in the previous section that dependent verbs take their status specification from the independent verb. This does not apply to subordinate verbs:

> *fu-mo d-mi-ma-da*   *u-gu-e*
> pig-TP 1SG U-give-SUB OTHER-3SG A go-UNREAL-DECL OTHER
> 'he gave me pork, and so I will go'

In this example, the subordinate verb is real, indicated by $\emptyset$, and the independent verb is unreal. This independent specification for status aligns subordinate verbs with independent verbs. The suffix *-ma* indicates a subordinate verb-form, in contrast to *-ga*, for different actor, and $\emptyset$, for same actor, dependent verbs. Like dependent verbs with *-ga* and $\emptyset$, the subordinate verb requires an anticipatory actor suffix, *-da* for third singular. This is found whether the verb is different actor, as above, or same actor:

> *fina-mo hu-pa-ta*   *fina-mo hu-gu-ne*
> fight-TP do-SUB 1PL-1PL A fight-TP do-UNREAL-DECL 1PL
> 'we have fought and we will fight'

This feature contrasts dependent and subordinate verbs with independent verbs, which never have anticipatory actor suffixes.

For illocutionary force the greatest differences in behaviour are found. Neither dependent nor subordinate verbs may be inflected for illocutionary force, but this disguises an important difference. Dependent verbs take their illocutionary force specification from the independent verb: whatever speech act is marked on the independent verb applies to the dependent verb as well.

> *fu-mo k-mi-ga-ka*   *da-pe?*
> pig-TP 2SG U-give-DA OTHER-2SG A eat 2SG-Q 2SG
> 'did he give you pork and did you eat it?'

Subordinate verbs are fundamentally different. While they too may never be inflected for illocutionary force, they are impervious to the illocutionary force specification of the independent verb, always remaining assertions:

> *fu-mo k-mi-ma-ka*   *da-pe?*
> pig-TP 2SG U-give-SUB OTHER-2SG A eat 2SG-Q 2SG
> 'he gave you pork, and so did you eat it?'

This difference in behaviour under the illocutionary force operator provides the fundamental clue to the function of subordinate clauses, as against dependent clauses. The illocutionary force of a subordinate clause may never be anything but a statement, but dependent clauses are not so restricted. Essentially, subordinate clauses represent given, presupposed information (Haiman 1978), a background to the ongoing discourse, while dependent clauses, like independent ones, are part of the ongoing development of the discourse, the focused and asserted progression of events. The independent selection of tense/status in subordinate clauses, but not in dependent ones, becomes explicable in light of this difference. Subordinate clauses, in providing background information out of the main line of discourse, need not be tied to the time of the discourse, and, further, in order to be sufficiently flexible in expressing kinds of background information, need to be able to select their own tense/status specifications. The time of a background event to a discourse need not be, and often is not, the same as the main time of the discourse. Dependent clauses, on the other hand, constitute the main, asserted lines of the discourse, all of which must occur in the same time frame as the independent verb, on which tense is marked. If the time of the narrative changes midstream, the sentence is closed with an independent verb, indicating tense, and a new sentence is started with a chain of dependent clauses before an independent verb indicating the new tense.

Nothing highlights the backgrounding function of subordinate clauses in Papuan languages more than their most common usage, the so-called tail–head linkage. When a sentence is terminated by an independent verb, the next sentence often begins with a subordinate clause recapitulating the information of the last clause of the previous sentence. This information was of course asserted in the previous sentence, and is now backgrounded, but the recapitulating subordinate clause provides a linkage between the previously asserted information and the new information to be asserted in its own sentence. Consider this example from Yimas:

> *ma-ŋariŋ ipa-wa-ntut*   *iraki*   *al-ik*
> other-day 1PL S-go-RM PAST wood-VIII SG cut-IRR
> 'another day we went to cut wood'
>
> *i-kay-wa-ka-al-ntuk-imp-in*
> VIII SG-1PL A-go-SEQ-cut-RM PAST-SEQ-SUB
> *i-kay-pay-pra-ntut*
> VIII SG-1PL A-carry-toward-RM PAST
> 'after we went and cut it, we carried it back'

The first sentence contains a main independent verb and a purposive complement, asserting 'we went to cut ...'. In the second sentence, the first verb, a subordinate verb, marked by the oblique nominal suffix -*n* functioning as a subordinator, recapitulates the events of the first sentence, 'after we went and cut it', before a following independent verb asserts the new information, 'we carried it back'. This use of subordinate clauses, often called tail–head linkage, is extremely common in Papuan languages, especially in narrative texts. Such texts are littered with dozens of examples of this usage.

Subordinate clauses in Papuan languages always function to background given information, and correspond to two different constructions in more familiar languages, adverbial clauses and relative clauses. Both of these constructions express background information in a sentence: adverbial clauses provide a temporal setting or a background condition or cause for the asserted new information in the main clause, e.g. *while I sat under the tree, an apple hit me on the head* or *if he comes, I will leave*; while relative clauses provide crucial background information for the identification of the referents of their head nouns: *the pig which has white spots* or *the pig which I killed*. The close relationship of these two types of subordinate clauses is readily apparent in many Papuan languages, in which they are formally very similar or even identical. In Iatmul (Staalsen 1972) the verbs of both adverbial clauses and relative clauses contain the subordinating suffix -*a*, which indicates that the material in the clause is already assumed:

> *yɨ-nt-ǝy-a-n*   *sɨ-kɨyǝ-wɨn*
> go-3SG M-UNREAL-SUB-if shoot-UNREAL-1SG
> 'if he goes, I will shoot him'

> *yɨ-lɨ-m-ǝy-a*   *vaalǝ*
> go-EXT-2SG M-UNREAL-SUB canoe
> 'the canoe that you will be going in'

The subordinate verbs only differ in the conditional suffix -*n* in the conditional adverbial clause. Bruce (1984) in fact identifies the cognate suffix -*a* in Alamblak, a distantly related language, as a 'presupposition' marker, stating that it marks clauses expressing background assumed information, such as adverbial clauses, relative clauses and content questions:

> *frëhm dhëhnay-w-a-m*
> who   sick-EXT-PRESUP-3PL
> 'who is sick?'

In such content questions, that someone is sick is assumed information, and what is really being questioned is 'who is that someone who is sick?'

Hua (Haiman 1980) also exhibits a close morphological similarity in the two types of subordinate clauses. The verbs in both types obligatorily occur with the subordinating suffix -*ma*:

> *fu-mo d-mi-ma-da*   *u-gu-e*
> pig-TP 1SG U-give-SUB OTHER-3SG A go-UNREAL-DECL OTHER
> 'after he gives me pork, I will go'

> *hefi-ma*   *za*
> break 3-SUB OTHER wood
> 'wood which is broken'

A further formal feature of subordinate clauses in a great many Papuan languages is their morphological behaviour as nominal phrases, i.e. they take some of the same inflections as nouns. The types of nominal phrase that subordinate clauses generally resemble are definite nominals. Definite nominals presuppose the prior identification of their referent: *the cat* is distinguished from *a cat* by the fact that, when the speaker uses it, he assumes the hearer can identify which cat he is referring to. Subordinate clauses presuppose the prior identification of the events they describe, so not surprisingly this similarity in function is paralleled by a similarity in form. Fore (Scott 1978) is a good exemplar of this feature. Like Hua, adverbial clauses and relative clauses have a similar formation: the subordinate verbs use a special set of suffixes for the person and number of the actor, distinguishing them from both dependent and independent verbs. To these subordinate verbs any one of a number of nominal suffixes may be added, resulting in different types of subordinate clauses. Consider first those corresponding to adverbial clauses in English:

> *a-ka-ʔkib-iʔ-pa*   *máe-ʔki-i-e*
> 3SG U-see-LIKELY-3SG A SUB-TP get-LIKELY-3SG A-DECL
> 'if he sees it, he will get (it)'

> *ago   y-iʔ-pa*   *ab-ew-e*
> already say-3SG A SUB-TP hear-3PL A-DECL
> 'as he has already spoken, they have heard'

> *na-ʔkib-éʔ-ka-na*   *i-i-e*
> eat-LIKELY-3PL A SUB-REF-3SG A eat-3SG A-DECL
> 'he talks about how they will eat'

> *kana-ʔt-á:meʔ-ká-na*   *iʔka:ʔ-pi-i-e*
> come-NR PAST-3DL A SUB-REF-3SG A buy-do-3SG A-DECL
> 'I buy because he came'

-pa and *-ka* are common suffixes for nominals. *-pa* is the topicalizing suffix, and *-ka*, the suffix for what may be termed the referential case (Grimes 1972), i.e. 'concerning, about'. Here they are used on subordinate verbs as subordinators. The actual range of these subordinators is rather wide. *-pa* as a topicalization suffix simply marks the subordinate clause as topical and given. The specific meanings range from temporal sequence to conditional to topic/comment to thesis/antithesis. See Scott 1978: 130–1 for further examples. The use of the topicalizing suffix to mark subordinate clauses is widespread in Papuan languages, being reported as well for Hua (Haiman 1980), Barai (Olson 1981) and Imonda (Seiler 1984). The use of the topic marker to indicate subordinate clauses is semantically appropriate because both topics and subordinate clauses express given information which set the frame of reference for the rest of the sentence. See Haiman 1978 for further discussion of this. *-ka* is a nominal case-marker meaning 'concerning'. In its use as a subordinator it too has a wide range of meanings, including reason and cause. *-ka* marked subordinate verbs differ from *-pa* verbs in that they require anticipatory actor marking, as in the above two examples.

Relative clauses in Fore occur either with a head nominal or without. When headless, they are indistinguishable from adverbial clauses:

> *a-egu-ʔt-óʔ-tí*   *w-aːn-ó*
> 3SG U-hit-NR PAST-1SG A SUB-ALL go-2SG A-Q
> 'are you going to where I hit him?'

> *máe-ʔte kana-ʔtá-iʔ-tasa*
> get-SEQ come-NR PAST-3SG A SUB-INSTR
> *a-egu-ʔtá-i-e*
> 3SG U-hit-NR PAST-3SG A-DECL
> 'he hit him with what he bought'

Here, the allative case-marker *-ti* 'to' and the instrumental case-marker *-tasa* 'with' are suffixed to subordinate verbs, just like the other nominal suffixes *-pa* and *-ka*. Formally, these headless relative clauses and the adverbial clauses are the same construction.

Relative clauses with expressed heads have the subordinate clause preceding them; any relevant case-markers occur on the nominal head:

> *a-ka-ʔt-ó*   *ntágara kána-i-e*
> 3SG U-see-NR PAST-1SG A SUB man   come-3SG A-DECL
> 'the man whom I saw is coming'

      a-egu-ʔtá-i   *ʔkasú mpáe-i-e*
      3SG U-hit-NR PAST-3SG A SUB club get-3SG A-DECL
      'he gets the club with which he hit him'

      mi-nt-i   *ʔkuma:ʔ-tá-sa kana-i-e*
      be at-RM PAST-3SG A SUB village-LOC-ABL come-3SG A-DECL
      'he came from the village in which he stayed'

The last example shows the case-markers fixed to the head nominal. The subordinate verbs here are like the previous two sets of examples, except here they lack nominal suffixes. They function as an embedded verbal modifier of the head noun; this modifier plus the head noun constitute the complete nominal phrase.

    In Yimas all relative and adverbial clauses are nominal phrases, but the two types are somewhat different in structure. Adverbial clauses are formed by suffixing the oblique case suffix *-n* to fully inflected verbs:

            mpu-ŋa-na-tay-nt-imp-in   *pu-ka-apan-kit*
            3PL A-1G U-now-see-PRES-SEQ-OBL 3PL U-1SG A-shoot-RM FUT
            'when they see me, I will shoot them'

            tuŋkuriŋ anti-ka-tay-nt-imp-in   *anti-ka-tu-r-ak*
            eye   POT-1SG A-see-PERF-SEQ-OBL POT-1SG A-kill-PERF-3SG U
            'if I had seen the eye (of the crocodile), I would have killed it'

Adverbial clauses express the background information which is the setting for the asserted information of the main clause. Yimas employs a straightforward way to indicate this by marking them with the same oblique case-marker used to mark other setting nominals such as locatives. Compare the following with the above:

            nam-in anti-ka-tu-r-ak
            house-OBL POT-1SG A-kill-PERF-3SG U
            'I would have killed him in the house'

The adverbial clauses are produced by replacing a nominal stem such as *nam* 'house' with a verb or clause. Nonetheless, the adverbial clause still functions as a nominal phrase, evidenced by the nominal suffix *-n*.

    All Yimas relative clauses are essentially headless. Yimas relative clauses are formed by suffixing one of the nominal class and number suffixes (see section 4.4) to a fully inflected verb. The suffix chosen is that of the class and number of the 'head noun', the nominal whose reference is restricted by the relative clause. The head noun need not be present, nor, if present, need it adjoin the relative clause. The relative clause is a full nominal phrase by itself, its class and number specifications being supplied by the final suffix. It and any adjoining 'head noun' are simply two juxtaposed nominal expressions which are coreferential, as indicated by the class and number markings. Unlike English and Fore relative clauses, Yimas relative clauses are not embedded: they are simply appositional nominals, rather like 'we, the people'. Consider the following example:

> *uranki*   *kia-mpu-ŋa-tɨkam-ɨt*   *mpu-yara-r-ɨŋki*
> coconut-VI PL VI PL-3PL A-1SG U-show-PERF 3PL A-get-PERF-VI PL
> 'they showed me the coconuts which they got'

The 'head noun' is *uranki* 'coconuts' and the relative clause *mpu-yara-r-ɨŋki* 'which they got'. The relative clause is marked by the suffix *-ŋki* VI PL, as befits one modifying a noun of that class and number. The only eligible noun is, of course, *uranki* 'coconuts'. Note that the relative clause and 'head noun' are not contiguous, being separated by the main verb of the sentence. Clearly, the relative clause is not embedded as a modifying phrase within a larger nominal phrase headed by a noun, as English and Fore relative clauses are. Rather, we have two independent nominal expressions which are indicated as coreferential because of the class and number morphology. The 'head noun' is not even necessary. If the 'head noun' is already well established in context, it will probably be omitted altogether, resulting in:

> *kia-mpu-ŋa-tɨkam-ɨt*   *mpu-yara-r-ɨŋki*
> VI PL-3PL A-1SG U-show-PERF 3PL A-get-PERF-VI PL
> 'they showed me those (coconuts) which they got'

The relative clause is still an independent nominal phrase, linked in this case to the prefix *kia-* on the main verb, which has the same gender and number specifications.

7

Problems of comparative
linguistics in Papuan languages

7.1 The comparative method and Papuan languages

As pointed out in Chapter 1, Papuan languages number around 750; and, given the
relatively small area (the island of New Guinea and adjacent small islands) and the
small total population of their speakers (approximately four million), the picture of
linguistic diversity they present is unparalleled on the globe. They provide a
challenge for the tools of comparative linguistics unmatched by any language family
or linguistic area. The methods of comparative linguistics were worked out in the
nineteenth century within the context of the unravelling of the prehistory of the
European peoples. In that case, some corroborating evidence existed for the results
of the methods, in the form of the early written documents of Greek, Latin and
Sanskrit; but, as Papuan languages remained unrecorded until the late nineteenth
and were not extensively recorded until the second half of the twentieth century, this
corroboratory evidence is lacking for them. As a result, the methods of comparative
linguistics are the only means available for investigating the earlier stages and
relations of Papuan languages.

In this feature Papuan languages are certainly not alone; the methods of
comparative linguistics have been applied successfully to other unwritten language
groups, for example Austronesian (Dempwolff 1933–8), Algonkian (Bloomfield
1946) or Athabaskan (Sapir 1949), but the very great diversity of Papuan languages
and their close contact with each over many millennia pose special difficulties not
present to the same extent in these other language groups. To see what these special
difficulties might be, let me investigate more closely the methodology of comparative linguistics.

The central tool of comparative linguistics is a procedure called the 'comparative
method'. This involves comparing the structures and, especially, the vocabularies of
a set of languages in order to group them into families, and to reconstruct features
and words of the ancestral parent language from which they descended. The
comparative method demonstrates that languages are related *genetically*, i.e.
descended from a common ancestor, and allows us to reconstruct that ancestor,

called the 'proto-language'. Consider the following few words from the Germanic languages of northern Europe (Bloomfield 1933) (the words have been re-spelt in a more systematic phonetic rendering):

	'house'	'mouse'	'louse'
English	*haws*	*maws*	*laws*
Dutch	*høys*	*møys*	*løys*
German	*haws*	*maws*	*laws*
Swedish	*hu·s*	*mu·s*	*lu·s*

I am only concerned with the vowel sounds in these words. Note that in all three words, English has /aw/, Dutch has /øy/, German /aw/, Swedish /u·/. English /aw/ then corresponds to Dutch /øy/, German /aw/, Swedish /u·/. This example introduces a notion of crucial importance to the comparative method, that of *sound correspondence*. The above data provide the following correspondence:

English	Dutch	German	Swedish
aw	*øy*	*aw*	*u·*

What is of fundamental importance to sound correspondences is their *regularity*. In the data, English /aw/ always corresponds to Dutch /øy/, German /aw/ and Swedish /u·/. We do not find a situation in which German sometimes has /aw/ corresponding to English /aw/ but at other times shows /u·/. It is the regularity of sound correspondences which provide the comparative method with its rigour. It is this regularity which allows us to impose order on the vocabularies of the languages, to select which words are related to each other or, in more technical language, which words are 'cognate'. Regular sound correspondences in cognate words are diagnostic proof that the languages being compared are genetically related. We can then reconstruct the forms of the proto-language. English, Dutch, German and Swedish are Germanic languages, and descend from a language called 'Proto-Germanic'. The above sound correspondence descends from a vowel sound *u· in Proto-Germanic (the asterisk indicates a reconstructed form), of which only Swedish preserves the original, although earlier stages of English, such as Chaucer's English, pronounced these words with a /u·/ as well. Thus, the forms in Proto-Germanic of these three words were: *mu·s, *hu·s and *lu·s.

English and all the languages of the Germanic family are related genetically in a still bigger language family called Indo-European, along with almost all the languages of Europe and many languages of Iran and India. Consider the following words in English and Latin:

English	*foot*	*fish*	*three*	*thin*	*hundred*	*head*
Latin	*ped-*	*pisc-*	*tres*	*tenuis*	*centum*	*caput*

which result in the following sound correspondences:

English	f	θ	h
Latin	p	t	k

Regular sound correspondences like these demonstrate that English and Latin are genetically related as Indo-European languages, and that both descend from Proto-Indo-European, as do Greek, Sanskrit, Russian and many other languages of Europe and Asia. But a further investigation of the vocabulary of English reveals a problem. English has a number of words of similar or related meaning which do not exhibit the proper sound correspondence, but resemble the Latin forms: *pedal, pedestrian; Pisces, piscatory, piscivorous; trinary, triceps, trice, triangle, triennium, trident; tenuous; cent, century, centimetre, centigrade; decapitate, capitulate, capital.* At first sight this would seem to present a problem for the principle of the *regularity* of sound change. Sometimes Latin /p/ corresponds to English /f/ and sometimes to English /p/; similarly, with /t/ and /k/. But there is no real problem here, and no exception to the principle of regularity. The English words with /p, t, s~k/ corresponding to Latin /p, t, k/, instead of the expected /f, θ, h/, are *borrowings*, not cognate words. Words with /f, θ, h/ descended directly into English from Proto-Indo-European, as did the Latin words with /p, t, k/. English words with /p, t, s~k/ have not descended directly from Proto-Indo-European: they are not cognates, but borrowings. They have been borrowed into English from Latin (or from French, a direct modern descendant of Latin) in the course of the last two thousand years because of its prestigious position in medieval culture and learning. Historical documents over this period will confirm this claim, but it is the irregularity of the sound correspondences which should first alert us to the special stature of these English words with /p, t, k/.

With English and other European languages the recognition of borrowed words is often not a problematic task because of the extensive written documentation we have of these languages. Borrowing has occurred on a massive scale in most European languages, but by a judicious blend of the use of the comparative method and the sifting of written documents, the sorting of cognates from borrowings has been largely accomplished. With Papuan languages we face a much more daunting assignment. Because there are no extensive written documents before the twentieth century, we cannot rely on these for help in sorting cognates from borrowings. Without these, the only way to distinguish these two is the irregularity of sound correspondences. But in order to sort the irregular sound correspondences from the regular ones, we would need to know which words would count as cognates, and which would not. So we find ourselves in a vicious circle. As this vicious circle is faced by any comparative linguist working with an unwritten language family, let us see how previous investigators in other unwritten language families have handled this dilemma.

The unwritten language families for which the most extensive comparative work has been undertaken are Austronesian, Algonkian and Bantu. All of these language families have a large number of languages spread over a very large territory, resulting in a very sharp fragmentation of the family. Words of similar form and meaning in languages at extreme ends of the territory of the family (such as Malay and Hawaiian in Austronesian, Blackfoot and Delaware in Algonkian, or Luganda and Zulu in Bantu) have a high probability of being cognate, for a word is less likely to be borrowed across such a wide area. This probability rises to near certainty if the word is not widespread in the intervening, but genetically related, languages.

The most common model of language change in fact assumes a historical scenario like that just sketched. It is called the 'family tree' model, and it assumes that the proto-language splits up sharply and neatly into its daughter languages, after which they develop independently of each other. So, for the Germanic languages we might have the family tree:

Any change in one daughter language is assumed to be independent of any change in another; so any developments in English are viewed in this model as having no connection with changes in German. As an abstraction this model may have some applicability to large language families spread over great areas. Given the enormous geographical areas between them, it seems a quite reasonable working assumption that, after the break-up of their ancestral proto-languages, Malay and Hawaiian, Blackfoot and Delaware or Luganda and Zulu have developed independently of each other.

When we then attempt to apply this model to Papuan languages, we run into immediate problems. Papuan language families are small and are generally spoken in small areas. The languages are usually contiguous, and have been so for millennia. None of the particular historical and geographical patterns necessary for the smooth application of the family tree model obtain in Papuan languages. Rather, as we shall see, Papuan languages normally exhibit a pattern of enormous cross-influence in all areas; so in no sense can the assumption that the daughter languages develop independently be taken as viable in this context. As the comparative method, with its sorting of cognates from borrowings, is deeply grounded in the family tree model, its application to Papuan languages is no mean problem, and suggests that some major rethinking of the method itself may be needed for these languages.

A common procedure followed when faced with the difficulty of sorting cognates from borrowings in unwritten languages is to assume that there is a core of basic words in a language that is relatively resistant to borrowing. This core of basic words consists of pronouns; nouns referring to body parts; simple kin relations; natural phenomena like the sun, moon, stars, rain, trees, fire, water, mountains; and verbs of body actions, like eating, hitting and giving. The sound correspondences assumed to be diagnostic of cognates are computed from these basic words, and the sound correspondences arrived at are used then to distinguish cognates from borrowings.

This can be a very valuable procedure (see, for example, a brilliant use of it in Dyen 1956), but its workabiliy does clearly depend on the assumption of a core of the vocabulary of a language that is resistant to borrowing. And it does seem that this assumption is of questionable value in Papuan languages. Within the southeast Asian area, pronouns have already been shown to be prone to borrowing: for example, the Indonesian pronoun *saya* 'I' is a borrowing from Sanskrit of *sahaya* 'slave', while Thai and Indonesian make use of the English pronouns *I* and *you* as neutral forms. I would argue that this type of borrowing is a possibility whenever two languages are in sufficiently intimate contact. Because of the multilingualism discussed in Chapter 2, Papuan languages are generally in a state of permanent intimate contact with each other. If one language is of greater prestige, this further increases its chances of being a source of borrowings. A good example of the borrowing of pronouns is found with the Sepik languages Iatmul (Staalsen n.d. b) and Kambot (Laycock and Z'graggen 1975).

	I	K	I	K
	SG	SG	PL	PL
1	*wɨn*	*nyɨ*	*nɨn*	*ne*
2M	*mɨn*	*wɨn*	*nkɨwt*	*nun*
F	*nyɨn*			
3M	*ntɨ*	*ma*	*ntɨy*	*le*
F	*lɨ*	*ga*		

Iatmul and Kambot are probably unrelated languages, and at best could only be very distantly related, yet the pronoun systems show a remarkable similarity. The Iatmul are a powerful and prestigious group along the Sepik, and this would suggest that their language is the donor language. The borrowing clearly seems the result of prolonged trading contact, with the following borrowings resulting: Iatmul *wɨn* 'I' has been borrowed as Kambot 'you', and Iatmul *nyɨn* 'you (F)' as Kambot *nyɨ* 'I'. In the plural, Iatmul *nɨn* 'we' has been borrowed as Kambot *nun* 'you (PL)'. A further, but more speculative, possibility is Iatmul *lɨ* 'she' appearing as Kambot *le* 'they'. The developments here in the first and second pronouns are common confusions in any multilingual contact situation, familiar to any linguistic fieldworker; first person is switched for second person, and vice versa. Kambot demonstrates borrowing of pronoun forms on an extensive scale, and indicates that in Papuan languages such forms are definitely not immune to borrowing, nor even particularly resistant.

Similar observations can be made about other areas of basic vocabulary. Several investigators (e.g. Wurm *et al.* 1975; Lynch 1981) have noted Austronesian (PAN) loan words corresponding to items of basic vocabulary in many Papuan languages. Consider the following examples:

'breast'   PAN *t'ut'u* Boazi *toto* Bedamini *tor* Awin-Pa *tutɛ*
           Nahu *susu* Naga *susu*
'ear'   PAN *talinga* Yenimu *turu* Telefol *tolooŋ* Tifal *tilaaŋ*
'leaf'   PAN *daun* Pisa *rõ* Nambu *rau* Kaeti-Wambon *ron*
'hair'   PAN *bulu* Kamoro *wiri*
'mouth'   POC *maŋa* Awyi *miŋgir* Kiwai *magota* Kati *moŋgot*
'skin'   PAN *kulit* Kaeti *kota* Kati *kat* Telefol *kaal* Kubo *kɔrɔ*
'bone'   POC *suɣi* Kiwai *soro* Kumukio *suwit*
'nose'   PAN *ijuŋ* Yoŋgom *kiriŋ* Komutu *kuruk*
'elder
sibling'   PAN *kaka* Gogodala *kaka* Ngaing *kak* Mape *kakaʔ*
'mother'   PAN *(t)ina* Kamoro *enea* Yoŋgom *ena*
'moon'   PAN *bulan* Kamoro *pura*
'star'   PAN *bituqen* Wambon *minduy* Yoŋgom *mindoŋ* Yaqay *mind*
           Tonda *bɔtɔge* Komutu *hituŋ* Timbe *pituŋ*
'water'   PAN *wayɔɣ* Gogodala *wi* Awin *wae* Gira *wai*

The loan words represented here cover a wide range of nouns typically assumed into basic vocabulary: body parts, kin terms and natural phenomena. These Austronesian loans in Papuan languages assume special importance. The Austronesian family is the only New Guinea language family with representative daughter languages outside New Guinea. This permits us to reconstruct the vocabulary of the proto-language without recourse to New Guinea area languages. Further, the reconstruction of the vocabulary of Proto-Austronesian is well advanced, and a significant body of Proto-Austronesian roots, of which the above are a small sample, is well established. Because of these two factors, it is relatively easy to isolate the Austronesian loans in a given Papuan language. Neither of these two conditions are met by Papuan language families: all are confined to the New

Guinea area, and none have reconstructed proto-languages. It is not therefore possible easily to discriminate borrowings from cognates in Papuan languages, and, as the above data on Austronesian loans clearly demonstrates, we cannot operate blindly with the working assumption that formal similarities in basic vocabulary reflect cognates. All formal similarities in vocabulary in Papuan languages must be regarded with suspicion.

All the above examples of loans in basic vocabulary involve nouns, and little work has been done to date on the likelihood of borrowing of basic verb-roots. My own impression is that these are somewhat more resistant to borrowing than basic nouns. This may be due to the extensive obligatory morphology associated with verbs in Papuan languages, which makes the isolation, and possible borrowing, of the root more difficult. Nouns often appear in uninflected forms in Papuan languages; verbs rarely do. In any case, while verbs may be more resistant to borrowing, they do not seem to be immune. In Yimas, there are two forms corresponding to 'come': *ya-* and *pura-. Ya-* is the form of the common middle Sepik root for 'come': Iatmul *yə-*, Yessan–Mayo *ya-*, Awtuw *yə-*, Mehek *ya-*, Abelam *ya-*, Kwoma *ya-. Pura-* is derived from the root *pu-* 'go' plus the suffix *-ra*, indicating reversed direction. Something like *pu-* is a common highland form for 'go': Awa *puk-*, Tairora *bu-*, Hua *vu-*, BenaBena *bu-*, Kuman *pu-*, Wahgi *pu-*, Kewa *pu-*, Huli *pu-*. In the Engan languages, which border Yimas to the south, 'come' is similarly derived from 'go': Enga *paegé* 'go', *e-pegé* 'come', Kewa *pu-* 'go', *i-pu-* 'come', Huli *pú-* 'go', *i-bu-* 'come'. It is not surprising that Yimas, occupying as it does the transitional fringe area between the Sepik basin and the central highlands, has verb-roots corresponding to both the Sepik and the highlands forms; but it is likely that one of these forms was borrowed. There is some rather weak evidence, too complex to present here, to suggest that the *pu-* based form is the older (and, therefore, original) form, and that the Sepik form *ya-* has been borrowed. But, whichever is the original root, the Yimas case does argue that basic verb-roots can be borrowed.

The case studies of the Kambot pronouns, the Austronesian loan words, and the Yimas roots for 'come' leave no doubt that the working assumption that basic vocabulary is resistant to borrowing cannot be applied blindly to Papuan languages. Such items may be *more* resistant than other words; but now we become involved in weighing probabilities and alternative hypotheses – a very complex proposition at any time, but especially problematic for Papuan languages, about which we know so little. Because of the extensive borrowing at all levels, the application of the comparative method to Papuan languages is a much more tricky undertaking than with some other language groupings. With languages which are closely related, the sheer weight of the evidence for genetic affiliation may be enough to silence doubts about the skewing effects of borrowing. And it does seem that relatively low-level genetic groupings of Papuan languages, roughly similar to the grouping of the Romance languages, are not too difficult to establish. However, genetic affiliations at a deeper level, where the evidence is much skimpier, are much more difficult to establish conclusively. The number of potential cognates is small, and consequently it is difficult to rule out borrowing as an explanation. Because of these problems, I have chosen to follow a rather conservative course in my delineation of Papuan language families in this book. I have only accepted as probable rather low-level genetic groupings of Papuan languages, on the order of Romance or Germanic. With this reckoning of relationship, there are over sixty Papuan language families. Without doubt some of these families will on further detailed research be combined into larger groupings, as Germanic and Romance have been combined into the Indo-European family; but I do not feel that the groundwork has yet been done to permit such wider groupings to be established on any large scale. Because of the great difficulty in applying the comparative method to Papuan languages, the evidence for larger groupings must be compelling, and the amassing of such evidence will be a slow process. There can be no short cuts to the classification of Papuan languages.

Given the extensive borrowing that has been demonstrated to be widespread among Papuan languages, the question of the meaning of genetic affiliation in these languages presents itself. Could borrowing proceed on such a scale that a language could be said to be 'mixed', composed of roughly equal portions of material from two unrelated language groupings? Of course, the ancestor of one particular language group would have been the starting point of any mixed language. Historical processes of borrowing and convergence would gradually have pushed the language toward members of a different language group, so that from a synchronic point of view it would present a mixed appearance with regard to genetic affiliation and be a 'mixed' language. Traditional approaches to comparative linguistics have claimed that the original starting point represents the genetic affiliation. This follows from the assumptions behind the family tree model of language change; but, since I have already stressed the problems Papuan languages may present for this model, we might also question this solution to the problem of 'mixed' languages. Of what use is it to say that language X belongs to family Y because Proto-Y was its ancestral starting point, if most of its vocabulary and structure actually come from family Z? To ignore all the features of Z found in X, just to get a simple yes/no classification of X in family Y, ignores the fundamental historical processes that have been at work in X. This suggests a number of complex issues that models of language change for Papuan languages must face. The question is surely not academic; there are convincing case studies of contact between Papuan and Austronesian languages which have resulted in what would qualify as

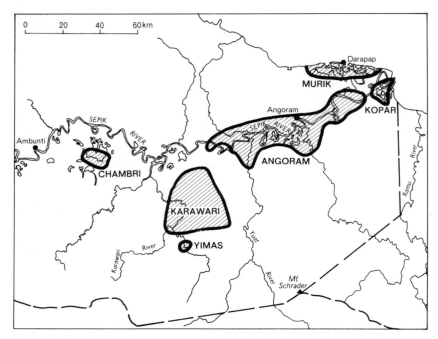

Map 5   Locations of languages of the Lower Sepik family

mixed languages (see Dutton 1976). As Austronesian languages are usually typologically very different from Papuan languages and comparatively well studied, these examples of language mixing are not too difficult to identify. Language mixing among Papuan languages, which are often typologically similar, is likely to be even more pervasive, but much more difficult to discover.

7.2   The Lower Sepik family: a comparative study

In this section I will take a detailed look at the Lower Sepik family, a family of six languages spoken in the Sepik basin, with a view to exemplifying how the specialized techniques of the comparative method may be applied to Papuan languages. The languages in this family are Yimas (250 speakers), Karawari (1,500 speakers), Angoram (7,000 speakers), Chambri (1,200 speakers), Murik (1,500 speakers) and Kopar (250 speakers). Map 5 gives the relative positions of the languages. Murik and Kopar are very closely related, almost dialects of the same language, so I will regard them as one for the purposes here. The source of data for each language is as follows: Yimas (own fieldnotes), Karawari (own fieldnotes), Angoram (own fieldnotes; Abbott 1977; and Laycock's fieldnotes of 1959 trip), Chambri (own fieldnotes and Pagotto 1976), Murik (Schmidt 1953; Abbott 1977; 1978; Abbott and Abbott 1978). Consider first the possible cognates in a basic word-list for the five languages shown in Table 2 (K after words in the Murik column indicates Kopar forms). A number of straightforward consonantal correspondences with reconstructed Proto-Lower Sepik (PLS) phonemes are presented in Table 3.

Table 2 *Lower Sepik family: basic word-list*

		Yimas	Karawari	Angoram	Chambri	Murik
1	'one'	mba-	mba-	mbia-	mbwia-	abe
2	'two'	-rpal	-ripay	-(lɨ)par	-ri	kompari(K)
3	'three'	-ramnaw	-rianmaw	-elɨm	-ram	kerongo
4	'person'	narmaŋ	yarmasɨnar		noranan	nor
5	'male'	panmal	panmari	pondo		puin
6	'female/ mother'	ŋay	asay	nuŋor	kaye	ŋai
7	'father'	apwi	anay	apa/ano	kanu	apa
8	'water'	arɨm	arɨm	alɨm	arɨm	arɨm
9	'fire'	awt	awi	aluŋ	ayɨr	awr
10	'sun'	tɨmal	sɨmari	mbwino	sɨnmari	akɨn
11	'moon'	mɨla	tuŋgwi	mɨle	mwɨl	karewan
12	'star'	awak	suŋgwincɨrɨm	arenjo	suŋkwi	moai
13	'canoe'	kay	kay	ke	ke	gain
14	'louse'	nam	yam	nam	kurɨr	iran
15	'village'	num	imuŋga	num	num	nomot
16	'breast'	nɨŋay	njay	ŋge	nɨŋke	niŋgen
17	'tooth'	tɨrɨŋ	sɨsɨŋ	sisiŋ	sraŋk	asarap
18	'blood'	yat	yay	ayakone	yari	yaran
19	'bone'	tanɨm	tanɨm	salɨŋ	anamp	sarɨŋib
20	'tongue'	mɨnyɨŋ	mumɨnyɨŋ	mɨnɨŋ	tɨbulanɨŋk	menɨŋ
21	'eye'	tuŋgurɨŋ	sambɨs	tambli	sisɨŋk	nabrin
22	'nose'	tɨkay	ipun	naŋim	wambusu	daur
23	'hair'	wapwi	wambi	mbwikmaley	yawi	dwar
24	'ear'	kwandumɨŋ	kwandukas	kwandum	kukunam	karekep
25	'egg'	awŋ	yawŋ	awŋ	awŋk	gaug
26	'leaf'	nɨmbrɨm	yimbrɨm	(nam)blum	nɨmpramp	nabirɨk
27	'tree'	yan	yuwan	lor	yuwan	yarar
28	'yesterday'/ 'tomorrow'	ŋarɨŋ	arɨŋ	nakɨmɨn	namasɨnɨŋ	ŋarɨŋ
29	'oar'	muraŋ	mɨnaŋ	inap	naŋk	inaŋ
30	'betelnut'	patn	payn	parɨŋ	muntikɨn	porog
31	'lime'	awi	as	awer	ayɨr	ayr
32	'pig'	numbran	imbian	imbar	numpran	(nim)bren
33	'crocodile'	manba	manbo	walami	ayi	oramen
34	'snake'	wakɨn	wakɨn	paruŋ	wan	wakɨn
35	'mosquito'	naŋgun	yaŋgun	wawarɨn	naŋgun	nauk/naŋgɨt(K)

Table 2 *(cont.)*

	Yimas	Karawari	Angoram	Chambri	Murik
36 'chicken'	nakwan	yakwan	kɨlɨkala	nakwan	goabar
37 'sago grub'	wun	wun	wurɨn	wun	kamur
38 'sago palm'	tɨnum	sɨmasum	(t)uli(no)	tɨnum	dun
39 'sago refuse'	tɨki	sikis	tikɨr		
40 'pound sago'	pan-	pan-	pan-	pun-	pon-
41 'wash sago'	tuku-	suku-	tuku-	tuku-	tokun-
42 'hear'	andɨ-	andu-	andɨ-	andɨ-	dɨn-
43 'hit'	tupul-	kurar-	ti-	dii-	di-
44 'eat'	am-	am-	am-	am-	mɨn-
45 'go'	wa-	kuria-	kal-	wa-	on-
46 'faeces'	mɨlɨm	mɨndi	mɨndi	munjar	mɨndɨn
47 'spine of leaf'	kɨnɨŋ	kɨnɨŋ	kɨnɨŋ	kɨnɨŋk	kɨnɨŋ
48 'leg'	pamuŋ	pamuŋ	namuŋ	namaŋk	namoŋ(K)
49 'big'	kɨpa-	kupa-	kupa-	wupa-	apo-
50 'cold'	tarɨk	sarɨk	popant	saruk	serɨpatin(K)

Table 3 *Lower Sepik phoneme correspondences: consonants*

PLS	Yimas	Karawari	Angoram	Chambri	Murik	Examples
*p	p	p	p	p	p	2, 5, 30, 40, 49
*m	m	m	m	m	m	3, 8, 10, 11, 14, 15, 20, 44, 46, 48
*w	w	w	w	w	w	25, 34, 37
*k	k	k	k	k	g/k	13, 24, 47, 50
*ŋ	ŋ		ŋ		ŋ	6, 28
*y	y	y	y	y	y	18, 27
*r	r	r	l	r	r	2, 3, 4, 8, 26, 28, 50
	t	y	r	r	r	2, 9, 18, 30, 32
		*r → Yt/#, ____ n *r → Ky/a				
		l/i				
*t	t	s	t	t	t	38, 39, 41
*s	r/t	s	s	s	s	10, 12, 17, 50
		*s merges with *r in Y and *t in K				
*n	n	n	n	n	n	5, 16, 32, 34, 37, 47
	n	y	n	y	n	4, 14, 15, 32, 35, 36
		*n → Ky/# ____				

The voiced stops and the homorganic nasal-plus-stop clusters present greater problems. Chambri has the most complex system of stops, contrasting plain voiced and voiceless stops and pre-nasalized voiced and voiceless stops, although the voiced pre-nasalized stops are rare in Chambri. In final position Chambri

Table 4 *Lower Sepik phoneme correspondences: pre-nasalized stops*

PLS	Yimas	Karawari	Angoram	Chambri	Murik	Examples
*mp	mb	mb	mb	mp	b	21, 26
	m	m		mp	b	19, 26
			*mp → Y, K, A *m*/ ___ #			
*mb	mb	mb	mb	mb	b	1
*ŋk	ŋg	ŋg	ŋg	ŋk	(ŋ)g	12, 16
	ŋ	ŋ	ŋ	ŋk	ŋ/g	17, 20, 25, 29, 30, 47, 48
			*ŋk → Y, K, A *ŋ*/ ___ #[a]			
*ŋg	ŋg	ŋg	–	ŋg	k/ŋg(K)[b]	35
(*nt)	no examples					
*nd	nd	nd	nd	nd	d/nd[c]	42, 46

[a] The split in Murik between *g* and *ŋ* for *ŋk* in final position is unexplained.
[b] Why Murik shows *k* rather than the expected *g* here is unclear.
[c] The alternations in the Murik reflexes could be the result of initial versus intervocal position; other examples of pre-nasalized reflexes are intervocalic: (16) 'breast' and (35) 'mosquito'.

neutralizes this to a simple plain versus pre-nasalized stop contrast, with the stop realized as voiceless. Yimas and Karawari are the simplest, contrasting a plain voiceless stop with a pre-nasalized stop which varies freely between voiced and voiceless. The contrast between Chambri pre-nasalized voiceless and voiced stops is neutralized in Yimas and Karawari: compare (12) 'star' with (35) 'mosquito'. As there is no apparent conditioning factor for this Chambri contrast, we must assume it reflects the situation in the proto-language.

Murik stops are intermediate in complexity. It contrasts plain voiceless and voiced stops, but has pre-nasalized voiced stops only. The plain and pre-nasalized voiced stops generally correspond to pre-nasalized stops in other languages. Consider the correspondences in Table 4. For the plain voiced stops the data are very sketchy. Only (43) 'hit' provides any evidence for a plain voiced stop in the proto-language. In this word Chambri and Murik show *d*, while Yimas and Angoram have a voiceless correspondent. The Chambri *d* is the crucial evidence; it is difficult to explain away. It could not arise from a pre-nasalized stop because in Chambri they do not undergo simplification. I tentatively reconstruct **d* for this correspondence:

PLS	Yimas	Karawari	Angoram	Chambri	Murik	Examples
*d	t	–	t	d	d	43

This is no evidence for *b and *g but given *d and *mb, *nd and *ŋg, it is likely they existed. I have now reconstructed the following consonantal system for Proto-Lower Sepik:

*p	*t	*k
(*b)	*d	(*g)
*mp	(*nt)	*ŋk
*mb	*nd	*ŋg
	*s	
*m	*n	*ŋ
	*r	
*w	*y	

This system is rather tentative. While the contrast in PLS between plain and pre-nasalized stops is certain, that between voiced and voiceless is much less certain. As mentioned, the evidence for the plain voiced stops is extremely skimpy, resting on one cognate, (43) 'hit'. The contrast in voiced versus pre-nasalized stops is a little more definite, but not much, as it rests on the Chambri reflexes in four cognates: (1) 'one', (35) 'mosquito', (42) 'hear' and (46) 'faeces'. If these are rejected as insufficient, the above system would simplify to:

*p	*t	*k
*mb	*nd	*ŋg
	*s	
*m	*n	*ŋ
	*r	
*w	*y	

– a system like that of modern Karawari. I will follow a conservative course and stick to the more complex system here; but further research may confirm the simpler Karawari system above.

Vowel correspondences are typically more complicated than those of consonants, and these languages are no exception. The vowel correspondences above exhibit many conditionings and irregularities that I do not have space to discuss here, but there is a basic pattern which I will elucidate. Typologically, the vowel systems of the five languages divide into two groups. One group, consisting of Murik, Chambri and Angoram, are six-vowel languages; the other, composed of Yimas and Karawari, are four-vowel languages:

M, C, A: Y, K:

i	ɨ	u
e		o
	a	

i	ɨ	u
	a	

Table 5 *Lower Sepik phoneme correspondences: vowels*

PLS	Yimas	Karawari	Angoram	Chambri	Murik	Examples
*a	a	a	a	a	a	1, 2, 3, 8, 9, 13, 14, 18, 19, 21, 24, 25, 28, 29, 31, 32, 34, 35, 36
*oᵃ	a	a	o	o	o	4, 5, 40
*eᵃ	no examples					
*ɨ	ɨ	ɨ	ɨ	ɨ	ɨ	8, 10, 16, 26, 28, 34, 38, 39, 42, 46, 47
*u	u	u	u	u	u	15, 24, 32, 35, 37, 38, 41, 48, 49
*i	i/ɨ	i	i	i	i	2, 17, 19, 20, 43
*aw	aw	aw	aw	aw	aw	9, 25
*ay	ay	ay	e	e	ay/e	13, 16

[a] Note that the mid vowels in PLS were comparatively rare: this may account for their loss in Yimas and Karawari.

Proto-Lower Sepik was clearly like Murik, Chambri and Angoram. While there are no correspondences illustrating *e, *o is fairly well established, and reasons of symmetry, as well as the testimony of Angoram, Chambri and Murik, justify a full six-vowel system. Yimas and Karawari have lowered the mid vowels to *a*. In addition, Yimas has undergone an extensive historical process of vowel centralization: the peripheral vowels, especially *i*, have been attracted to the central *ɨ*. This applies also, to a lesser extent, to Karawari and Angoram. The basic vowel correspondences with their reconstructed proto-phonemes are given in Table 5.

The reconstructed forms in Proto-Lower Sepik for most of the above words are given in Table 6 (the vowels in some forms are still problematic).

With the sound correspondences and these reconstructions a number of borrowings can be identified. For example, the Karawari forms for (11) 'moon' and (19) 'bone' are borrowings, probably from Yimas, for they exhibit *t* for *s, rather than the expected Karawari reflex *s*. *t* is, of course, the normal Yimas reflex for *s, suggesting these Karawari forms are Yimas loans. A second example is the Chambri form for (21) 'eye', *sɨsiŋk*, which is unrelated to the proto-form *tambri and the forms in other languages. This is probably a corruption of a Iatmul loan, as the Iatmul form is *mɨnisɨkŋ*. The sources of many of the other non-cognate forms have not been established, as, with the exception of Iatmul, the languages surrounding the family are poorly known.

Now consider the nonsingular pronouns in the five languages given in Table 7. Not all languages make the same set of distinctions. Yimas, Chambri and Murik have the richest system: dual, paucal and plural are distinguished; while Angoram has the simplest, with only a simple plural. Yimas and Murik are the furthest separated geographically, which may suggest that the proto-language also made a three-way distinction; but there is further evidence that clinches this proposal. First of all, Chambri has a paucal form for the first person with a cluster *ŋk*, present in all

Table 6 *Proto-Lower Sepik: reconstruction of basic word-list*

1	*mb(w)ia-	'one'	27	*y(uw)an	'tree'
2	*ri-pa-	'two'	28	*ŋariŋ	'yesterday/tomorrow'
3	*ram	'three'	29	*(mɨ)naŋk	'oar'
4	*nor	'person'	30	*poriŋk	'betelnut'
5	*pon	'male'	31	*awi-r	'lime'
6	*ŋay	'female/mother'	32	*numpran	'pig'
8	*arɨm	'water'	34	*wakɨn	'snake'
9	*aw-r	'fire'	35	*naŋgun	'mosquito'
10	*sɨnmari	'sun'	36	*nakwan	'chicken'
11	*m(w)il	'moon'	37	*wun	'sago grub'
12	*suŋkwi	'star'	38	*tɨnum	'sago palm'
13	*kay	'canoe'	39	*tɨk-	'sago refuse'
14	*nam	'house'	40	*pon-	'pound sago'
15	*num	'village'	41	*tuku-	'wash sago'
16	*nɨŋkay	'breast'	42	*and-	'hear'
17	*sisiŋk	'tooth'	43	*di-	'hit'
18	*ya-r	'blood'	44	*am-	'eat'
19	*sariŋamp	'bone'	46	*mɨndi	'faeces'
20	*miniŋk	'tongue'	47	*kɨniŋk	'spine of leaf'
21	*tambri	'eye'	48	*namuŋk	'leg'
24	*kwandum	'ear'	49	*(k)upa-	'big'
25	*awŋk	'egg'	50	*sarɨk	'cold'
26	*nɨmpramp	'leaf'			

Table 7 *Lower Sepik nonsingular pronouns*

	Yimas	Karawari	Angoram	Chambri	Murik
'we' (DL)	kapa	kapa	–	kɨpi	gai
'you' (DL)	kapwa	kupa	–	kɨbwi	gau
'we' (PAUC)	paŋkɨt	–	–	yipiŋk	agi
'you' (PAUC)	paŋkɨt	–	–	–	agu
'we' (PL)	ipa	apia	paŋgɨr	yipi	e
'you' (PL)	ipwa	ipa	ipwe	yibwi	o

the paucals in Yimas and obviously related to the *g* of Murik. Furthermore, the Angoram plural pronouns are an obvious conflation of older paucal and plural pronouns, with the first person pronoun *paŋgɨr* clearly cognate to the paucal form *paŋkɨt* in Yimas. Thus, we can reconstruct a form *ŋk* for paucal pronouns in Proto-Lower Sepik.

These nonsingular pronoun forms are especially interesting, in that the second person pronouns are clearly derived from the first in all but Angoram and Murik by adding a high back quality to the first person form: Yimas *kapa* 1DL, *kapwa* 2DL,

Chambri *yipi* 1PL, *yibwi* 2PL (the *p* is voiced before the *w* in Chambri). The same high back quality is associated with the nonsingular forms in Murik: *gau* 2DL, *agu* 2PAUC. Murik also shows a high front quality associated with the first person: *gai* 1DL, *agi* 1PAUC. The Murik plural forms arise by contraction of forms built by suffixing these glides to a stem *a*: *e* < *a* + *i* 1NSG and *o* < *a* + *u* 2N-SG. Yimas also has a 1PL form *ay*: *ay-wa-n* 1PL-go-IMP 'let's go'. The Murik paucal forms are built on this same *a* plus *g* PAUC < PLS *ŋk* PAUC plus *i* or *u* for first or second person. Finally, the dual forms are transparently a dual stem *ga*- plus *i* or *u*: The Murik nonsingular pronouns may be summarized as:

	DL	PAUC	PL
	DL + Person	PL + PAUC + Person	PL + Person
1	*ga* + *i*	*a* + *g* + *i*	*a* + *i*
2	*ga* + *u*	*a* + *g* + *u*	*a* + *u*

The Murik dual stem *ga* is undoubtedly cognate to the dual stem *ka*- in Yimas and Karawari and *kɨ*- in Chambri. Initial *k* in Yimas, Karawari and Chambri may correspond to *g* in Murik: see (13) 'canoe' in the earlier word-list. I reconstruct a PLS dual stem **ka*. All the languages but Murik have the additional nonsingular stem **pa*, to which is added a person marker. In Yimas, Angoram and Chambri, the person marker occurs between the consonant and vowel of the **pa* stem: Y *kap-w-a* 2DL, A *ip-w-e* 2PL, C *yib-w-i* 2PL. Parallel formations are presumably the source of the first person forms: Y **kap-y-a* 1DL, **ip-y-a* 1PL, C **yip-y-a* 1PL. These have been simplified in the modern languages to *kapa*, *ipa* and *yipi* respectively, but supporting evidence for the reconstruction is found in the Karawari 1PL form *apia*, in which a high front vowel following the *p* is still present.

The only remaining problem concerns the stem *(y)i*- found in the plural of all languages but Murik, which has a plural stem in *a*-. Karawari *apia* 1PL also has this plural stem, indicating that it must be assigned to the proto-language, but as there is no convincing evidence that the other four languages form a subgroup, *(y)i*- must be assigned to it as well. Both **(y)i*- and **pa*- have a similar distribution, missing in Murik, but present in the other four languages. Further research may provide evidence for a subgrouping in which these are shared innovations, but on present data we must assume both in the proto-language. What distinguished **a*- from **(y)i*- is at this point unknown.

The nonsingular pronouns for first and second person in Proto-Lower Sepik can be reconstructed as follows:

	DL	PAUC	PL
1	**ka-(pa)-i*	**(pa)ŋk-i*	**a/(y)i-(pa)-i*
2	**ka-(pa)-u*	**(pa)ŋk-u*	**a/(y)i-(pa)-u*

The comparative method need not stop at the establishment of sound correspondences and the reconstruction of the sound system and basic vocabulary (including pronouns) of the proto-language, but can also involve grammatical comparison and reconstruction. I wish to turn now to this task, attempting a reconstruction of some of the noun-class system of Proto-Lower Sepik. The reader is advised to glance again at section 4.4 on Yimas noun classes to familiarize himself with the basic data. Here I will write the Yimas clusters *mp*, *nt* and *ŋk* as *mb*, *nd*, *ŋg* respectively, to ease comparison with the other languages. Of the five Lower Sepik languages, only Murik lacks noun-classes. It does have number inflections on nouns and number concord with adjectives, a likely vestige of an earlier noun-class system: 'big person' SG *nor apo*, DL *norimbo apaabo*, PAUC *norigi apaara*, PL *normot apak*; 'bad house' SG *iran moago*, DL *irambo moagaabo*, PAUC *iramoara moagaara*, PL *iranmot moak*. Only a few human nouns take the nominal paucal suffix *-gi*; all other nouns take *-moara*. The Murik number system may be summarized as:

	N	Adj
SG	$\emptyset$	*-o*
DL	*-mbo*	*-abo*
PAUC	*-gi*/*-moara*	*-ara*
PL	*-mot*	*-k*

The other four languages have full noun-class systems, parallel to Yimas. Tables 8, 9 and 10 present the data for the classes corresponding to Yimas classes V–VII. The abbreviations used and the explanation of the arrangement of the tables follows:

NOUN   the form of the sample noun in each language inflected for number
POSS   the noun plus the first singular possessor, e.g. Yimas *wun ama-na-kin* 'my sago grub'
ADJ   the noun modified by the adjective 'big' in each language
NUM   the noun modified by a given numeral, 'one' for SG, 'two' for DL and 'three' for PL
VERB   the noun agreeing as the third singular subject of an intransitive verb: as for example *tumukit* 'fall' in Yimas or *kibran* 'break' in Chambri

In most cases the words from each language in each class are cognate; if not, they are cognates of other Yimas words in the same class.

The first major observation is that not all languages make the same number distinctions. Angoram never provides a distinct dual, while Karawari does so only in class VI. Also, with the exception of Angoram, all languages exhibit the same pattern for concord affixes as Yimas: suffixes for adjectives and prefixes for verbs. The numerals are more complex. In all languages, 'one' agrees as an adjective but 'two'

Table 8 Comparative data for Lower Sepik class V

		Yimas	Karawari	Angoram	Chambri
SG	NOUN	wun 'sago grub'	sɨkɨr 'chair'	wurɨn 'sago grub'	wun 'sago grub'
	POSS	wun ama-na-kɨn	sɨkɨr ama-na-n	wurɨn ami-na-kɨna	wun amɨ-na-n
	ADJ	wun kɨpa-n	sɨkɨr kupa-n	wurɨn kupa-na	wun wupa-n
	NUM	wun mba-n	sɨkɨr mba-n	wurɨn mbia-n	wun mbwia-n
	VERB	wun na-tumukɨt	sɨkɨr mɨn-puŋiar	wurɨn ikolondɨka-na	wun an-cɨcɨrɨn
DL	NOUN	wundrɨm			wunasɨm
	POSS	wundrɨm ama-na-ndrɨm			wunasɨm amɨ-na-sɨm
	ADJ	wundrɨm kɨpa-ndrɨm			wunasɨm wupa-sɨm
	NUM	wundrɨm tɨm-pal			wunasɨm wu-sɨm
	VERB	wundrɨm tɨma-tumukɨt			wunasɨm ari-cɨcɨrɨn
PL	NOUN	wunɨt	sɨkɨrɨŋar	wurɨŋar	wunar
	POSS	wunɨt ama-na-ra	sɨkɨrɨŋar ama-na-kia	wurɨŋar ami-na-klea	wunar ami-na-r
	ADJ	wunɨt kɨpa-ra	sɨkɨrɨŋar kupa-ya	wurɨŋar kup-lea	wunar wupa-r
	NUM	wunɨt tamunum	sɨkɨrɨŋar sɨm-ianmaw	wurɨŋar sum-elim	wunar sammenamp
	VERB	wunɨt ya-tumukɨt	sɨkɨrɨŋar maya-puŋiar	wurɨŋar ikolondɨka-ne	wunar ar-cɨcɨrɨn

Table 9 *Comparative data for Lower Sepik class VI*

		Yimas	Karawari	Angoram	Chambri
SG	NOUN	tɨrɨŋ 'tooth'	sɨsɨŋ 'tooth'	sisiŋ 'tooth'	sraŋk 'tooth'
	POSS	tɨrɨŋ ama-na-ŋ	sɨsɨŋ ama-na-k	sisiŋ ami-na-ŋga	sraŋk amɨ-na-ŋk
	ADJ	tɨrɨŋ kɨpa-ŋ	sɨsɨŋ kupa-ŋ	sisiŋ kupa-ŋga	sraŋk wupa-ŋk
	NUM	tɨrɨŋ mba-ŋ	sɨsɨŋ mba-ŋ	sisiŋ mbia-ŋ	sraŋk mbwia-ŋk
	VERB	tɨrɨŋ kɨ-tumukɨt	sɨsɨŋ ŋgɨ-puŋgiar	sisiŋ ikolondɨka-ŋ	sraŋk aŋkɨ-kɨbran
DL	NOUN	tɨrɨŋɨl	sɨsɨŋgri		sraŋkɨkri
	POSS	tɨrɨŋɨl ama-na-ŋgɨl	sɨsɨŋgri ama-na-kŋgri		sraŋkɨkri amɨ-na-ŋkɨkri
	ADJ	tɨrɨŋɨl kɨpa-ŋgɨl	sɨsɨŋgri kupa-ŋgri		sraŋkɨkri wupa-ŋkɨkri
	NUM	tɨrɨŋɨl kɨ-rpal	sɨsɨŋgri k-ripay		sraŋkɨkri k-ri
	VERB	tɨrɨŋɨl kɨla-tumukɨt	sɨsɨŋgri ŋgri-puŋgiar		sraŋkɨkri ari-kɨbran
PL	NOUN	tɨrɨŋgi	sɨsɨŋgi	sisiŋgli	sraŋkɨr
	POSS	tɨrɨŋgi ama-na-ŋgi	sɨsɨŋgi ama-na-k-ŋgi	sisiŋgli amɨ-na-ŋglia	sraŋkɨr amɨ-na-r
	ADJ	tɨrɨŋgi kɨpa-ŋgi	sɨsɨŋgi kupa-ŋgi	sisiŋgli kupa-ŋglia	sraŋkɨr wupa-r
	NUM	tɨrɨŋgi k-ramnawt	sɨsɨŋgi k-rianmaw	sisiŋgli kl-elim	sraŋkɨr kia-ram
	VERB	tɨrɨŋgi kia-tumukɨt	sɨsɨŋgi ŋgi-puŋgiar	sisiŋgli ikolondɨka-ŋgli	sraŋkɨr ar-kɨbran

Table 10 *Comparative data for Lower Sepik class VII*

		Yimas	Karawari	Angoram	Chambri
SG	NOUN	*tanɨm* 'bone'	*tanɨm* 'bone'	*mɨnɨm* 'neck'	*anamp* 'bone'
	POSS	*tanɨm ama-na-m*	*tanɨm ama-na-m*	*mɨnɨm ami-na-kamba*	*anamp ami-na-mp*
	ADJ	*tanɨm kɨpa-m*	*tanɨm kupa-m*	*mɨnɨm kupa-mba*	*anamp wupa-mp*
	NUM	*tanɨm mba-m*	*tanɨm mba-m*	*mɨnɨm mbia-m*	*anamp mbwia-mp*
	VERB	*tanɨm pɨ-tumukɨt*	*tanɨm mbu-puŋgiar*	*mɨnɨm ikolondika-m*	*anamp ampi-kɨbran*
DL	NOUN	*tanɨmbɨl*	*tanɨmbri*		*anampri*
	POSS	*tanɨmbɨl ama-na-mbɨl*	*tanɨmbri ama-na-mbri*		*anampri ami-na-mpri*
	ADJ	*tanɨmbɨl kɨpa-mbɨl*	*tanɨmbri kupa-mbri*		*anampri wupa-mpri*
	NUM	*tanɨmbɨl pɨ-rpal*	*tanɨmbri p-ripay*		*anampri p-ri*
	VERB	*tanɨmbɨl pɨla-tumukɨt*	*tanɨmbri mbu-puŋgiar*		*anampri ari-kɨbran*
PL	NOUN	*tanɨmbat*	*tanɨmbas*	*mɨnɨmbar*	*anabar*
	POSS	*tanɨmbat ama-na-ra*	*tanɨmbas ama-na-kia*	*mɨnɨmbar ami-na-kumbra*	*anabar ami-na-r*
	ADJ	*tanɨmbat kɨpa-ra*	*tanɨmbas kupa-ya*	*mɨnɨmbar kupa-mbra*	*anabar wupa-r*
	NUM	*tanɨmbat p-ramnawt*	*tanɨmbas p-riamnaw*	*mɨnɨmbar pl-elim*	*anabar pia-ram*
	VERB	*tanɨmbat ya-tumukɨt*	*tanɨmbas maya-puŋgiar*	*mɨnɨmbar ikolondika-mbɨr*	*anabar ar-kɨbran*

and 'three' as verbs. Even in Angoram, in which concord affixes are generally suffixes, the affixes for 'two' and 'three' are prefixes. All of this clearly demonstrates the antiquity of the split system. For Proto-Lower Sepik we can conclude that adjectival concord was suffixal, while verbal was prefixal, with 'one' behaving as an adjective, and 'two' and 'three' as verbs.

Let me start with class VI, as it is the most straightforward. The mark of this class on nominals is clearly *ηk, as preserved by Chambri. The other three languages have simplified the cluster in final position to η, following the cluster simplification rule discussed above; but the original clusters emerge in the dual and plural forms, in which number suffixes are attached to the noun stem: Yimas SG *tɨriŋ*, DL *tɨriŋgɨl*, PL *tɨriŋgi*. The dual is marked by *-ŋgɨl* in Yimas, *-ŋgri* in Karawari, *-ŋgli* in Angoram (the plural is clearly the old dual) and *-kri* in Chambri. *l* in Yimas is a palatalized lateral which corresponds with, and clearly developed from, an earlier *-ri*, which is the form of the dual marker in Proto-Lower Sepik, preserved as such in Karawari and Angoram. Chambri has innovated in this class by simply suffixing the numeral 'two', *-ri*, inflected for this class with the verbal prefix *k-*. This was aided no doubt by the transparent relationship between the numeral two and the dual suffix.

The plural is formed by suffixing *-i* in Yimas and Karawari, but *-r* in Chambri. Chambri has innovated, having neutralized most class distinctions in the plural by suffixing *-r* to all classes. Yimas and Karawari reflect the original situation with different forms of plural suffixes for different classes. More evidence for this view will be presented below. The form of the plural suffix for this class in PLS then is *-i*.

The possessive and adjective concord suffixes are transparently formed by suffixing the class marker *ηk plus the number marker (*$\emptyset$ for singular, *-ri for dual and *-i for plural) to the possessive form of the pronoun in *-na or to the adjective stem. Chambri shows the same developments here as with the nouns, while Angoram has added a demonstrative stem *-a* to the concord suffixes. The only complication here is the Karawari forms which show an intrusive *-k* in the possessive forms. This is very likely by analogy with the forms in class V which have a possessive concord suffix *-kɨn* (cf. Yimas and Angoram forms for class V), which may have been analysed as *-k* POSS plus *-n* class V marker. Extending by analogy into class VI, Karawari would have derived SG *-k-ŋg-$\emptyset$ DL *-k-ŋg-i PL *-k-ŋg-i. The dual and plural are the attested forms, but the singular underwent cluster simplification: *-kŋg > -k.

The verbal prefixes present a more complex case. We find the following correspondence in the singular: Y *kɨ-*, K *ŋgɨ-*, A *-ŋ*, C *aŋkɨ-*. The Chambri and Karawari forms show close agreement: they seem to be simply the class marker *ηk prefixed to the verb (the Chambri forms are prefixed by *a-*). Prima facie, this would seem the best reconstruction for the proto-language, with Angoram analogizing the verbs to the suffixal concord forms of the adjectives and possessives and Yimas undergoing cluster simplification. But a closer look leads us to suspect this reconstruction. Remember the point made earlier that the numerals 'two' and 'three' behave like verbs. Looking at these numerals, we find that the prefix in all four languages is k-, the same form as the Yimas verbal prefix. The only plausible explanation is that the verbal prefix for this class is in fact *k-, preserved by Yimas and the numerals in all four languages. The other three languages have innovated, Angoram by extending the adjectives and possessive concord suffixes to verbs as well, and Karawari and Chambri by taking the nominal class marker as basic and prefixing it to the verb. The dual and plural verbal prefixes are formed with the verbal class marker *k plus a number marker *ri- or *i- plus a nonsingular verbal prefix *a-. While Yimas is the only language to have preserved this *a-, the Chambri form for 'three' *kia-ram* < k- class VI + i- PL + a- NSG leaves no doubt as to its antiquity. Chambri exhibits the same neutralization of class distinctions in the verbal inflection of the plural as it did in the nominals and adjective concord affixes, but it also extends this to the dual category. Only the numerals in Chambri preserve the original class distinctions in the dual and plural.

Class VII is on the whole quite parallel to class VI. Here the class marker is *mp, and the same rules and combinations found with class VI *ηk apply here as well. The only major difference is found in the plural. Instead of the expected *mp-i, we find *-mp-r with normal phonological developments in all four languages. As discussed in section 4.4, Yimas plurals in -t < *r are always associated with an adjective/ possessive suffix in -ra and a verbal prefix in ya-. This holds true in the other languages which preserve class distinctions in the plural, Karawari and Angoram, and must therefore be reconstructed (remember *r > K y/a). Interestingly, Angoram has analogized, spreading the class marker -mb < *mp into the plural, resulting in an adjective concord suffix -$mbra$. All languages show a prefix form p- in the numerals, demonstrating again the conservatism of Yimas in the verbal prefix system.

Class V is rather different from classes VI and VII. There is no overt nominal class marker; any nominal ending in p, t, k, m, n, η, r or l belongs to this class. Different nouns take different forms of the plural suffix, depending on their final segment. In Yimas, nouns ending in n take -t or -ra, those in t or r take -ηgat, those in -k take -i or -ra etc. Similar rules apply in the other languages, although Chambri again has neutralized most distinctions, applying -ar to mark the plural of most nouns. As the above example involves *-r plurals (Yimas t), they will be associated with a suffix *-ra and a prefix *ya- < $\emptyset$- class marker + *i- PL + *a- NSG. The dual is only distinct in Yimas and Chambri, and is marked by an affix *sim (Y r < *s). This *-sim is suffixed as an adjective/possessive concord marker and prefixed as a verbal concord marker (Y r > $t/\#$). Note also that it is used as the numeral prefix to 'three' in Karawari and

Angoram, while the Chambri and Yimas forms are suppletive. As the Chambri and Yimas suppletive forms are clearly cognate, it is likely that the suppletive variant was the form in the proto-language for this class, with Karawari and Angoram analogizing on the basis of other classes.

The basic class marker for class v exemplified by the singular concord suffixes is *-n*. This is prefixed as *n(a)-* for the verbal concord marker. The only complication concerns the intrusive *-k* in the possessive forms. This is found in the singular in Yimas, in the plural in Karawari, and in both singular and plural in Angoram. It is lacking in Chambri but, as Chambri has a rule dropping *k* in such environments ('snake' PLS *wakɨn* > C *wan*), we are justified in reconstructing it in the proto-system, at least in the singular.

The reconstructions of the systems of classes v–vii in Proto-Lower Sepik are given in Table 11. While the data and these reconstructions leave no doubt as to the presence of the noun-class system in the proto-language of these four languages, the assignment of this system to PLS requires Murik to be considered. While Murik currently lacks a noun-class system, it does bear unmistakable traces of something like the above system. We have already seen in our reconstruction that the numerals 'two' and 'three' seem to be the most conservative forms. Cognate forms for these in Murik–Kopar (2 and 3 in Table 2) are 'two' *kompari* and 'three' *kerongo*. These undoubtedly descend from *k-* class vi marker plus *-pa* 'two' and *-ram* 'three' plus *-ri* DL and *-ŋk* PAUC. These are the invariable numerals in Murik. An interesting question is why the numeral forms for class vi ultimately became the basic unchanging number forms for Murik. I have no good explanation for this, except to point out that when Yimas children are learning to use their own highly complex number system they almost invariably use the class vi form as the unmarked form. I have no doubt that, if Yimas were to lose its noun-class system, the class vi numerals in Yimas would also become the basic numbers. Another vestige of the earlier noun-class system in Murik is the paucal adjective concord suffix *-ara*. This is clearly cognate with the plural adjective concord suffix *-ra* for classes v and vi.

I have now applied the comparative method to a number of areas in the languages of the Lower Sepik family: basic vocabulary, pronouns and noun-class systems. The attempt has been very encouraging; I have reconstructed for the proto-language a basic vocabulary of some forty items, some pronoun forms and the inflectional system for three of the noun classes. But the Lower Sepik family is a relatively closely related one, roughly on the level of Germanic, and this is the depth to which I claimed we could expect to apply the comparative method successfully. Beyond this the number of cognates will drop significantly, and it will become increasingly difficult to establish sound correspondences. It is my contention, however, that comparison and reconstruction on the grammatical level, such as I attempted with

Table 11 *PLS noun-class systems*

		Class v	Class vi	Class vii
SG	NOUN	$\emptyset$	*-ŋk	*-mp
	POSS	*-k-n	*-ŋk	*-mp
	ADJ	*-n	*-ŋk	*-mp
	NUM	*-n	*-ŋk	*-mp
	VERB	*n(a)-	*k-	*p-
DL	NOUN	*-sɨm	*-ŋk-ri	*-mp-ri
	POSS	*-sɨm	*-ŋk-ri	*-mp-ri
	ADJ	*-sɨm	*-ŋk-ri	*-mp-ri
	NUM	*sɨm-	*k-	*p-
	VERB	*sɨm-	*k-ri-a-	*p-ri-a-
PL	NOUN	*-r etc.	*-ŋk-i	*-mp-at
	POSS	*-ra	*-ŋk-i	*-ra
	ADJ	*-ra	*-ŋk-i	*-ra
	NUM	*samnenump	*k-(i-a-)	*p-(i-a-)
	VERB	*$\emptyset$-i-a-	*k-i-a-	*p-i-a-

the noun-classes, may still yield useful and conclusive results even when the number of cognates may be insufficient to prove anything. If, for example, the cognates among the above five languages were insignificant, but the verbal prefixes and numerals still showed the relations above, this would argue for a genetic relationship, as the odds against borrowing such a complex system are very great indeed. If the cognates between German and English were minimal, the relationships *good*: *better*, *gut*: *besser* and *is*: *was*, *ist*: *war* would prove genetic relationship, again because borrowing is not plausible here. The major point is that all traditional uses of the comparative method can be applied to Papuan languages at a relatively shallow level, but as relations of a deeper level become the centre of interest, grammatical comparison and reconstruction must assume a progressively greater role in establishing genetic relations. This does not include superficial typological grammatical similarities, as these are easily diffused, but detailed grammatical parallelism with shared forms, especially suppletive forms, of the type exemplified by the lower Sepik noun-classes. This is a fundamental problem to which I will return in section 7.4, which discusses deep-level genetic relations among Papuan languages.

7.3 Survey of major Papuan language families

The geographical position of the families discussed below is presented in Map 6. For a more detailed survey of Papuan language families see Wurm (1975), from which

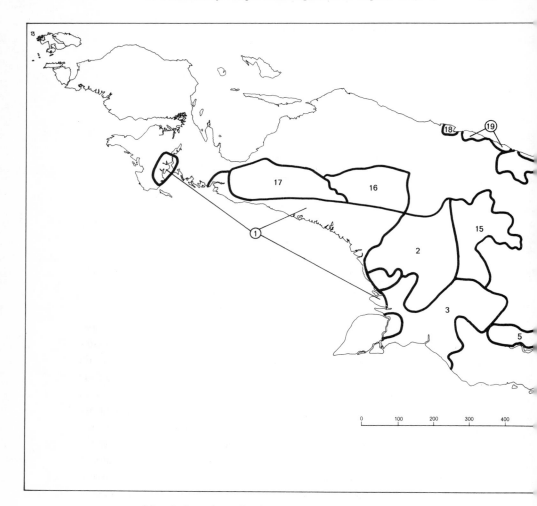

Map 6   Locations of major Papuan language families

1. Asmat family
2. Awyu family
3. Marind family
4. Kiwaian family
5. Suki-Gogodala family
6. Eleman family
7. Goilalan family

8. Koiarian family
9. Binanderean family
10. Angan family
11. Kainantu family
12. Gorokan family
13. Chimbu family
14. Engan family

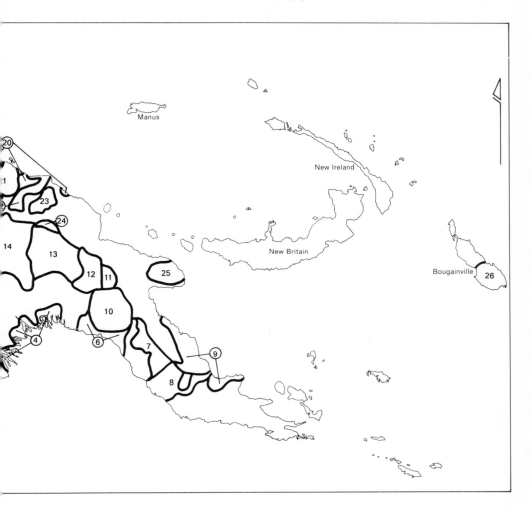

15. Ok family
16. Dani family
17. Wissel Lakes family
18. Sentani family
19. Sko family
20. Torricelli family

21. Ndu family
22. The Lower Sepik family
23. Grass family
24. Kalam family
25. Huon family
26. South Bougainville family

language listings and population figures below are drawn. Population growth in recent years in certain areas of New Guinea has been on the order of three per cent a year, suggesting that, for some of the languages discussed below, the population of speakers at present (1985) may be up to thirty per cent higher than the figure given.

7.3.1 The Asmat family

This is a small, closely related language family. It is spread over a large area of southern Irian Jaya, roughly from Etna Bay in the west to the Sirac (Eilanden) River. The four languages in the family with their population figures are:

Iria–Asienara	1,600	Sempan	1,000
Kamoro	9,000	Asmat	40,000

Little is known of Iria–Asienara. Kamoro and Sempan probably form a subgroup as against Asmat. The two larger languages, Kamoro and Asmat, have extensive dialect differentiation (Voorhoeve 1975a).

Kamoro and Asmat are among the better known of Papuan languages. Drabbe 1953 is a grammar of Kamoro, while there are two grammars of Asmat, Drabbe 1959a on the central coast dialect and Voorhoeve 1965 on the Flamingo Bay dialect. In addition, for Asmat there is a dictionary (Drabbe 1959b) and a comparative study of three of the dialects (Drabbe 1963). Voorhoeve (1969) proposed some evidence linking Asmat to Sentani on the north coast of Irian Jaya. While not conclusive, the evidence is tantalizing. Voorhoeve (1980) is a comparative study of Asmat dialects.

7.3.2 The Awyu family

This family is of average size for a Papuan language family and is spoken between the Sirac (Eilanden) River and the Digul, or between the areas of the Asmat and Marind families. Languages and their population figures are:

Sawuy	2,000	Wambon	1,000
Syiagha–Yenimu	3,000	Kaeti	4,000
Pisa	3,500	Waŋgom	1,000
Aghu	3,000	Kotogüt	1,000
Airo–Sumagaxe	2,000		

A deeper relationship between this family and the Asmat family (7.3.1) and the Ok family (7.3.15) seems possible, but is not yet proven.

Thanks to the work of Drabbe, this family is reasonably well known. Drabbe 1950 is a comparative study of Syiagha–Yenimu and Pisa, while Drabbe 1957 is a full grammar of Aghu, incorporating some sample texts. Drabbe 1959c is a grammatical sketch of Wambon, with texts in both Kaeti and Wambon. Healey 1970 attempts a reconstruction of the phonology of the proto-language of this family.

7.3.3   *The Marind family*

This family occupies southern Irian Jaya close to the border of Papua New Guinea, and spreads into Papua New Guinea in the Lake Murray area of Western Province. It roughly occupies the area between the Awyu and Kiwaian families. There are six languages, with the following population figures:

Boazi	2,000	Bian	900
Zimakani	1,500	Yaqay	9,000
Marind	7,000	Warkai	400?

The indefatigable Drabbe is responsible for much of our information on these languages. He provided grammatical notes and a comparative vocabulary for Boazi (Drabbe 1954), notes on Bian verb structure (Drabbe 1954), and a full detailed grammar with texts of the Gawir dialect of Marind (Drabbe 1955). Drabbe's (1955) grammar of Marind also contains comparative word-lists for other dialects of Marind in which dialect differentiation is considerable, as well as lists for Bian, Boazi and Yaqay. Marind is one of the best known Papuan languages. In addition to Drabbe's (1955) grammar, there is an earlier grammar by Geurtjens (1926), as well as two Marind dictionaries (Kolk and Vertenten 1922: Geurtjens 1933). Other sources for languages in this family are Voorhoeve's (1970a) study of Boazi and Zimakani and Drabbe's (1954) word-lists and notes on Yaqay. Finally, materials in English, based on Drabbe's Dutch studies, for all three language families discussed thus far, Asmat, Awyu and Marind, as well as for other language families in southern Irian Jaya, can be found in Boelaars 1950.

7.3.4   *The Kiwaian family*

The languages of this family are spoken along the coast of the Western and Gulf Provinces, from the mouth of the Fly River eastwards. The languages of this family are:

Southern Kiwai	9,700	Kerewo	2,200
Wabuda	1,700	Northeastern Kiwai	3,700
Bamu	2,850	Arigibi	700
Morigi	700		

The Kiwai presented in Ray's (1933) standard grammar is Island Kiwai, a dialect of Southern Kiwai. Other materials on the Kiwaian family may be found in Ray 1923;

Riley and Ray 1930–1; and Wurm 1951; 1973. Wurm 1973 is an especially good survey of this language family.

7.3.5   *The Suki–Gogodala family*
This family is spoken in two languages, Suki and Gogodala, found on either side of the Fly River. The population figures are as follows:

Suki   1,000   Gogodala   10,500

Gogodala is spoken in two dialects: Gogodala proper with 7,000 speakers and Waruna with 3,500 speakers.

A comparative study of Suki and Gogodala can be found in Voorhoeve (1970b).

7.3.6   *The Eleman family*
This is a small, very closely related language family, spoken along the coastal and inland areas of the Gulf Province. Member languages include:

Toaripi	20,200	Keuru	4,600
Uraipi	2,500	Orokolo	6,400
Opao	1,200		

For a comparative study of this family, see Brown 1973. Brown 1968 is a dictionary of the largest language of the family, Toaripi.

7.3.7   *The Goilalan family*
This language family is spoken in the mountainous area of the northern Central Province, spilling over into adjacent areas of southern Morobe and western Oro Provinces. It consists of five languages:

Weri	3,500	Tauade	8,700
Biangai	900	Fuyuge	10,000
Kunimaipa	8,000		

Kunimaipa is the best known of these languages. Pence 1966 presents a phonological analysis, while Geary 1977 is a detailed grammar. Fuyuge is dialectally quite diverse: an early elementary grammar of it is Ray 1912. For Weri, see Boxwell and Boxwell 1966; Boxwell 1967; 1980. Only a phonological analysis is available for Biangai (Dubert and Dubert 1973).

7.3.8   *The Koiarian family*
This is one of the best known Papuan language families. It includes Barai, a language mentioned previously many times. The Koiarian family is from Port

Moresby inland to the Owen Stanley Range, over the range and into Oro Province. It includes six languages:

Koita	2,500	Barai	3,500
Koiari	1,200	Ömie	1,200
Mountain Koiari	4,000	Managalasi	4,000

Sketch grammars of Koita, Mountain Koiari, Barai and Ömie are found in Dutton 1975. Koiari is described in Dutton 1969. Olson 1981 is a detailed grammar of Barai, while Austing and Austing 1977 further treats Ömie grammar. Managalasi is the largest language, with extensive dialect differentiation; a dictionary (Parlier and Parlier 1980) as well as a short paper on verb inflections (Parlier 1964) has been published.

7.3.9 *The Binanderean family*
This is one of the largest Papuan language families. It is spoken along the coast and hinterland of Oro Province, and numbers fourteen languages:

Suena	1,400	Hunjara	4,300
Yekora	300	Notu	10,000
Zia	3,300	Yega	900
Binandere	3,000	Gaina	130
Ambasi	1,200	Baruga	1,100
Aeka	2,000	Dogoro	120
Orokaiva	25,000	Korafe	4,200

A few of these languages have been studied in depth. Orokaiva is the largest language, with a number of dialect divisions. Larsen and Larsen 1977 describes the phonology of the language, while Larsen and Larsen 1980 is a pedagogical grammar. Wilson 1974 is a detailed grammar of Suena. An early, but still useful, grammar of a Binanderean language is King's (1927) grammar of Binandere, whose analysis of the verb is systematized in Capell 1969. Materials on Korafe include a phonological study (Farr and Farr 1974) and a grammatical sketch (Farr and Farr 1975). A preliminary comparative study of the entire family is presented in Wilson 1969a.

7.3.10 *The Angan family*
This is a relatively large family spoken in the mountainous country at the junction of the Eastern Highlands, Morobe and Gulf Provinces, and down into lowland areas of the Gulf Province to within twenty-five kilometres of the coast. These are the languages of the so-called 'Kukukuku' peoples:

Simbari	2,400	Ankave	1,500
Baruya	4,900	Ivori	400
Ampale	3,500	Lohiki	850
Kawacha	30	Menya	12,000
Kamasa	50	Kapau	32,300
Yagwoia	6,100	Angaataha	1,000

An overall comparative study of this family is Lloyd 1973. Angaataha is the most divergent language; a discussion of its verb inflection can be found in Huisman 1973. Other sources for this family are Oates and Oates 1968 for Kapau and West 1973 for Ampale. The phonological systems of Angan languages are especially complex. Papers dealing with the phonologies of various languages in the family have been collected in Healey 1981.

7.3.11   *The Kainantu family*
This is a small but well studied family spoken in the Eastern Highlands Province around Kainantu. It consists of four languages:

Gadsup	19,500	Tairora	9,600
Auyana	7,500	Awa	1,500

Dialect differentiation in all but Awa is quite great, and some of these dialects may constitute separate languages. Almost all the published material relevant to the Kainantu family has been collected in McKaughan 1973. There has also been published a separate dictionary of Awa (Loving and Loving 1975).

7.3.12   *The Gorokan family*
This family, spoken in the Eastern Highlands Province round Goroka, is somewhat larger than the Kainantu family, but is equally well studied. Both Fore and Hua, languages mentioned many times previously, belong to this family, which includes the following:

Gende	9,000	BenaBena	15,000
Siane	16,000	Kamano–Yagaria	84,000
Yabiyufa	4,900	Fore	13,000
Gahuku–Asaro	23,000	Gimi	19,000

Dialect differentiation in a number of these languages, especially the larger ones, is very great, and this creates problems in classification. The problem is essentially caused by dialect chain. For example, in Kamano–Yagaria the dialects at the extreme ends of the chains clearly constitute different languages, but dialects in the middle show about equal relationship to both ends of the chain. Hence there is no non-arbitrary way to draw a line separating the two languages (see Wurm and Laycock 1961 for further discussion of this problem). Hua is one of the dialects in the Yagaria end of this chain.

Grammars are available for most of the languages of this family. For Gende, see Aufenanger 1952 and Brandson (in preparation). Siane is described in James (ms) and Haiman 1980. Deibler 1976 is a grammar of Gahuku, while parts of Asaro grammar are presented in Strange 1965 and Strange 1973. Young 1971 discusses BenaBena verb inflection. Kamano–Yagaria dialects are well represented. At the Kamano end, descriptions of Kamano (Payne and Drew 1966) and Kanite (McCarthy 1965), have been published, while Renck 1975 and Haiman 1980 discuss the Move and Hua dialects of Yagaria respectively. Fore is analysed in the much quoted grammar of Scott (1978). Gimi is discussed rather briefly in Haiman 1980. In addition, dictionaries exist for Fore (Scott 1980) and the Move dialect of Yagaria (Renck 1977a). Comparative material in this family is available in Scott 1978.

The Gorokan and Kainantu families are clearly related at a deeper level of genetic relationship. I will present evidence for this in section 7.4, while discussing the problems involved in proving deeper levels of relationship among Papuan language families.

7.3.13   The Chimbu family

This language family is spoken in Chimbu and Western Highlands Provinces. In terms of numbers of speakers this is the largest Papuan language family. One language alone, Chimbu, has 133,000 speakers. As might be expected, dialect divisions are very great, so it is practicable to distinguish a number of distinct 'languages' within Chimbu, including Kuman, Golin, Salt–Yui and Sinasina. The languages within this family are:

Chimbu dialects:	133,000	Wahgi	45,000
Kuman	66,000	Nii	9,300
Dom	9,300	Narak	3,600
Golin	26,700	Maring	8,000
Salt–Yui	8,000	Medlpa	69,000
Sinasina	19,000	Kaugel	31,000

The languages of this family are typologically very different from those of the Gorokan and Engan families on either side of them. Wurm (1961, 1975) has claimed that the Chimbu family is related to these two families, but no evidence has ever been presented and, in view of the divergence of this family, I remain sceptical. In Wurm's (1961; 1975) classification, the Chimbu family bears the same level of genetic relationship to the Gorokan family as does the Kainantu family. I do not believe this to be the case. The Kainantu family is unquestionably related to the Gorokan family, while the relationship with the Chimbu family, if any, is much more distant. Detailed comparative work will be necessary to prove any deeper relationships of the Chimbu family; many similarities it does share with neighbouring groups may be the result of diffusion.

Sources for this family include: Kuman grammars (Bergmann 1953, Piau 1985) and a dictionary (Nilles 1969); grammars of Golin (Bunn 1974), Salt–Yui (Irwin 1974) and Sinasina (McVinney and Luzbetak 1954); a phonology (Swick 1966) and a study of medial verbs in Chuave (Thurman 1975); a phonological study (Luzbetak 1956) and a grammar of Wahgi (Luzbetak 1954), as well as a phonology and morphology of the same language (Phillips 1976); a phonology of Nii (Stucky and Stucky 1973); a grammar of Medlpa (Strauss n.d.); and articles on the phonology and verbal inflection of Kaugel (Blowers 1970, Blowers and Blowers 1970).

7.3.14 *The Engan family*

This language family is spoken in Enga Province and adjacent areas of East Sepik Province and Southern Highlands Province. It includes the Papuan language with the largest number of speakers, Enga, which is spoken in a number of quite divergent dialects, some of which may constitute distinct languages. Dialect differences are also considerable in the other large languages of the family, especially Mendi and Kewa. The composition of this family is as follows:

Enga	157,000	Huli	65,000
Nete	1,000	Mendi	55,000
Iniai	200	Kewa	43,000
Ipili	6,000	Sau	2,500

Nete, Iniai and Ipili are closely related to Enga and form a group, as do Mendi, Kewa and Sau. This family has been claimed to be related to the Chimbu, Gorokan and Kainantu families. This may or may not be the case, but evidence according to rigorous methods of comparative linguistics has yet to be provided. This is discussed in detail in section 7.4.

Materials on Enga include a dictionary containing a grammatical sketch (Lang 1973), as well as a study of the verbal system (Lang 1975). Kewa is the best known of the Engan languages. In addition to a grammar (Franklin 1971), there are some phonological studies (Franklin and Franklin 1962; Franklin 1975b), a compendious dictionary (Franklin and Franklin 1978) and a dialect study (Franklin 1968). Rule (1977) is a comparative study of Kewa and Huli. Other comparative studies in the family are Franklin 1974 and 1975a.

7.3.15   *The Ok family*

This family takes its name from the word for 'water' in these languages. It is located in the mountainous central hub of New Guinea, spilling down into the adjacent lowland areas of Western Province and Irian Jaya. The family is divided into two branches, Lowland Ok and Mountain Ok (A. Healey 1964b):

Lowland Ok:		Mountain Ok:	
Southern Kati	4,000	Telefol	4,000
Northern Kati	8,000	Tifal	2,500
Yoŋgom	2,000	Kauwol	500
Iwur	1,000	Faiwol	3,000
Niŋgirum	4,000	Setaman	200
		Bimin	1,000
		Mianmin	1,500
		Warabai	500
		Ngalum	18,000

This family presents a complex picture as to genetic affiliation. Structurally, these languages show a similarity to the languages of the central highlands, such as those of the Engan or Gorokan families. The family also exhibits links, primarily in vocabulary, but also in structural features, to the languages of southern Irian Jaya, especially the languages of the Asmat and Awyu families. Detailed comparative work will be necessary to determine conclusively the genetic position of the Ok family.

Materials available on the languages of this family include Drabbe (1954) for Northern and Southern Kati; A. Healey 1964a and 1974, and P.M. Healey 1964, 1965a, b and c and 1966, and Healey and Healey 1977 for Telefol; Steinkraus 1969 and Healey and Steinkraus 1972 for Tifal; Mecklenburg 1974 for Faiwol; and Smith 1977, Weston 1977 and Smith and Weston 1974a and b for Mianmin. A. Healey (1964b) presents some basic comparative work on this family.

7.3.16   *The Dani family*

This is a closely related family with over 220,000 speakers. It is located around the valley of the Balim River in the central highlands of Irian Jaya. Languages of the family include:

Grand Valley Dani	75,000	South Ngalik	5,000
Western Dani	100,000	Nduga	10,000
North Ngalik (Yaly)	35,000	Wano	1,500

Both Grand Valley and Western Dani have a number of quite divergent dialects. Bromley 1961 is a phonological study of these Dani dialects. Bromley 1981 provides a detailed grammatical study of the dialect termed Lower Grand Valley Dani. Another morphological study of Grand Valley Dani is available (Stap 1966). Comparative work in this family is only preliminary. Bromley 1967 is a basic classificatory study of Dani family languages, while Fahner 1979 offers a comparative analysis of the morphology of Grand Valley Dani and North Ngalik (Yaly).

7.3.17   *The Wissel Lakes family*

This family is also spoken in the central highlands of Irian Jaya, from Wissel Lakes eastward to the border of the Dani family. While not as large as the Dani family, it still has around 90,000 speakers:

Ekagi (Kapauku)	60,000	Moni	12,000
Wodani	3,000	Uhunduni	12,000

For this family published materials are only available for Ekagi and Moni. These include grammatical studies (Drabbe 1952, Doble 1962 and Steltenpool and van der Stap 1959 for Ekagi, and Larson and Larson 1958 for Moni), as well as two dictionaries for Ekagi (Doble 1960 and Steltenpool 1969). The only comparative work is a short lexicostatistical study (Larson and Larson 1972).

7.3.18   *The Sentani family*

This family is spoken on the north coast of Irian Jaya, immediately to the west of Jayapura, around Lake Sentai and westward. Its composition is as follows:

Sentani	6,000	Tanah Merah	3,200
Nafri	?		

Sentani is the only language for which published material is available. This includes a short grammar and glossary (Cowan 1965), a phonological study (M. Hartzler 1976), an article on verb morphology (D. Hartzler 1976) and a set of texts (Cowan 1951–2, 1952).

7.3.19   *The Sko family*

This family is spoken on the north coast of New Guinea, straddling the border between Irian Jaya and Papua New Guinea. It is spoken from immediately to the east of Jayapura, eastward past Vanimo, half-way to Aitape. It includes eight languages:

Sko	350	Krisa	350
Sangke	200	Rawo	500
Wutung	410	Puari	370
Vanimo	1,400	Warapu	3,000

Vanimo is the best known of these languages. Ross 1980 presents a discussion of the phonology and a grammatical sketch of the language. Other data include grammatical notes on Sko (Voorhoeve 1971) and brief notes on Warapu (Laycock 1973b).

7.3.20 *The Torricelli family*

This is a large language grouping, first proposed in Laycock 1973a, spoken in the Torricelli Ranges between the north coast and the Sepik River, eastward through the hills north of the Lower Sepik area into the Madang Province. It consists of 47 languages, grouped into subfamilies. Whether all these families are in fact related in one large grouping remains an open question. Laycock published his classification (1973a; 1975) but no supporting data, and no comparative work has since been undertaken. Still, the languages of this proposed grouping do share a number of unusual typological features: svo word-order, complex noun-class systems with phonological shape being a determining factor, unusual pronoun prefixes to the verb, simple morphological structure for verbs, and irregular plurals for nouns. Noun-classes based on phonological shape and irregular nominal plurals are salient features of the Lower Sepik family as well, but this is definitely not related to the Torricelli family. These unusual features of so-called Torricelli languages may of course be simply due to diffusion, but they may also reflect genetic links. The genetic relations of these Torricelli languages are clearly not settled, but Laycock's (1973a) classification represents to me a reasonable hypothesis, which it is hoped that further work will confirm.

Because of the very large number of languages in this family, I only list the most important or more studied languages:

One	2,200	Kombio	2,150
Olo	10,820	Mountain Arapesh	10,300
Au	4,000	Southern Arapesh	10,650
Yil	2,130	Kamasau	790
Valman	700	Monumbo	450

The Arapesh languages are the best known of the family. Fortune 1942 is a detailed grammar with texts of Mountain Arapesh; Gerstner 1963 is a second grammar of the same language. Alungun *et al.* 1978 discusses Southern Arapesh grammar. Conrad

1978b is a comparative study of the Arapesh languages. Materials in other languages include McGregor and McGregor 1982 on Olo phonology and grammar; Scorza (1974; in press) on Au grammar; Martens and Tuominen 1977 on Yil phonology; Schmidt and Vormann 1900; Spölgen and Schmidt 1901; and Klaffl and Vormann 1905 for Valman; Sanders and Sanders 1980b; 1980c for a phonological study and dialect survey of Kamasau; and Sanders and Sanders 1980a for a comparative study of Kamasau with closely related Torricelli languages; and Vormann and Scharfenberger 1914 on Monumbo.

7.3.21   *The Ndu family*

This is the family to which the much quoted Iatmul belongs. It has the largest number of speakers of any family in the Sepik basin and is constituted as follows:

Abelam	39,290	Sawos	9,000
Boiken	30,530	Kaunga	230
Iatmul	9,840	Ngala	140
Manambu	2,060		

Laycock (1973a) has proposed a larger grouping of Sepik languages called the Sepik sub-phylum which takes the Ndu family as its core. This also includes languages up-river on the Sepik such as Yessan–Mayo, Iwam and Abau; languages north of the Sepik such as Kwanga, Kwoma, Mehek and Namie; and a large language family of fifteen languages (which includes Alamblak) called the Sepik Hill family, spoken in the swampy and hilly country between the Sepik and the central highlands. Whether all these languages are related to the Ndu family is problematic, but it seems probable that at least some are, the most likely candidates being Kwoma and Kwanga and the Sepik Hill languages. Detailed and careful comparative work will be necessary to ascertain these wider relations of the Ndu family.

This family is the best studied in the Sepik area. Laycock 1965 is a comparative study of the family and includes a sketch grammar of Abelam and notes on the other languages. Other studies on Abelam include a detailed grammar (Wilson 1980), an analysis of sentence and paragraph structure (Wilson 1973) and a dialect survey (Wilson 1976). For Boiken, there is a phonological study (Freudenburg and Freudenburg 1974) and a dialect survey (Freudenburg 1976). Staalsen has contributed a series of articles on Iatmul, including a phonology report (Staalsen 1966), a dialect survey (Staalsen 1969) and an article on verbal inflection and clause linkage (Staalsen 1972). Staalsen 1975 presents material on Sawos. For the other languages the only published materials are brief notes in Laycock 1965.

7.3.22   The Lower Sepik family

This has already been discussed in 7.2.

7.3.23   The Grass family

This family is spoken in the swampy area between East Sepik and Madang Provinces, between the Keram and Ramu Rivers. It consists of five languages:

Kambot	5,740	Aion	770
Gorovu	50	Banaro	2,570
Adjora	2,350		

It is probable that this family is related to other language families of the border area between East Sepik and Madang Provinces and lowland western Madang Province, especially around the Ramu River. This larger grouping has been termed the Ramu sub-phylum (Laycock and Z'graggen 1975).

There is no detailed published material on any of these languages, but Laycock and Z'graggen 1975 present some notes on Kambot.

7.3.24   The Kalam family

This consists of three languages, spoken on the northern slopes of the central highlands at the junction of Madang and Western Highlands Provinces:

Kalam	13,000	Gants	1,900
Kobon	3,000		

The relationship of Gants is somewhat unclear.

Kalam and Kobon are both relatively well studied. For Kalam we have Biggs 1963 on the phonology and Pawley 1966 as a full grammar. In addition there is a very detailed dictionary in preparation by Bulmer, Biggs and Pawley. For Kobon we have Dawson and Dawson 1974 on phrases, and a series of papers by Davies dealing with all aspects of Kobon: a detailed phonology (Davies 1980a), an article on semivowels (Davies 1980b), a study of clausal syntax (Davies 1981a) and a full grammar (1981b).

7.3.25   The Huon family

This is a large language family spoken in the Huon Peninsula. It is divided into two branches, eastern and western:

Eastern Huon:		Western Huon:	
Kâte	6,130	Ono	4,650
Mape	4,860	Sialum	640
Dedua	4,730	Nomu	810
Sene	10	Kinalakna	220
Momave	370	Kumukio	550
Migabac	1,030	Selepet	6,350
Kube	5,800	Timbe	11,279
		Komba	12,350
		Tobo	2,870
		Yaknge	2,080
		Kosorong	1,460
		Burum	4,190
		Momolili (Mesem)	1,700
		Nabak	9,840

These languages are probably related to other language families to their west, in the Finisterre Range. This larger grouping is called the Finisterre–Huon family (McElhanon 1975).

This family contains two of the best known Papuan languages. Kâte has been used as a *lingua franca* by the Lutheran Mission, and materials available for it include two grammars (Pilhofer 1933, Schneuker 1962), two dictionaries (Keysser 1925, Flierl and Strauss 1977) and comparative dialect studies (Pilhofer 1928, 1929). McElhanon has been indefatigable in providing data on Selepet: these include phonological studies (McElhanon 1967b; 1970a; 1970d), a study of verbal morphology (McElhanon 1970b), one on pronominal elements (McElhanon 1970c), a detailed grammar of words and phrasal constructions (McElhanon 1972) and a dictionary (McElhanon and McElhanon 1970). Other languages are much more poorly documented. For Ono, there is Wacke's (1931) grammar sketch, and for Nabak, only a short paper on morphophonemics (Fabian *et al.* 1971). Comparative work in this family is the labour of McElhanon; publications include McElhanon 1967a; 1970e; 1971; 1973; 1975.

7.3.26   *The South Bougainville family*
This family is spoken in the southern third of Bougainville Island. It consists of four fairly closely related languages:

Nasioi	11,600	Buin	9,500
Nagovisi	5,000	Siwai	6,600

This family as a whole is probably related to another small family of Papuan languages, the North Bougainville family, spoken to its north, although this relationship is not close, and careful work will be necessary to validate it.

Nasioi is one of the better known Papuan languages. Rausch (1912) is an early grammar, but in addition there is a pedagogical grammar (Hurd and Hurd 1966), an article on verbal morphology (Hurd and Hurd 1970) and another on noun classification (Hurd 1977). For Buin, there is an article on language play (Laycock 1969) and one on directionals (Griffin 1970). A grammatical sketch with a detailed dictionary of Buin by Laycock is forthcoming.

7.4 An exploration of deeper genetic relationships

In this section I will be looking in some detail at language families of the central highlands with a view to establishing their wider genetic affiliations. These families are well suited for this task, as they are among the most completely studied. My purpose here will be to develop a methodology which will be useful in establishing genetic relationships among Papuan languages which are only distantly related. Central to this task will be determining which areas of Papuan languages are most conservative, i.e. which are likely to be most amenable to the application of the tools of comparative linguistics. I have already pointed out in 7.2 that I believe that cognate morphology is most useful in diagnosing distant relationships. The earlier reconstruction of Lower Sepik noun-classes vindicated this point of view. The Lower Sepik languages are unusual among Papuan languages in having highly complex nominal morphology. More generally, nouns are morphologically simple; it is the verbs that carry most of the morphological complexity. Hence, it would seem that the verbal morphology is the place to look in determining these deeper relations. Lexical evidence is important as well, but because of their greater likelihood of being borrowed, formal similarities in words do not carry as much weight as such similarities in bound morphology, especially when these morphemes fit into similar overall morphological patterns.

A relationship between the Kainantu and Gorokan families was first suggested in Capell (1948–9), and has been maintained by Wurm in a number of publications (Wurm 1961; 1964). As these families have complex verbal morphologies and are well known, this seems a good place to start. Scott (1978) provides a comparative list of basic words in Gorokan languages from which the list in Table 12 is drawn. The correspondences and proto-phonemes for Proto-Gorokan (PG) shown in Tables 13 and 14 can be deduced from this set of cognates.

Table 12 *Gorokan family: basic word-list*

		Gende	Siane	BenaBena	Kamano–Yagaria	Fore
1	'two'	*ogondrari*	*lele*	*loe*	*lole*	*tara*
2	'man'	*vei*	*we*	*vo*	*ve*	*wa*
3	'water'	*nogoi*	*no*	*nagami*	*ni(na)*	*wani*
4	'fire'	*tuva*	*yo*	*logo*	*hali*	*yakuʔ*
5	'tree'	*izo*	*ya*	*yafa*	*yava*	*yaː*
6	'leaf'	*kuruma*	*aila*	*haya(ʔa)*	*haeya*	*aʔyeʔ*
7	'root'	*tovaya*	*lufawa*	*lufusa(ʔa)*	*havu*	*aubu*
8	'house'	*nomu*	*numu(na)*	*no(hi)*	*yo(na)*	*naːmaʔ*
9	'breast'	*ami-*	*ami(na)*	*amiha(ʔa)*	*ami(maʔa)*	*nono*
10	'tooth'	*va(iza)*	*auma*	*yogo(ʔa)*	*(ä)veʔ*	*(a)wa*
11	'bone'	*yami-*	*auma*	*felisa(ʔa)*	*(a)pu(va)*	*(a)yaːmpu*
12	'ear'	*ka-*	*ka(la)*	*(e)kesa(ʔa)*	*(ä)geta*	*(a)ge*
13	'hair'	*yogo*	*yowa(la)*	*oka(ʔa)*	*(a)yokaʔ*	*(a)yaːʔ*
14	'leg'	*kia-*	*kiya(na)*	*gigusa(ʔa)*	*(a)gia*	*(a)gisaː*
15	'blood'	*mamia-*	*wanu*	*golaha(ʔa)*	*gola(na)*	*koraːʔ*
16	'hand'	*ya*	*a(na)*	*yaha(ʔa)*	*(ä)ya*	*ya*
17	'egg'	*mura*	*mula*	*mu(ʔa)*	*mu(na)*	*amuʔ*
18	'sun'	*po*	*fo*	*yafi*	*yafo*	*yaːbu*
19	'axe'	*tu*	*luna*	*lu*	*lu*	*tuʔ*
20	'netbag'	*ko*	*owo*	*gu(ʔi)*	*gu(na)*	*koʔ*
21	'eat'	*na-*	*n-*	*na-*	*no-*	*na-*
22	'die'	*pri-*	*fol-*	*fili-*	*fili-*	*puri-*
23	'say'	*ti-*	*l-*	*li-*	*hi-*	*i-*
24	'give'	*imi-*	*om-*	*m-*	*mi-*	*mi-*
25	'big'	*namba*	*namba*	*napa*	*legepa*	*tabe*

Table 13 *Gorokan phoneme correspondences: consonants*

PG	Gende	Siane	BenaBena	Kamano–Yagaria	Fore	Examples and notes
*p	p	f	f	f	p/b	18, 22 *p→F *b*/V__V
*p	v	f	f	v	b	7 *p→G, K-Y *v*/V__V
*m	m	m	m	m	m	9, 17, 24
*t	t	l	l	l	t	1, 15, 19
	r	l	l	l	r	1, 17?, 22 *t→G, F *r*/V__V
*n	n	n	n	n	n	4, 8, 21

Table 13 *cont.*

PG	Gende	Siane	BenaBena	Kamano–Yagaria	Fore	Examples and notes
*s[a]	t	l	l	h	∅	7, 23
*k[b]	k/g	k/g	g	g	k/g	12, 13, 14, 15, 20 *k→ G, F g, S w/V__ V
*w	v	w	v	v	w	2, 10
*y	y	y	y	y	y	5, 13

[a] *s merges with *t in G, S and B. This is a highly tentative construction, but there seems to be no conditioning factor for assigning this correspondence to *t.

[b] The lenition of *p, *t, *k to v/b, r, g in G and F strongly indicates that such a pattern was present in the proto-language (see Brandson ms a and Scott 1978 for a discussion of this in modern Gende and Fore).

The data presented in Table 13 result in the following consonantal system:

$$
\begin{array}{ccc}
*p & *t & *k \\
*m & *n & \\
 & *s & \\
*w & *y & \\
\end{array}
$$

Table 14 *Gorokan phoneme correspondences: vowels*

PG	Gende	Siane	BenaBena	Kamano–Yagaria	Fore	Examples and notes
*a[a]	a	a	a	a/e/o	a	5, 9, 10, 11, 14, 15, 16, 21, 25
*i	i	i	i	i	i	9, 14, 22, 23, 24
*u	u	u	u	u	u	7, 17, 19
*e	e	e	e	e	e/a	1, 2, 12
*o	o	o	o	o	o/a	3, 8, 13

[a] a becomes a mid-vowel sporadically in K–Y (see 10, 21)

The data presented in Table 14 yield a normal five-vowel proto-system:

with the reconstructed forms for PG shown in Table 15.

Table 15 *Proto-Gorokan: reconstructed word-list*

1	'two'	*tote*	15	'blood'	*kota*
2	'man'	*we*	16	'hand'	*ya*
3	'water'	*no(k)*	17	'egg'	*mut*
5	'tree'	*ya*	18	'sun'	*po*
7	'root'	*supa*	19	'axe'	*tu*
8	'house'	*nom*	20	'netbag'	*ko*
9	'breast'	*ami*	21	'eat'	*na-*
10	'tooth'	*wa*	22	'die'	*puti-*
11	'bone'	*yampu*	23	'say'	*si-*
12	'ear'	*ke/a*	24	'give'	*mi-*
13	'hair'	*yoka*	25	'big'	*(n)ampa*
14	'leg'	*kia*			

Table 16 *Gorokan family: pronouns*

		Gende	Siane	BenaBena	Kamano–Yagaria	Fore
SG	1	*na*	*na(mo)*	*na(ni)*	*na(gaya)*	*na(e)*
	2	*ka*	*ka(mo)*	*ka(i)*	*ka(gaya)*	*ka(e)*
	3	*ya*	*a(mo)*	*a(i)*	*a(gaya)*	*a(e)*
PL	1	*ta(ri)*	*la(mo)*	*la(li)*	*ta(gaya)*	*ta(e)*
	2	*ta*	*ina(te)*	*len(ali)*	*tapa(gaya)*	*ti(ge)*
	3	*ya*	*a(mo)*	*en(ali)*	*apa(gaya)*	*i(ge)*

Turning now to the pronouns, the basic sets in these languages are given in Table 16. The pronoun system in PG is straightforwardly reconstructable from these data. The only complications are the second and third plural forms, in which no obvious proto-form suggests itself. Note that, in all languages but Siane, the second plural is derived from the third plural by compounding the latter with the first plural form. This suggests that for PG there was no distinction between second and third person in the nonsingular. These distinctions are later innovations in the languages. For Gende, the PG second/third plural has also become the third singular form, while for Siane the third singular has extended to the plural. The pronoun system of PG seems to have been as follows:

	SG	PL
1	*na	*ta
2	*ka	*ya
3	*a	

The verbal morphology of all languages in the Gorokan family is very similar, and is typified by Fore and Hua as described in Chapter 5. The undergoer is indicated by a verbal prefix, closely related in form to the independent pronouns as shown in Table 17. While the evidence does not strongly suggest *a- for third singular, this reconstruction is confirmed by the form a- for the third singular undergoer prefix in Gahuku (Deibler 1976), a language closely related to BenaBena. The languages with ∅ have simply lost this prefix from.

Table 17 *Gorokan family: undergoer prefixes*

		PG	Siane	BenaBena	Kamano–Yagaria	Fore
SG	1	*na-	n-	na-	na-	na-
	2	*ka-	k-	ka-	ga-	ka-
	3	*a-	∅	∅	∅	a-
PL	1	*ta-	r-	la-	l-	ta-

Table 18 *Gorokan family: verbal inflections for actor (A)*

		Hua (Haiman 1980)	BenaBena (Young 1971)	Gende (Brandson ms b)
SG	1	do-e	ho-be	minu < *minu-e
	2	da-ne	ha-ne	mina-ni
	3	de < *de-e	ha-be	mina-e
DL	1	do-ʔe	ho-ʔibe	minu-ri
	2/3	da-ʔe	ha-ʔibe	mina-ri
PL	1	do-ne	ho-ne	minu-ni
	2/3	da-e	ha-be	mina-e
		'I ate' etc.	'I hit' etc.	'I stay' etc.

The actor is normally indicated by suffixes. Many of these languages indicate the person and number of the actor by the complex interaction of vowel alternations of the verb-stem with allomorphs of the illocutionary force suffixes, as described for Hua (of the Kamano–Yagaria dialect chain) in Chapter 5. Compare the forms in Table 18. The close relationship of these three inflectional patterns cannot be doubted. All three languages exhibit the same complex pattern of allomorphy for the declarative suffix:

	2SG, 1PL	DL	OTHER
Hua	-ne	∼ -ʔe	∼ -e
BenaBena	-ne	∼ -ʔibe	∼ -be
Gende	-ni	∼ -ri	∼ -e

The vowel alternations of the verb-stems themselves are also closely related: first person of this *o* stem verb is associated with *o* (*o* > *u* in Gende) and non-first person with *a* (Hua has the additional complication of *e* for the third singular, accounted for below).

Table 19 *Gorokan family: verbal inflections for actor (B)*

		Siane (Haiman 1980)	Fore (Scott 1978)
SG	1	*sino-o-e*	*na-u-e*
	2	*sino-a-ne*	*na-a:-ne*
	3	*sino-i-e*	*na-i-e*
DL	1	*sino-o-ie*	*na-u-se*
	2/3	*sino-a-ie*	*na-a:se*
PL	1	*sino-o-ne*	*na-u-ne*
	2/3	*sino-a-e*	*na-a:-e*
		'I get up' etc.	'I eat' etc.

The verbal inflections for Siane and Fore are slightly different, but again clearly related. In these languages an invariable set of person and number morphemes are suffixed to the verb-stem, followed by the illocutionary force suffixes (Table 19). Siane and Fore exhibit the same alternation of the illocutionary force suffix as the other three languages:

	2SG, 1PL	DL	OTHER
Siane	-ne	∼ -ie	∼ -e
Fore	-ne	∼ -se	∼ -e

allowing at least a reconstruction of the declarative illocutionary force suffix as *-ne* 2SG, 1PL ∼ *-e* OTHER. Evidence for a reconstruction of the dual form is insufficient. Siane and Fore also provide the clues to the origins of the complex vowel alternations of the verbal stems of the other languages. These have arisen by simplification of the vowel clusters formed by suffixing the vowels associated with the person of the actor to the vowel-final verb-stem. In some cases the vowel of the stem remained: Hua stem *-o* + *u* first person > *o*; but in others the vowel of the actor remained: stem *-o* + *a* second person > *a*. Finally, the Hua third singular form in *e* comes from stem $-o+i$ third person $> e$, a natural phonetic process. Thus, the vowels associated with the person of the actor in PG were:

　1　　*-u*
　2　　*-a*
　3　　*-i*

-i was, of course, restricted to the singular; in the nonsingular there was no distinction between second and third person, so the *-a* suffix was present there.

A further question to be considered is the origin of the curious alternation of the illocutionary force suffixes between a form for 2SG, 1PL and OTHER. Besides the reconstructed declarative suffix *-ne* 2SG, 1PL $\sim$ *-e* OTHER, the languages exhibit parallel alternations in the interrogative suffixes:

	2SG, 1PL		OTHER
Hua (Haiman 1980)	-pe	$\sim$	-ve
BenaBena (Young 1971)	-pi	$\sim$	-fi
Gende (Brandon ms b)	-no	$\sim$	-wo
Fore (Scott 1978)	-no	$\sim$	-o

In the Fore and Gende forms, as with the declarative, the same *n* appears in the 2SG, 1PL suffix. This suggests a recurring partial associated with person, the second person, now reconstructed as *-an*. The 1PL then derives from a combination of the first and second person forms: *-u*+ *-an*> *un*. Thus, the declarative may now be reconstructed simply as *-e*, with the alternation due to a re-analysis of *-an*+ *e* and *-un*+ *e* as *-a*+ *ne* and *-u*+ *ne* respectively. The form of the interrogative suffix in PG was probably *-o*, witnessed by Gende and Fore, but reflexes of *-pe* are widespread in the highlands, requiring PG *-pe* as well. Hua and BenaBena have innovated new forms based on *-pe*. The initial consonant of this suffix underwent lenition in the OTHER form to Hua *-ve* because it was intervocalic, but did not do so in the 2SG, 1PL form because it followed the *-n* of the person/number suffix of the actor: *-u*+ *pe* 1SG and *-a*+ *pe* 2/3 PL $>$ Hua *-u*+ *ve* and *-a*+ *ve*, but *-an*+ *pe* 2SG and *-un*+ *pe* PL $>$ *-a*+ *pe* and *-u*+ *pe*. Thus the revised reconstructions of the verb suffixes are:

person/number of actor				illocutionary force	
SG 1 *-u*		PL 1 *-un*		declarative	*-e*
2 *-an*			$+$		
		2/3 *-a*		interrogative	*-o*, *-pe*
3 *-i*					

These person/number markers are identical to the forms reconstructed in Pawley 1966.

A verbal construction widespread in Gorokan family languages, and presumably present in PG, is the indication of a benefactive core nominal by a serial verb construction involving 'give' or, more typically in this family, 'put', as illustrated by Hua in Chapter 4. Compare the following examples:

Hua:
(Haiman 1980)

>   *zuʔ   ki-na   d-te*
>   house build-SA 3SG 1SG U-put 3SG DECL
>   'he built me a house'

BenaBena:
(Young 1971)

>   *hu   ke-to-ʔohu-be*
>   do   2SG U-put?-be 1-DECL OTHER
>   'I did it for you'

Fore:
(Scott 1978)

>   *pu-na-ʔta-i-e*
>   do-1SG U-put-3SG A-DECL
>   'he did it for me'

This evidence suggests that a periphrastic benefactive construction in which the undergoer prefix is affixed to the verb **to-* 'put' should be reconstructed for PG. A construction like this seems good evidence for genetic relationship, as such a highly specific construction is unlikely to be borrowed in quite this form.

Now let me turn to a deeper genetic relationship and compare the Gorokan family with its neighbour to the east, the Kainantu family. The proposed relation between these two families can be summarized thus:

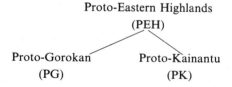

Proto-Eastern Highlands
(PEH)

Proto-Gorokan   Proto-Kainantu
(PG)   (PK)

Since Capell (1948–9) these two families have been claimed to be related, but no strong evidence has ever been supplied for this claim. Compare the twenty-five words in languages of the Kainantu family given in Table 20 with the earlier list for the Gorokan languages (Kainantu family data from McKaughan 1973). The proper way to proceed from here would be to work out correspondences and proto-forms for the Kainantu family and compare these to those of the Gorokan family, but

Table 20 *Kainantu family: basic word-list*

		Awa	Auyana	Gadsup	Tairora
1	'two'	tɔtare	kaiʔa	kaantani	taaraʔanta
2	'man'	wɛ	waiya	banta	bainti
3	'water'	no	nomba	nomi	namari
4	'fire'	ira	irama	ikai	iha
5	'tree'	ta	taima	yaani	katari
6	'leaf'	ɔnɔ	anama	anai	mare
7	'root'	anuʔ	anuʔa	anuʔi	tuʔa
8	'house'	nɔ	naamba	maʔi	naabu
9	'breast'	nɔ	naamba	naami	naama
10	'tooth'	awɛ	awaiyamba	abakuni	aabai
11	'bone'	ayɔnta	ayaantamba	ayampai	buhaarima
12	'ear'	ɔre	aʔa	aakami	aato
13	'hair'	(a)yɔra	aayara	-nyoi	kauhi
14	'leg'	ai	aisamima	akani	aiʔu
15	'blood'	nɛe	naema	naarei	naare
16	'hand'	ayɔnobeh	ayamba	aayaami	kauʔu
17	'egg'	au	auma	amuʔi	auru
18	'sun'	popoʔhah	aabauma	ikona	kauri
19	'axe'	konaro	koraroba	kuntaʔi	kaarima
20	'netbag'	unɔ	unaamba	unaami	uta
21	'eat'	nɔno	nare	naano	naana
22	'die'	pukire	pukai	pukono	ʔutubiro
23	'say'	iraruwo	siyo	seʔu	tiena
24	'give'	awiʔ	ami	ameno	amina
25	'big'	aanotɔ	anomba	inoʔha	nora

limitations of space prohibit this approach. Rather, in Table 21 I compare forms from the Kainantu languages directly with PG reconstructions, and in the case of cognates propose proto-forms for the proto-language of both these families, Proto-Eastern Highlands. These data and the possible reconstructions leave no doubt as to the genetic affiliations of the Gorokan and Kainantu families. One significant difference between the two families is the presence of an initial *a* in many of the cognates of the Kainantu languages (see numbers 10, 11, 16, 17, 24, 25). This is not normally present in the languages of the Gorokan family, except in some cases in words of Kamano–Yagaria and Fore, the Gorokan family languages adjoining the Kainantu languages (see 10, 11, 12, 13, 14, 17). This is unquestionably the prefix *a*-for third singular possessors and undergoers used on inalienably possessed nouns and transitive verbs. I have not reconstructed it for PEH, assuming this prefixation to be a productive process in PEH.

Verbal inflection in Kainantu languages is very similar to Gorokan languages. The undergoer of a verb is also indicated by a prefix, as shown in Table 22. Of the Kainantu languages, only Awa exhibits any distinction in number in the first person

Table 21 *Eastern Highlands: reconstruction of word-list*

1	'two'	PG **tote* Aw *tɔtare* T *taara-* PEH **tata*
2	'man'	PG **we* Aw *wɛ* Au *waiya* T *bainti* PEH **way*
3	'water'	PG **no(k)* Aw *no* G *nomi* T *namari* PEH **nok(ami)*
7	'root'	PG **supa* T *tuʔa* PEH **supa*
		*p > Tʔ is regular: see 22, 'die'
8	'house'	PG **nom* Aw *nɔ* Au *naamba* T *naabu* PEH **no/am*
9	'breast'	PG **ami* Aw *nɔ* G *naami* T *naama* PEH **(n)ami*
10	'tooth'	PG **wa* Aw *awɛ* Au *awai-* T *aabai* PEH **way*
11	'bone'	PG **yampu* Aw *ayɔnta* Au *ayaantamba* G *ayampai* PEH **ya(nta)mpV*
13	'hair'	PG **yoka* Aw *yɔra* Au *aayara* G *-nyoi* PEH **yo(k/t)a*
16	'hand'	PG **ya* Aw *ayɔ-* Au *ayampa* G *aayaami* PEH **ya*
17	'egg'	PG **mut* G *amuʔi* PEH **mut*
21	'eat'	PG **na-* Aw *nɔno* Au *nare* G *naano* T *naana* PEH **na-*
22	'die'	PG **puti-* Aw *puki-* Au *pukai-* G *puka-* T *ʔutu-* PEH **puti-*
23	'say'	PG **si-* Aw *i-* Au *si-* G *se-* T *ti-* PEH **si-*
24	'give'	PG **mi-* Au *ami-* G *ame-* T *ami-* PEH **mi-*
25	'big'	PG **(n)ampa* Au *anomba* PEH **(a)nompa*

Table 22 *Eastern Highlands: undergoer prefixes*

		PG	Awa	Usarufa	Gadsup	Tairora	PEH
SG	1	**na-*	*ni-*	*ti-*	*ti-*	*ti-*	**na-*
	2	**ka-*	*a-*	*a-*	*a-*	*a-*	**ka-*
	3	**a-*	*a-*	*a-*	*a-*	*a-*	**a-*
PL	1	**ta-*	*i-*	*ti-*	*ti-*	*ti-*	**ta-*

Table 23 *Eastern Highlands: actor suffixes*

		PG	Awa	Usarufa	Gadsup	Tairora	PEH
SG	1	**u*	*-uʔ*	*-un*	*-u*	*-u*	**-u*
	2	**-an*	*-onaʔ*	*-an*	*-ona*	*-an*	**-an*
	3	**-i*	*-iʔ*	*-i*	*-i*	*-i*	**-i*
PL	1	**-un*	*-unaʔ*	*-unata*	*-u*	*-un*	**-un*
	2/3	**-a*	*-oʔ*	*-a*	*-o*	*-a*	**-a*

Table 24 *Proto-Eastern Highlands: declarative and interrogative suffixes*

	PG	Awa	Usarufa	Gadsup	Tairora	PEH
DECL	**-e*	*-e*	*-e*	*-e*	*-ma*	**-e*
Q	**-o, *-pe*	*-o, -po*	*-o*	*-ap*	*-e*	**-o, *-p*

Table 25 Eastern Highlands: pronoun systems

PG	SG	PL	Awa	SG	PL	Usarufa	SG	PL	Gadsup	SG	PL
1	*na	*ta	1	ne		1			1	te	mayau
2	*ka	*ya	2	are	ite	2	e	ke	2	e	ike
3	*a		3	we	se	3	we	ye	3	be	ye/ mayau

Tairora	SG	PL	PK	SG	PL	PEH	SG	PL
1	te		1	*ne	*te	1	*na	*ta
2	are	be	2	*a	*ye	2	?	*ya
3	bi		3	*we		3	?	

undergoer prefixes: in all the other languages the old plural form functions also as the undifferentiated first person form. An innovation diagnostic of all Kainantu family languages is the ousting of the old second singular prefix by the third singular, which now functions in both persons (that this is an innovation is supported in further reconstruction work below).

Verbal suffixes indicate the person and number of the actor and illocutionary force. The actor suffixes compared with those of PG are shown in Table 23. The fit between the reconstructions for PG and the Kainantu forms is very close. Gadsup has lost the contrast for number in the first person, following the pattern of the undergoer prefixes, while Usarufa has replaced the old first singular with the first plural and innovated a new first plural by compounding this with the independent form *ta. Also, Awa and Gadsup show a sound shift *a > o in the second person forms.

The declarative and interrogative suffixes are given in Table 24. Again, the match is very close; only Tairora is innovative.

The independent pronoun forms in Kainantu languages show rather more radical divergence from those of PG than do the bound forms. Consider the independent pronoun system shown in Table 25. Only Awa preserves the distinction of number in the first person with reflexes of *na and *ta; the other three languages have neutralized the distinction and use the old plural form as a first person pronoun, generally undistinguished for number (Gadsup is the exception here; mayau 1/3PL is a strange, unexplained innovation). Usarufa ke 1SG, 1/2PL, is likely from *ta 1PL, as is Gadsup ike 2PL; for k < *t is a common sound shift in these languages (see 22, 'die' in the earlier word list for Kainantu languages). The Kainantu languages sharply diverge from the Gorokan languages in the singular second and third persons, having *a instead of *ka for the second singular and a distinct *we for the third singular. The PG form **ya* 2/3PL corresponds to PK **ye* 2/3PL, preserved in Usarufa and Gadsup *ye* 3PL and possibly Awa *se* 3PL. The wide divergence between the PG and PK systems makes it impossible to reconstruct PEH forms for singular non-first persons. I will return to this problem when I consider still deeper genetic relationships below.

All the Kainantu languages parallel the Gorokan languages in having benefactive constructions involving periphrastic verbal constructions:

Awa:	*keri-ri-t-ɛʔ*
	burn-3PL U-BEN-3SG A NR PAST
	'he burned it for them'
Auyana:	*na-si-nka-i*
	eat-1 U-BEN-3SG A
	'he eats for me/us'
Gadsup:	*kumu-ti-nk-a*
	descend-1 U-BEN-3SG A
	'he descends for me/us'
Tairora:	*rumpa-ti-mi-te-ro*
	tie-1 U-give-PERF-3SG A PAST
	'he tied it for me'

The constructions in all these languages show a close relation to the corresponding one in the Gorokan languages. Only Tairora shows any real difference, in using the verb *mi-* 'give' instead of the reflex of the expected **-to* 'put'. The Auyana and Gadsup forms in *k* are normal developments from **-to* by the common sound shift **t > k*. This evidence from Kainantu languages leaves no doubt that the benefactive periphrastic construction with **-to* 'put' should be assigned to PEH.

I now wish to turn to potential genetic relations of a still deeper level by comparing our PEH reconstructed forms with two languages each of the Engan and Huon families, as well as Dani and Ekagi from the central highlands of Irian Jaya. Consider first the word-list of possible cognates from these six languages (Table 26). Data sources are as follows: Enga – Lang 1973; Franklin 1975a; Kewa – Franklin 1971; 1975a; 1978; Kâte – Pilhofer 1933; Flierl and Strauss 1977; McElhanon 1967a; Selepet – McElhanon 1967a; 1970e; 1972; 1975; Dani – Bromley 1967; 1981; and Ekagi – Doble 1962; Larson and Larson 1972; Steltenpool 1969. Comparing these languages with each other and with the Gorokan and Kainantu forms, the cognate findings are very unimpressive, to say the least. While the genetic relationship between Enga and Kewa is readily apparent, the relationship of these six languages to each other and to the Eastern Highlands family is by no means so apparent. The possible cognates are given in Table 27. This, too, is not a very impressive list. Given

Table 26 *Proto-Highlands: basic word-list*

		Enga	Kewa	Kâte	Selepet	Dani	Ekagi
1	'two'	rama	laapo	yaheʔ	yɔhɔp	bite	wiya
2	'man'	akari	ali	ŋiʔ	lok	ap	yame
3	'water'	ipa	ipa	opɔ	to	i	uwo
4	'fire'	ita	repona	dzoʔ		idu	bodiya
5	'tree'	ita	are	yɔʔ	nak	e	piya
6	'leaf'	yoko	yo	rehaʔ-	esen-	ega	iye
7	'root'	pingi	pitaa	gɔtɔ-	gihit-	omagen	mani
8	'house'	ada	ada	fiʔ	opon	o	owaa
9	'breast'	adu	adu	mɔŋ	nam-	edak	ama
10	'tooth'	nege	agaa	miʔ-	sɔt-	aik	ego
11	'bone'	kori	kuli	sieʔ-	hahit	-oak	mitoo
12	'ear'	kare	kale	hatseʔ-	ɔdɔp-	-atuk	gapa
13	'hair'	iti	iri	dzɔwɔ-	somot-	-eti	iyo
14	'leg'	kape	aa	kike-	kɔi-	-esok	bo
15	'blood'	kupapu	kupaa	soʔ-	hep-	mep	emo
16	'hand'	ruma	ki	me-	bɔt-	-egi	gane
17	'egg'	kapa	yaa apaa	munduŋ	bon-	tewe-gen	napo
18	'sun'	nita	nare	dzoaŋ	dewutɔ	mo	tani
19	'axe'	patama	rai	araŋ	unam	posiye	
20	'netbag'	nuu	nu	hɔfɔhe		su	agiya
21	'eat'	ne-	na-	nɔ-	ni-	na-	nai-
22	'die'	kumi-	koma-	homo-	mu-	kagi-	bokai-
23	'say'	re-	la-	mu-	y-	i-	tii-
24	'give'	mai-/gi-	gi-	re-	gi-	et-	mai-
25	'big'	adake	adaa	kɔʔgbene	pato	gok	ebo

Table 27 *Proto-Highlands: possible cognates*

3	'water'	Enga, Kewa *ipa* Kâte *opɔ* Ekagi *uwo*
4	'fire'	Awa *ira* Auyana *irama* Enga *ita* Kâte *dzoʔ* Dani *idu*
5	'tree'	PG *ya* Kâte *yɔʔ* Dani *e* Ekagi *piya*
6	'leaf'	Enga *yoko* Kewa *yo* Ekagi *iye*
9	'breast'	PEH *(n)ami* Kâte *mɔŋ* Selepet *nam* Ekagi *ama*
10	'tooth'	Enga *nege* Kewa *agaa* Dani *aik* Ekagi *ego*
12	'ear'	PG *ke/a* Enga *kare* Kewa *kale* Ekagi *gapa*
13	'hair'	PEH *yo(k/t)a* Ekagi *iyo*
14	'leg'	PG *kia* Enga *kape* Kâte *kike* Selepet *kɔi*
17	'egg'	PEH *mut* Kâte *munduŋ* Selepet *bon*
21	'eat'	PEH *na-* Enga *ne-* Kewa *na-* Kâte *nɔ-* Selepet *ni-* Dani *na-* Ekagi *nai-*
22	'die'	PEH *puti* Ekagi *bokai-*
23	'say'	PEH *si-* Enga *re-* Kewa *la-* Selepet *y-* Dani *i-* Ekagi *tii-*
24	'give'	PEH *mi* Enga *mai-/gi-* Ekagi *mai-* OR
		PEH *ki-* Enga *mai-/gi-* Kewa *gi-* Selepet *gi-*

Table 28 *Proto-Highlands: pronoun systems*

	PG			Enga			Kewa	
	SG	PL		SG	PL		SG	PL
1	*na	*ta	1	na(ba)	nai(ma)	1	ni	niaa
2	*ka		2	e(ba)		2	ne	nimi
3	*a	*ya	3	baa	nyaka(ma)	3	nipu	nimu

	Kâte			Selepet			Dani			Ekagi	
	SG	PL		SG	PL		SG	PL		SG	PL
1	no	nɔ(ne)	1	nɔ	nen	1	an	nit	1	ani	inii
2	go	ŋo(ne)	2	gɔ	yen	2	kat	kit	2	aki	iki
3	e	ya(ne)	3	yɔk	yɔkyen	3	at	it	3	okai	okei

the small number of phonemes and the short words, the apparent resemblance of these forms could be put down to chance. Only the verbs 'eat' (21) and 'say' (23) are at all convincing in their similarity to the PEH forms. A few nouns such as 'fire' (4), 'breast' (9), 'tooth' (10), 'ear' (12) and 'leg' (14) are good candidates for cognates, but the evidence is certainly not compelling. I must conclude that, on the basis of cognates in basic vocabulary, the evidence for a genetic relationship between these languages and those of the Eastern Highlands family is insufficient.

Now let me consider grammatical evidence. The independent pronoun series in these six languages are compared with that of PG in Table 28.

The pronoun systems of the two Engan family languages, Enga and Kewa, are the most innovative here; only the PEH first singular form *na has clear reflexes in the Engan languages. The Enga form *e(ba)* 2SG may be related to the PK form *a 2SG, but the evidence is insufficient to assert this. In any case, the other four languages all show second singular forms with an initial velar, clearly all related to the PG form *ka. The pronoun systems of the two Huon languages, Kâte and Selepet, exhibit the greatest similarity to that of PG. These languages have clear reflexes of PEH *ya- 2/ 3PL, as Kâte *ya(ne)* 3PL and Selepet *yen* 2PL and *yɔkyen* 3PL. The Kâte form *e* 3SG may be a cognate of *a. Dani and Ekagi are more divergent, but agree in a morpheme -*i* to show plural. This interestingly tallies with McElhanon's (1975) reconstruction of a morpheme *-*i* to mark nonsingular number in the Huon languages, e.g. Selepet *yen* < *ya- 2/3 PL + -*i* N-SG + -*n* PL. One feature in which all of these languages differ from PEH is the first plural form in *n*, most likely *ni. Given a genetic relationship between most of these languages, it would seem that PEH was innovative here, by replacing *ni with a form *ta.

Turning to patterns of verbals, again it is the two Engan languages which are aberrant. The Engan languages lack verbal affixes to mark undergoer, while the other two languages have prefixes closely parallel in form to those of PEH, as shown

Table 29 *PH: undergoer prefixes*

		PEH	Kâte	Selepet	Dani	Ekagi
SG	1	*na-	n-	n-	n-	na-
	2	*ka-	g-	g-	k-	ka-
	3	*a-	∅	∅	∅	e-
PL	1	*ta-	nɔ-	ni-	ni-	ni-

Table 30 *PH: actor suffixes*

		PEH	Enga	Kewa	Kâte	Selepet	Dani	Ekagi
SG	1	*-u	-o	-o	-pe	-an/m	-i	-a
	2	*-an	-e	-e	-(me)	-t/n	-in	-e
	3	*-i	-a	-a	-o	-p	-e	-i
PL	1	*un	-(a)ma	-ma	-nan	-in	-u	-e
	2/3	*-a	-(a)mi	-me	-nin	-i	-a	-a

in Table 29. Again, the four languages differ from PEH in a form *ni- 1PL, rather than *ta-, presumably a PEH innovation. Only Ekagi here exhibits an overt prefix e- for 3SG, plausibly related to PEH *a-. As in the Gorokan family, most of the languages have lost the prefix, although a possible alternative hypothesis is to suggest an original zero form with independent innovations in PEH and Ekagi. This seems less likely, but there is no convincing evidence to refute it, except perhaps the Dani independent third singular pronoun in a; $at < $ *a- 3SG + -t pronoun formative.

All six languages follow the EH pattern in marking the person and number of the actor with suffixes. The actor suffixes in comparison to PEH are given in Table 30. The fit with the PEH forms is much less close with the actor suffixes than with the undergoer prefixes. In this case it is the Huon languages which are the most different; neither Kâte nor Selepet exhibit a single obvious cognate morpheme with PEH, although the Selepet -an 1SG may come from *-an 2SG by semantic shift and the n in the first plural forms could be related to *-un. But this is sheer speculation; there is no evidence for linking the Huon forms to those of PEH. The Engan languages fare little better; only the form -o 1SG is transparently relatable to the PEH form. Interestingly it is the geographically most distant languages, Dani and Ekagi, which present forms closest to those of PEH. Ekagi is closest of all; -i 3SG and -a 2PL are clearly related to PEH *-i 3SG and *-a 2/3PL. Further, Ekagi exhibits the distinctive 2SG/1PL crossover pattern found in the Gorokan languages in their illocutionary force suffixes and traced to the n in the actor suffixes, PEH *-an 2SG and *-un 1PL. Note Ekagi has the same form -e for both 2SG and 1PL. This may be chance, or it could reflect a shared earlier morphological pattern. The Dani forms are perhaps not quite so impressive, but still fairly close: -*a* 3PL is clearly related to PEH *-*a* 2/3PL, and -*e* 3SG is plausibly connected to PEH *-*i* 3SG. Either PEH *-*u* 1SG or *-*un* PL could have given rise to Dani -*u* 1PL; the connection is certainly not too far-fetched. Finally, the *n* in -*in* 2SG may be descended from PEH *-*an*; the *n* is clearly associated with 2SG as the form -*in* is in opposition to a form -*ip* 2PL.

Turning finally to the benefactive construction, this is a feature of all six languages, as the following examples show:

Enga: *akáli dokó-mé mená dóko namba-nyá pya-k-e-á*
man the-ERG pig   the   1SG-BEN   hit-BEN-PAST-3SG
'the man killed the pig for me'

Kewa: *ní-ná   méá-á-ri-a*
1SG-BEN get-BEN-PAST-3SG
'he got it for me'

Kâte: *yopa-n-ale-ʔ*
hit-1SG U-give-2SG IMP
'hit (them) for me!'

Selepet: *kat-n-ihi-a-p*
put-1SG U-give-IM PAST-3SG A
'he put it away for me'

Dani: *hakki   pa-n-akeik-h-e*
bananas cut-2SG U-put-REAL-3SG A
'he cut bananas for me'

Ekagi: *nota ni-ya-dok-ii*
yam 1PL U-BEN-carry -IMP
'carry the yams for us!'

The benefactive construction in the Engan languages is clearly not related to that of PEH, while in the other four languages it is very similar. In the Engan languages, the benefactive is not indicated by the undergoer prefix (absent in the Engan languages in any case), but appears as a nominal suffixed with a benefactive case-marker (the same form as the possessive suffix). The verb is simply affixed with a benefactive suffix indicating the benefactive relation. In the other four languages, the benefactive construction is exactly parallel in form to that of PEH: the benefactive argument appears as the undergoer prefix followed by the benefactive morpheme, usually the verb 'give' or 'put'. In Kâte, Selepet and Dani these periphrastic constructions are part of a general periphrastic verbal conjugation system with

Table 31 *Proto-Highlands: grammatical evidence*

	Enga	Kewa	Kâte	Selepet	Dani	Ekagi
pronouns	√	√	√√√	√√√	√√	√√
undergoer prefixes			√√	√√	√√	√√√
actor suffixes	√	√			√√√	√√√
benefactive			√√√	√√√	√√√	√√√

verbs like 'give', 'put', 'see' and 'hit', as discussed in section 5.3. In Dani there are three different verbal stems which may be used in periphrastic constructions to express a benefactive relation. Either the PEH benefactive construction is a vestige of an earlier richer periphrastic conjugation system, as in Kâte, Selepet and Dani, or the latter systems are the result of new constructions formed analogically with the benefactive construction. Either seems plausible, although Ekagi (which has the periphrastic benefactive construction, but no general periphrastic verbal conjugations) may suggest that the PEH system is older: for although Ekagi, if anything, is most closely related to Dani, it exhibits here the PEH pattern, rather than that of Dani.

The grammatical evidence for genetic relations between these six languages and PEH are summarized in Table 31 (the number of checks reflects the strength of the evidence). While the evidence in basic vocabulary for genetic links between these six and the EH languages is very weak, on the grammatical level some of the languages fare much better. However, even on the grammatical level there is little convincing evidence for a genetic link with the Engan languages; and we must conclude that, on present evidence, they are unrelatable to the EH languages. For the other four languages the grammatical evidence does suggest a genetic link. Perhaps most surprisingly of all, it is the geographically most distant languages from the Eastern Highlands, Dani and Ekagi, which turn out to be most closely related, at least on the above evidence. The Huon languages seem a bit more distant, but nonetheless clearly related. The above data suggest a very tentative family tree as follows:

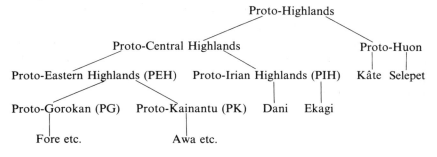

Further research will be necessary to ascertain whether Dani and Ekagi form a subgroup in themselves or whether both are equal sisters of PEH; but the above can be accepted provisionally.

The main lesson to be drawn from this exercise in deep genetic relationships in Papuan languages is the importance of shared grammatical morphemes in establishing such relationships. In the case of establishment of the Gorokan family, cognates in basic vocabulary clearly established the genetic relationship, and the cognate grammatical forms merely confirmed this. The genetic relationship of the Gorokan family to the Kainantu languages is less obvious in basic vocabulary, but still unquestionable, and again the grammatical evidence plays a largely confirmatory role, albeit an important one. But in investigating deeper relations as between the Eastern Highlands and the Huon or Irian Highlands languages, the role of grammatical evidence becomes central. In general, where such distant relationships are concerned, the number of cognates is wholly insufficient to establish genetic affiliation. Because of this, cognates in bound grammatical morphemes assume the primary diagnostic function.

Papuan languages often seem to be subject to a more rapid turnover in basic vocabulary than in basic morphology. What could be the explanation for this? Consider again the quote in section 2.2 from Mead (1938), discussing a Sepik village as 'an aggregation of widely diffused traits peculiar to it' and 'a center of many lines of diffusion'. I believe that this characterization can be applied generally to Papuan languages. A major source of diversification in Papuan languages is borrowing and diffusion. Independent words, whether basic vocabulary or not, are much more subject to borrowing than are bound morphemes, which are part of an entire paradigmatic system. Words are easily isolatable, and hence amenable to borrowing, whereas bound morphemes are not. A word containing the morpheme may be borrowed, in which case it will be analysed simply as part of the stem, or the entire paradigmatic system may be taken on wholesale. But borrowing a whole paradigmatic system would doubtless be a much more complex task than borrowing a word, and this difficulty would be reflected in the relative rarity of such morpheme borrowing as opposed to word borrowing. Hence, bound morphemes would be more resistant than words to borrowing, and in this context cognate morphemes will be of high diagnostic value for genetic affiliation.

It is important to emphasize that it is bound morphemic forms that I am claiming are relatively resistant to borrowing, not general morphological patterns. The diffusion of morphological patterns is a widespread feature of Papuan languages, and this is a problem to which I now turn.

7.5 **Areal features and diffusion**

In this section I will investigate some structural features of Yimas in comparison to those of two neighbouring but unrelated languages, Alamblak (Bruce 1984) and Enga (Lang 1973). Alamblak adjoins Yimas to the west and Enga to the south. To the north of Yimas is the related language Karawari and, to its east, the poorly known and unrelated Arafundi language. On present knowledge, Alamblak and Enga are unrelated to Yimas, and if further research should demonstrate a genetic affiliation to one or the other or both, the relationship will be of necessity so distant as not to affect the conclusions drawn here.

Phonology

1 *Consonantal inventories*

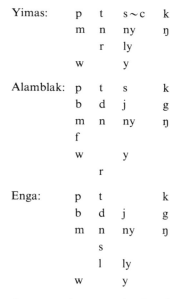

Yimas:
p	t	s∼c	k
m	n	ny	ŋ
	r	ly	
w		y	

Alamblak:
p	t	s	k
b	d	j	g
m	n	ny	ŋ
f			
w		y	
	r		

Enga:
p	t		k
b	d	j	g
m	n	ny	ŋ
	s		
	l	ly	
w		y	

All three languages have a palatal series; such phonemes are not generally common in Papuan languages, but are reasonably so in the Sepik area. Such a series was a feature of Proto-Engan (Franklin 1975a), but is clearly innovative in Yimas and Alamblak. In both languages this has been a recent phonological development by palatalization with an adjoining high front vowel or glide, which then disappears:

Yimas: *tay-ntut > tanycut*
see-RM PAST

Alamblak: *bari + -t > bars*
hornbill-3sɢ F

Clearly, palatals are an areal feature of the south Karawari River region, possibly as a result of diffusion from Enga, the language in which this feature is most archaic.

2 *Vocalic systems*

Yimas			Alamblak			Enga	
i	ɨ	u	i	ɨ	u	i	u
			e	ʌ	o	e	o
	a			a			a

Enga has the typical five-vowel system of highlands languages, while Yimas and Alamblak present the typical Sepik pattern of a predominance of central vowels. The similarity of Yimas and Alamblak is not due to diffusion but is the result of direct inheritance from their respective proto-languages.

Morphology

1 *Nominal*

1 *Case suffixes*   Enga is typical of highlands languages in having a number of suffixes to mark case relations, including an ergative suffix. Yimas lacks nominal case-marking except for a general, all-purpose oblique suffix, *-n*. Alamblak parallels Yimas in lacking case-marking for core relations, but has a number of suffixes for peripheral notions. Like Yimas, it does, however, have a rather general oblique suffix *-n*.

2 *Possessive morphology*   All three languages may form possessives in the same way, by suffixing a possessive morpheme to the possessor:

Yimas: *ama-na ' pamuŋ*
1SG-POSS leg
'my leg'

Alamblak: *nan-ho   wurat*
1SG-POSS foot
'my foot'

Enga: *namba-nyá mená*
1SG-POSS   pig
'my pig'

While all three languages have parallelism of structure, Yimas and Enga appear to have related possessive morphemes, Yimas *-na*, Enga *-nya*. These forms may be traced back to their respective proto-languages; **-na* is the Proto-Lower Sepik possessive, present in all daughter languages, and *-n(y)a* is the Proto-Engan form (compare Kewa, Huli *-na* POSS). This feature, then, cannot be the result of recent diffusion between Enga and Yimas, but may indicate a very distant genetic relationship or, more probably, contact between the two proto-languages, with important implications for the original homeland of these language families.

3 *Gender* Enga, typical of highlands languages, lacks any overt gender marking on its nouns. Alamblak has the simple two-gender system common in the middle Sepik area, opposing a masculine *-r* and a feminine *-t* in the singular, but neutralizing it in the nonsingular, *-f* DL and *-m* PL. Yimas has a full and complex noun-class system, discussed in 4.4. While the Alamblak and Yimas systems are overall very different, note that the Alamblak plural form *-m* and the Yimas adjective concord suffix for classes I and III (male human and higher animals) *-um* are very similar. This may be the result of diffusion, as both languages form pronouns with this suffix: Yimas *m-um* PRO-PL 'they', Alamblak *rë-m* PRO-PL 'they'.

2 *Verbal*

1 *Tense* All three languages have complex tense systems, distinguishing a number of past tenses. Enga and Alamblak are simpler; they have a future, a present, and three past tenses: immediate past (earlier in the day), near past (yesterday) and remote past (before yesterday). To this Yimas adds a distinction in the future, near future (later today, tomorrow) versus remote future (after tomorrow), as well as another past tense, far past (day before yesterday to about five days prior). These tense systems are highly similar and plausibly the result of diffusion. Such a five-tense system can be reconstructed for Proto-Engan (Kewa has the same system (Franklin 1971)) and for the ancestor of Alamblak (data in Bruce 1979), but probably not for Proto-Lower Sepik. It would seem, then, that Yimas may be the borrowing language here.

2 *Verb compounding* Both Yimas and Alamblak have very elaborate verb serialization constructions resulting in single words, hence the more apt term 'verb compounding'. The verbs in the compound take the person/number affixes of the core nominals as a whole rather than individually.

> Yimas: *na-mpɨ-yakal-tantaw-antɨ-ntut*
> 3SG U-3DL A-EXT-sit down-hear-RM PAST
> 'they both sat down listening to him'

> Alamblak: *muh-hambrë-më-r-r*
> climb-search-RM PAST-3SG M A-3SG M U
> 'he climbed searching for him'

3 *Adverbial incorporation* Both Yimas and Alamblak incorporate bound adverbial forms directly into the verbal complex:

Yimas: *pu-kwanan-kulanaŋ-tut*
3PL-aimlessly-walk-RM PAST
'they walked about aimlessly'

Alamblak: *yënr nur-nheh-mër-r*
child cry-feignedly-RM PAST-3SG M
'a child cried feignedly'

Both features 2 and 3 are highly diagnostic of Yimas and Alamblak verbal structures. As such elaborate structures are not present in sister languages of Yimas, they are probably the result of diffusion from Alamblak. Nothing similar is present in Enga.

4 *Causatives* Yimas has a number of ways of forming causatives. The most restricted is by affixing *-(a)sa* to a small set of intransitive process verbs:

na-n-kumprak-asa-t
3SG U-3SG A-break-CAUS-PERF
'he broke it'

Enga has an exactly parallel form, with the same restrictions:

énda dóko kuma-sá-py-á
woman the die-CAUS-NR PAST-3SG
'he made the woman die'

This may be a rare example of the borrowing of a bound form, but more likely it is the result of the later affixation of a form borrowed as an independent word. Enga *-sa* is the descendant of the Proto-Enga verb 'put' *sa-* (see Kewa *sa-* 'put'). In Enga it came to be used in a periphrastic verbal construction for causatives and at this stage was borrowed into Yimas (the Yimas verb 'put' is *ta-* ? < *sa-*). The verb lost its meaning and became an affix independently in the two languages.

Yimas has two other causative constructions, both involving verb compounding, one for physical manipulative causation with *tal-* 'hold', and the other for indirect causation with *tɨmi-* 'say':

na-ka-tal-kwalca-t
3SG U-1SG A-hold-arise-PERF
'I woke him up'

yan   na-mpu-tɨmi-wapal
tree-VSG VSG U-3PL A-say-climb
'they made him climb the tree'

The first Yimas construction above has a direct parallel in an Alamblak construction involving compounds with *kak-* 'get',

kat-kkah-më-t-a
get-hot-RM PAST-3SG F A-1SG U
'it made me hot'

This is one of four Alamblak causative constructions; two involve verb compounding, and two bound affixes. The second Yimas construction has a parallel in the second Enga causative construction with *lá-* 'say':

énda   dóko Wápaka pe-ná l-é-a
woman the   Wabag go-3SG say-IM PAST-3SG
'he caused the woman to go to Wabag'

Thus, Yimas shares constructions with both Alamblak and Enga, while Alamblak and Enga have nothing in common with respect to this feature.

Syntax

1 *Switch reference*

Enga has the typical sentence structure of highlands languages with complex clause chaining and switch-reference morphemes. Yimas and Alamblak have simpler sentence structures, with generally shorter sentences. Yimas has no switch-reference morphology, but Alamblak has:

Enga: *nambá p-e-ó-pa   baa-mé kalái p-i-á*
          I   go-PAST-1SG-DA he-ERG work do-IM PAST-3SG
          'I went and he worked'

Alamblak: *na hingna-më-t-a   mëfha-t fa-më-t-a*
          I work-RM PAST-DA-1SG head-F eat-RM PAST-3SG F A-1SG U
          'I worked, and my head hurt me'

The Enga and Alamblak forms are similar in adding an invariable different-actor suffix to an otherwise normally inflected independent verb. As different-actor dependent verb forms are not very common in the Sepik area languages, diffusion of this feature from Enga into Alamblak is possible.

2 Temporal adverbial clauses

Yimas and Alamblak share a distinctive manner of forming temporal adverbial clauses. They are formed by suffixing the oblique suffix -*n*, used to mark locatives, temporals and other setting nominals, to a fully inflected verb:

Yimas: *mpu-ŋa-tay-nt-ɨmp-ɨn*   *pu-ka-apan-kit*
            3PL A-1SG U-see-PRES-SEQ-OBL 3PL U-1SG A-shoot-RM FUT
            'when they see me, I will shoot them'

Alamblak: *nërwit gur-haym-et-r-n*   *yarim-fɨnah-më-m*
            drum beat-PROG-POSS-3SG M A-OBL toward-arrive-RM PAST-3PL
            'while he was beating the drum, they arrived'

This feature is widespread among Sepik area languages, so whether it results from contact between Yimas and Alamblak or is part of a wider diffusion area is impossible to say. Enga is quite different here, exemplifying a typical highlands pattern with the topic suffix -*mo* for adverbial clauses.

In this section I have identified a number of shared features in the phonology, morphology and syntax of Yimas, Alamblak and Enga, which may be the result of diffusion. The sheer number of these features (and I have by no means listed them all) suggests a very heavy role for diffusion in the linguistic prehistory of these languages. Extended to Papuan languages generally, it is easy to see the immense problems such diffusion can create for determining the genetic affiliations and the prehistory of Papuan languages. I have tried in this chapter to develop rigorous methods of comparative linguistics which attempt partially to circumvent these problems by concentrating on bound morphology; but even here, as the Yimas causative construction in -*(a)sa* cautions, we must be wary of being too confident in our procedures. We must always be aware in Papuan comparative and historical linguistics of the pervasive presence of borrowing, for fundamentally, to paraphrase Mead (1938), each Papuan language is a sink of many lines of diffusion, an aggregation of widely diffused traits peculiar to it.

8

Papuan languages and New Guinea prehistory

8.1   Introduction

The span of New Guinea history for which there exists historical documentation is very short, only a hundred years; and for certain areas, such as the central highlands, it is briefer still: less than fifty years. Thus, the history of New Guinea prior to the historical period of a hundred years belongs properly to prehistory. In the study of the prehistory of various regions of the world, two major tools are available. The first is the methodology of comparative linguistics, as presented in the previous chapter. This has not yet been applied in any thoroughgoing fashion to Papuan languages, but a few preliminary studies such as those in the previous chapter are available. The second is the methodology of archaeology. This too has only recently made its debut in New Guinea studies – within the last twenty-five years. Archaeological studies in New Guinea have not been systematic, the vast majority of digs being concentrated in the central highlands area of Papua New Guinea and the Papuan coast. Irian Jaya is almost totally unknown archaeologically, while the lowland areas of Papua New Guinea fare only a little better. The findings of comparative linguistics and of archaeology must be combined in piecing together the prehistory of a region. In this chapter, I will be comparing the findings in the New Guinea area of these two disciplines to try to reconstruct some of the prehistory of the region: the settlement and migration patterns of the speakers of the ancestors of modern Papuan languages.

8.2   Is there a link between Australian and Papuan languages?

It is now well established that up until about 8,000 years ago Australia and New Guinea were joined together into a larger continental mass called Sahul (White and O'Connell 1982). This was the result of the much lower sea levels during the last ice age. During the period of the lowest sea levels (about 17,000 years ago), the present-day Arafura Sea was a flat plain connecting what is now New Guinea to Australia. As the sea levels rose from 16,000 to 6,000 years ago, this plain was slowly flooded, until New Guinea was cut off from Australia with the formation of Torres Strait.

The earliest dates for human habitation in the region are around 25–30,000 years ago from Lake Mungo in Australia and 26,000 years ago from Kosipe in Papua New Guinea (White and O'Connell 1982). Both of these dates clearly fall into the period in which New Guinea and Australia were joined as Sahul. The earlier of these dates, 25–30,000 years ago, comes from Lake Mungo in New South Wales, in the southeast corner of Australia. It is generally assumed that humans coming to Sahul would of necessity have migrated from southeast Asia, especially Indonesia, the large western islands of which were themselves joined to the Asian land-mass in a peninsula called Sunda, also a result of the lower sea levels. There is clear evidence of human habitation in the Indonesian area well before 40,000 years ago (Bellwood 1978). Indeed, Java man, an example of *homo erectus* rather than *homo sapiens*, dates from at least a million years ago (Bellwood 1978). Other *homo erectus* remains date from between one million and 300,000 years ago. An especially interesting fossil record is Solo man from central Java, possibly dating from 100,000 years ago. This individual seems intermediate between *homo erectus* and *homo sapiens*, prompting different researchers to assign it to different species. Some scholars (Thorne 1980) regard Solo man as the direct ancestor of modern Australoid populations. Be that as it may, the fossil record clearly demonstrates human occupation in the immense area to the northwest of Sahul to be very ancient indeed. Further, this region is the only possible population source for Sahul, as the small Oceanic island world to its east was not populated until much later, with the arrival of the Austronesians around 5,000 years ago (Pawley and Green 1973).

Given that the population migrating to Sahul came from Asia, a quick glance at a map demonstrates that the likely migration route would be from Sunda, through the many small islands of Wallacea (present-day eastern Indonesia), to the northwest coast of Sahul, several thousand kilometres distant from Lake Mungo. A population in Sahul sufficient to reach Lake Mungo around 25–30,000 years ago would suggest an initial arrival in the northwest well before that date; 40,000 years ago does not seem too far-fetched. Indeed, there is a possible earlier date of 45,000 years ago from the Huon Peninsula (Swadling 1981); and Jones (1979) suggests a date of 50,000 years ago for human habitation in Sahul.

Fifty thousand years is a very long time, and if the present-day populations in the Sahul region descend directly from this period, then the extreme linguistic diversity found here, especially in New Guinea, finds a ready historical explanation. Furthermore, if the split between Australian language groups and Papuan languages dates from a period anywhere approaching this date, then certainly all traces of an earlier unity would have been long obliterated. Note that I am operating here with the assumption that modern New Guinea and Australian populations trace their ancestry back to a single immigrant population. This is a simplifying assumption, to be sure, but I see no convincing reason to abandon it. The many differences between these populations today may be merely the result of genetic drift and divergence over many tens of thousands of years. Genetically, Australians and Papuans have many features in common (Kirk 1980), and the differences between Papuans and Australians in many ways do not loom much greater than those between two Papuan groups.

While 50,000 years would erase any linguistic evidence for a link between Australian and Papuan groups, it is by no means necessary for them to have diverged so long ago. Physical contact between Australia and New Guinea remained possible until 8,000 years ago, when the Torres Strait was formed. 8,000 years is also a very long time, and a time depth which may present many problems for the application of the methods of comparative linguistics. But, unlike 50,000 years, 8,000 years may not present insurmountable problems. The Austronesian languages have a time depth of at least 6,000 and possibly 7,000 years, but have been subjected to a very successful application of the rigorous methods of comparative linguistics, resulting in a detailed reconstruction of Proto-Austronesian. For a number of reasons, Austronesian languages are relatively slow-changing, and we would be expecting too much to replicate the results of comparative Austronesian linguistics in the much more complex sphere of Papuan genetic linguistics. But the Austronesian example should be enough to hearten us, so that even with a minimum time depth of 8,000 years, sufficient evidence could be found to make some sort of case for a link between Australian languages and a group of Papuan languages.

This is not a new idea; a number of investigators have considered this possibility before, but no-one has previously made any case for it. There were two reasons for this. The first is that previous investigators looked in the wrong place, the south coast of New Guinea, immediately above the Torres Strait and the Arafura Sea. This is the logical place to look – the area closest to Australia – but unfortunately none of the languages spoken there today display any evidence of a link to Australian languages. Rather, I will show that it is the languages of the highlands of New Guinea which show the closest links to Australian languages. The second is that, until very recently, almost nothing was known of Proto-Australian. Only with the publication of Dixon 1980 was a good case made for the genetic unity of Australian languages, and detailed evidence presented.

The main evidence Dixon (1980) offers for the genetic unity of Australian languages is the presence of a number of monosyllabic verb-stems with a final suffixed sonorant acting as a conjugation marker. Most words in Australian languages are disyllabic, so these monosyllabic verb-stems are a highly diagnostic feature, and these forms tend to be cognate right across the continent. Dixon (1980) lists nearly twenty of these monosyllabic verb-stems for Proto-Australian. It was the presence of plausible cognates for these monosyllabic verbs in Eastern Highlands languages that first alerted me to their possible relationship to Australian languages. Other reconstructions Dixon (1980) offers for Proto-Australian are forms for first and second person pronouns. In addition, earlier researchers (e.g. Capell 1956; Hale 1976) pointed out a number of common forms in the basic vocabulary of Australian languages; some of these also have clear counterparts in Eastern Highlands languages.

Typologically, Australian and Eastern Highlands languages are very different, and this is nowhere more apparent than in the phonology. Of course, this does not preclude genetic relationship; English, Hindi and Russian are all very different typologically, yet nonetheless related genetically. Australian languages have quite complex consonantal inventories with up to six places of articulation, each with a corresponding nasal and often a liquid as well. Proto-Australian (Dixon 1980) had four places of articulation; besides labial and velar, the peripheral places of articulation, it distinguished apical from laminal in the non-peripheral, each stop with a corresponding nasal:

labial	apical	laminal	velar
p	t	th	k
n	n	nh	ŋ
	l	lh	
	rr, r		
w		y	

As the above table details, Proto-Australian also had two laterals, an apical and a laminal, as well as two rhotics, a trill (*rr*) and a retroflex approximant (*r*). Note that Proto-Australian had no voicing contrast in stops, and this is true of the vast majority of the modern languages.

The Eastern Highlands languages display a considerable degree of variation in their consonantal systems, but what is common to all can be represented as follows:

p	t	k
m	n	
	s	
w	y	

This is probably the system of PEH and is essentially that of modern Fore (Scott 1978); see section 3.1. No Eastern Highlands language contrasts apicals and laminals; there is always a single dental/alveolar non-peripheral place of articulation. Eastern Highlands languages lack a phoneme /ŋ/, but do have /s/. Unlike the Australian languages with their complex inventories of laterals and rhotics, these features are lacking in the Eastern Highlands languages where [r ~ l] is merely an intervocalic allophone of /t/.

The vocalic systems of both language groupings are simple. Eastern Highlands languages have a simple five-vowel system /i e a o u/ and Australian languages, a three-vowel system /i a u/. Proto-Australian did, however, have a length distinction in its vowels, lost in most modern languages (Dixon 1980). Vowel length is not a contrastive feature in most Eastern Highlands languages, and seems not to have been so in the proto-language.

I now turn to presenting the evidence – the possible cognates between Proto-Australian and Eastern Highlands languages. One important point that must be borne in mind is the great simplicity of the Eastern Highlands consonantal system as opposed to Proto-Australian (PA). A large number of distinctions in Proto-Australian collapse in Eastern Highlands languages; this is relevant in the correspondences below.

The monosyllabic verbs are the best evidence for Proto-Australian, so I will start with them. The conjugation markers of Australian languages have no reflexes in Papuan languages.

1 'hit/do'   PA *pu-m   PEH *pu-   Fore *pu-*   Gahuku *pV(l)-*   Kamano *he-*
Hua *hu-*   Siane *(o)fo-*   Tairora *ʔuʔu-*   (*p > ʔ* is regular in Tairora). The Hua and Kamano reflexes *h < *p* are irregular, so there is some doubt concerning these forms' cognacy.

2 'get/take' PA *maa-n   PEH *ma-   Fore *mae-*   Awa *me-*   Auyana *ma-*
Gadsup *ma-*. Moni of the Irian Highlands languages has a cognate causative prefix, plausibly derived from an earlier verbal compounding with *ma-* 'get/take'.

3 'put'   PA *thu-n   PEH *to-   Fore *ʔta-*   BenaBena *to-*   Hua *to-*   Awa *t-*   Gadsup *daa(na)-*   Tairora *(ba)taa(na)-*

4 'eat'   PA *ŋa-l   PEH *na-   Fore *na-*   Gende *na-*   Siane *na-*   Yagaria *no-*   Awa *nɔ-*   Auyana *na-*   Tairora *naa-*

5 'stand'   PA *tha(a)-n   PEH *ti-   Gende *oro-*   Gahuku *t-*   BenaBena *ti-*   Yagaria *ti-*   Fore *(a)si-*   Awa *(i)ri-*   Auyana *(usa)si(na)-*

Now compare the pronoun systems of PA (Dixon 1980) and PEH, as shown in Table 32. PA had a minimal/augmented pronoun system (Dixon 1980) in which the first inclusive form *ŋali* 'you and I' behaves like a singular paradigmatically. The only clear cognate here is PA *ŋay* PEH *na* 1SG. However, remember that in section 7.4 I pointed out that *ta* 1PL was an innovation in PEH, and that the earlier Proto-Highlands form was *ni* 'we'. This form *ni* 1PL shows a transparent relationship formally to PA *ŋin* 2SG, although the meaning difference is problematic. But I have

Table 32 *PA and PEH pronoun systems*

| | PA | | PEH | |
	Minimal	Augmented	SG	PL
1 incl.	*ŋali	*ŋanh-	1 *na	*ta
excl.	*ŋay	*ŋana		
2	*ŋin	*nhurra	2 *ka	*ya
3	no clear PA forms		3 *a	

already pointed out example after example in Eastern Highlands languages of an interrelationship between 2sG and 1PL forms (see section 7.4). In view of this it seems reasonable to propose an earlier 2sG form *ŋi (as in PA) becoming re-analysed as 1PL.

Finally, there are a good number of words of basic vocabulary with related forms in a number of Australian languages (probably in PA) with clear cognates in Eastern Highlands languages:

6 'what'   PA *ŋhaa/*naa PEH *na Fore *na:(na)* Gahuku *na(na)*
BenaBena *(he)na* Awa *(a)neʔ* Gadsup *ne(pi)* Tairora *nana*

7 'two'   PA *kuthara PEH *tata Fore *tara* Yagaria *lole* Awa
(tɔ)tare Tairora *taara-*

8 'breast'   PA *ŋama PEH *nami Gende *ami* Siane *ami(na)* Gadsup
naami Tairora *naama*

9 'water'   PA *ŋuku PEH *nok(ami) Gende *nogoi* Siane *no*
BenaBena *nagami* Awa *no* Tairora *namari*

10 'dead/rotten' PA *puka 'die' PEH *puti Fore *puri-* Gende *pri-*
BenaBena *fili-* Awa *puki-* Auyana *pukai-* Gadsup *puka-*
Tairora *ʔutu-* Ekagi *bokai-*

This form was reconstructed with a *t in PEH with a common sound-shift *t > k in some Kainantu languages. However, the Ekagi form also suggests a *k, thus PEH *puki, bringing the Highlands form into closer alignment with the PA reconstruction. A t/k alternation in the historical phonologies of highlands languages is a major problem that awaits solution.

11 'eye'   PA *mil 'egg' PEH *mut Fore *(a)muʔ* Gende
mura Siane *mula* Gadsup *(a)muʔi*. 'Eye' and 'egg' are
sometimes associated in Papuan languages (McElhanon
and Voorhoeve 1970), usually through the intermediate
'fruit' and 'ball'.

12 'vegetable food' PA **mayi* 'meat' PEH **ma(ʔi)* BenaBena *m me(ʔa)* Yagaria *me* Auyana *(a)maʔa* Gadsup *(a)maʔi* Tairora *mati*

13 'head' PA **kata* PG **ko(n)to* Gahuku *goto* Yagaria *geno(pa)* Gende *koi-*

14 deictic particle PA **pa* topic marker PEH **pa* Fore *-pa* Hua *-ve* Awa *-po*

15 'cough' PA **kuntul* PEH **kutu* Asaro *gutu* Gahuku *gulu* BenaBena *kuhu* Yagaria *gatu* Gimi *kotu*. This may simply be sound symbolism in both Australian and Eastern Highlands.

This is the sum total of evidence collected to date. It is not strongly compelling, but it is only the result of a relatively cursory look. More careful research may turn up more cognates, or provide arguments against any genetic relationship between Australian and Eastern Highlands languages. A major weakness in the above is that many examples of the sound correspondences involve mergers in the Papuan languages, e.g. PA **n, nh, ŋ* PEH **n*, PA **t, th, l, lh, rr, r* PEH **t*. This of course, increases the likelihood of chance resemblances, making the evaluation of the evidence more difficult.

It must be emphasized again that the above evidence in no way constitutes *proof* of a genetic relationship between Australian and Eastern Highlands languages. At this point fewer than twenty possible cognates have been assembled, and some of these have problems in the sound correspondences. Much more detailed and careful research needs to be done before a convincing proof is provided, and, given the time depth, that may never be possible. Rather, the above data represent a first attempt at marshalling some evidence for a genetic link between Australian and Papuan languages. The task for the future is to refine our reconstructions both of PA and of PEH, and compare these proto-languages in detail. Only then can a more conclusive answer be supplied to the question which began this section.

8.3 Papuan languages and New Guinea prehistory

Setting aside now the question of genetic links to Australian languages, no Papuan language family has been demonstrated to have any genetic affiliation outside the immediate New Guinea area. The extreme linguistic complexity of New Guinea (over sixty language families plus some isolates) must be assumed to have developed *in situ*. Given the archaeological record which indicates a minimum of human habitation in New Guinea of 26,000 years and a likely date of more than 40,000 (considering also Swadling's (1981) date of 45,000 years from the Huon Peninsula), there is ample time indeed for great language diversity to develop, as pointed out in section 1.3. With this great time depth and the particular social and cultural conditions of Papuan groups discussed in Chapter 2, the extreme linguistic fragmentation of New Guinea becomes readily explicable.

The prehistory of New Guinea properly divides into two spheres, that of the highlands and that of the lowlands. The archaeological record for the central highlands of Papua New Guinea is more extensive than for any other area in New Guinea. Archaeological finds in the Western Highlands indicate human habitation by 20,000 years ago (Golson, personal communication). Whether these ancestral humans bear any direct relationship to present-day inhabitants is impossible to say, and the same, of course, applies to whatever languages these humans spoke.

One of the most remarkable stories of New Guinea prehistory is the very early advent of agriculture in the valleys of the central highlands of Papua New Guinea, as reported in depth in Golson 1977. Golson provides strong evidence for the appearance of agriculture in the highlands about 9,000 years ago, based on his excavations in a swampy valley in the Western Highlands. What domesticated plants or animals were associated with this very early agriculture is unknown. At around 6,000 years ago, these swampland gardens betray distinctive features thought to be associated with the cultivation of taro, a plant often held to be of southeast Asian ancestry (Golson 1977). This development is roughly contemporaneous with the expansion in the highlands record of remains of the pig (Hope *et al.* 1983). The cultivation of the taro would have permitted the domestication and husbandry of pigs on a larger scale than would previously been possible, and this development may have been a crucial step in the formation of the distinctive character of highlands societies.

The growth of agriculture gave rise to significant shifts in the ecology of the highlands valleys. Early agriculturalists in the highlands probably practised slash-and-burn agriculture – cutting down the forest, burning it, growing a few seasons' crops on the land until the nutrients were exhausted, and then moving on to repeat the process. Although regrowth would occur on the land, it would not exhibit the richness of the primary forest because of the degraded state of the soil. After repeated cycles of slash-and-burn agriculture and consequent regrowth, the regrowth itself would become increasingly degraded, resulting in the grasslands so familiar in the highlands valleys today (Golson 1977). This process was probably intensified by the continual population increase made possible by agriculture. As the population grew, more and more land came under agricultural use, with the ultimate consequence of an increasing spread of the grasslands.

Unlike forests, grasslands are not amenable to slash-and-burn agricultural techniques. The disappearance of much of the forest and the proliferation of the grasslands required the highland agriculturalists to devise new agricultural techniques fitted to the changed ecosystem. It has long been recognized that modern highland agricultural techniques are well designed for productive cultivation in grasslands (Brookfield and Hart 1971). With the arrival, according to the orthodox theory, of the sweet potato from South America in highland New Guinea about 400 years ago, these techniques were found to be highly effective, promoting increased yields from land kept continuously in production. These techniques in association with the sweet potato allowed a veritable population explosion in the central highlands, building up to the very dense population found at European contact.

Golson (1982) makes the crucial observation that, given what is known of the performance of crops like taro in the highlands, there would have been great differences in the productive capacities of different communities, depending on soil conditions and altitude. Those communities on the valley floors with access to swamplands would have been among the most advantaged. This would have resulted especially in higher population increases in these areas, and also allowed the maintenance of large holdings of pigs, increasing the differential advantages and prestige of these communities still further. This concentration of large, well fed prestige populations, often on the valley floor, opposed to smaller, weaker populations higher on the slopes, has important implications for the movement of peoples in the highlands.

Today the central highlands are largely occupied by speakers of three language families, the Eastern Highlands, Chimbu and Engan families. All of these families are spoken by very large populations; the Chimbu and Engan families both have over 300,000 speakers. The speakers of these languages are clearly well adapted to the highland environment and sophisticated in highland agricultural techniques. All the linguistic evidence points to their being settled in the highlands for at least a couple of millennia.

When we attempt to trace the origins of the speakers of these languages, the picture becomes more obscure. Of the three, only the Eastern Highlands family has clear genetic links outside its immediate area, to the Irian Highlands and the Huon languages, as demonstrated in section 7.4. The Eastern Highlands languages have a number of probable Austronesian loan words, including the important PEH *ta* 1PL replacing the earlier form *ni* 1PL, suggesting an earlier habitation site close to Austronesian speakers. The closest such area is the Markham Valley, immediately to the west of the Eastern Highlands area, and this is the probable area from which speakers of the Eastern Highlands languages migrated, possibly as a result of pressure from an aggressive and expanding population of headhunting Austronesian speakers.

The Engan family is more confusing. It shows a number of lexical links – but almost no grammatical links – to Eastern Highlands languages, as documented in 7.4. It has quite a large number of Austronesian loan words (Lynch 1981), more than Eastern Highlands languages. Finally, it shows a significant number of structural links to languages of the Sepik basin. It is impossible to determine at this point whether or not the Engan family is intrusive into the highlands, but a migration into the highlands from the Sepik is not entirely implausible, a point I will return to below.

Of the three language families, then, only the Chimbu family remains without any potential genetic links outside the highlands. Further, of the three language families, the languages of the Chimbu family are typologically the most aberrant. They have some unusual phonemes for Papuan languages, and quite distinctive morphological patterns in verbs. This evidence leads me to suggest that the speakers of the Chimbu family are the oldest of the present-day inhabitants of the central highlands. Note that these people occupy the area of the earliest agricultural sites, and are today the most populous of all highlands peoples. It would be pure conjecture to suggest that these people descend from those early agriculturalists; but the speakers of the Chimbu family must have been in their present area for a long time, at least 3,000 years. This is a minimal linguistic time depth for the intrusive Eastern Highlands family. Whether present-day speakers of Chimbu languages descend from these early agriculturalists or not, they clearly received agricultural techniques from them, and probably promulgated them among Eastern Highlands and possibly Engan speakers coming into the highlands.

Given the time depth of at least 20,000 years for human habitation in the highlands, it is almost impossible that the present situation of three relatively closely related families represents anything like the earlier situation; rather, we would expect a much greater degree of linguistic fragmentation. The important idea of Golson (1982) concerning differences of land tenure in a community's success provides the clue here. The people who occupied the most favourable sites, especially the swampy valley floors, would have expanded faster, and at the expense of those in less favourable sites. With the ancestors of speakers of Chimbu family languages in their present position, they would be greatly advantaged indeed, and would have expanded rapidly. As they expanded, smaller and less advantaged groups would have been absorbed or pushed out of their lands. With the arrival of Eastern Highlands and Engan speakers and their adoption of highlands agricultural techniques and seizure of favourable lands, the same process would have been repeated to the east and west of the Chimbu family area. As the populations of these three families continued to grow and seize land, more and more groups would have become refugees from the central highlands, spilling down into the highland fringe areas and adjacent lowlands (see Pain and Scott 1981 for a discussion of this process in Enga Province). The end result of this process would be the demographic picture we see today: any glance at a linguistic map shows relative language homogeneity in the central highlands, but much greater linguistic fragmentation in highland fringe areas and adjacent lowlands.

Nowhere in New Guinea is linguistic fragmentation greater than in the drainage areas of the Sepik and Ramu Rivers. According to a recent account (Swadling 1984), this area may have had an especially interesting prehistory. According to this view, during the last ice age the Sepik–Ramu basin had much the same area as today, although downcut much lower; but with the rise of the sea at the end of the ice age, the sea would have began to encroach on the plain. By 5–6,000 years ago, when sea levels reached their present height, the Sepik–Ramu basin may have been a huge salt-water inlet. To the south of this inlet were the foothills of the mountains of the central highlands, and to its north the low mountains of the Prince Alexander and Torricelli Ranges. Gradually, the present-day flood plain was formed by infilling of the basin with sediment carried down by the rivers. Finally, Swadling (1984) claims that by 2,000 years ago this flood plain was largely in place.

This exceptional geomorphological history would give rise to an extremely complex demographic picture, and Swadling's (1984) account does provide a scenario in which a number of disparate and puzzling facts about the linguistic situation of the Sepik–Ramu basin and adjacent areas find a ready explanation. Although we have no dates for human habitation in the Sepik–Ramu basin earlier than European contact in the nineteenth century, there can be no doubt that actual habitation was much earlier, given the antiquity of the dates elsewhere in New Guinea. The proposed drowning of the basin by the sea 6,000 years ago would have caused massive population disruption, with people fleeing their flooded village sites to gain the higher ground to the north and south, presumably putting great pressure on any groups already resident there.

In the northern high ground consisting of the Torricelli and Prince Alexander Ranges is found the large Torricelli language family, with forty-seven languages and over 70,000 speakers (Laycock 1975). This family is highly distinctive typologically, having a cluster of structural features shared by no other typological group. They are spread over a large area of the northern Sepik high ground, from Lumi in the west to beyond Angoram in the east. It seems reasonable to conclude that these people have occupied the area for a long time, and are the descendants of people occupying a northern section of the ice-age Sepik flood plain.

The situation in the southern high ground would be vastly more complicated. The Sepik–Ramu refugees withdrawing to higher ground from their flooded villages in the proposed salt-water inlet would here come into contact with highlands refugees being pushed out into the fringe areas by the incessantly increasing populations of the highlands language families. The result is a demographic nightmare for the prehistorian, with a very complex scenario of population mixing occurring about 4–5,000 years ago. To cap it all, the date 4–5,000 years coincides with the arrival of the Austronesians in the northern Papua New Guinea area. And a large open salt-water inlet (as the Sepik–Ramu basin may then have been) would seem an ideal colonization site to arriving Austronesians. Thus, to this stew of Sepik and highlands populations in the southern high ground, we need to add the possibility of Austronesian arrivals as well.

All of this may help in explaining the complex picture provided by the Engan language family. I mentioned above that, in addition to a number of features typical of Sepik languages, Engan languages have a large number of Austronesian loan words, but today occupy an area very far from any Austronesian speakers. If the ancestors of Engan speakers were resident in the southern high ground of the Sepik basin, as are speakers of aberrant dialects of Enga today, then these features become explicable. Perhaps the speakers of Proto-Engan were early casualties of the rapidly expanding Chimbu speakers, forced from the highlands into the fringe area of the Sepik southern high ground. Here they came into contact with Sepik and Austronesian languages, with resultant language interference, and then migrated back into the highlands, but to the west of the expanding population of Chimbu speakers. This is speculation, but it does explain the picture the Engan languages present today.

As the present-day Sepik–Ramu flood plain was formed from sediment carried down by the rivers, people living along the southern high ground would have spread out to colonize the plain. Some of these colonizing groups would have been original highlands dwellers. Some present-day Sepik groups have clear traditions of having come down from the highlands. The Yimas, now located in the Sepik swamps, but just adjoining the southern high ground, make this claim; and if it is true, then the population of the entire Lower Sepik family may originate from the highlands.

The largest language family in the Sepik is the Ndu family, with about 100,000 speakers. It may form part of a still larger language grouping, including other languages of the middle and upper Sepik (such as Yessan–Mayo, Kwanga, Yerakai), as well as the languages of the Sepik Hill family, spoken in hills of the southern high ground from the Karawari to the Wogamush rivers. This area of the present-day Sepik Hill languages is very possibly the original site for the ancestors of the speakers of the Ndu languages, a proposal first broached in Laycock 1965. Accepting this proposal, the Proto-Ndu population would have moved north down the southern tributaries of the Sepik, fanning out along the main river. From there they would have spread along the north bank of the river, moving into the foothills of the Torricelli and Prince Alexander Mountains, the present territory of the Abelam and Boiken languages of the Ndu family.

Among the Abelam, historical processes similar to those of the highlands have occurred. Agriculturalists dependent on the yam, these people have been subject to increasing population pressure, resulting in their pushing the Arapesh people of the Torricelli family into more marginal land, where they amalgamated with resident populations. Large areas of the Abelam territory are grasslands, probably anthropogenic (Haantjens *et al.* 1965) as in the highlands, the result of human slash-and-burn agricultural techniques.

8.4 Papuan and Austronesian contact

Of all language families in New Guinea, the Austronesian family is the only one which is clearly immigrant, having come from southeast Asia in the last 5,000 years. Today there are around 200 Austronesian languages spoken in the New Guinea area, many in close proximity to Papuan languages, and there are a number of very interesting cases of Papuan and Austronesian language interference.

The Austronesians had clearly arrived in New Guinea by 5,000 years ago (Pawley and Green 1973). It has been claimed that they brought with them to New Guinea a number of innovations and re-introductions such as pottery; domesticated animals, such as chickens, pigs and dogs; and a number of crops of southeast Asian ancestry, such as some yam and banana types (Pawley and Green 1973). Very many Papuan languages have words for 'pig' closely related in form to the Austronesian word for 'domesticated pig', **mporo*, very probably a borrowing in these languages. The intrusive Austronesian population may have possessed technological superiority over the indigenous Papuan groups in a number of areas, suggesting that borrowing from the prestige population in both language and culture would occur. This has, in fact, occurred extensively, especially in the vocabulary; consider the Austronesian loan words in the basic vocabulary of Papuan languages, discussed in 7.1. But the opposite has also happened; there are a number of cases of extensive influence on Austronesian languages by Papuan languages. These cases tend to manifest themselves most strongly at the structural level.

Austronesian languages in Oceania are characterized by a very different grammatical typology from Papuan languages. They are svo in word-order and use prepositions to indicate functions of oblique nouns, as in this example from Tolai of New Britain (Capell 1976a):

> *a   tutuna i   ga   oe   ra davai livuan ta ta   uma*
> the man   3SG PAST plant a   tree   middle at the garden
> 'the man planted a tree in the middle of the garden'

Note that the actor *tutuna* 'man' precedes the verb *oe* 'plant', and the object *davai* 'tree' follows. The oblique locative noun *uma* 'garden' is marked by prepositions *ta* 'at' and *livuan* 'middle'. These features are true of Austronesian languages generally; Indonesian, for example, agrees in these particulars with Tolai.

Many Austronesian languages of the New Guinea area have undergone a fundamental shift in their typological characterization, so that they come to resemble the typical Papuan languages, with SOV word-order and postpositions. Motu, an Austronesian language of the Port Moresby area, typifies these languages (Capell 1976a):

> *tau   ese au-na   imea   bogarai-na-i vada e   hado*
> man A   tree-the garden middle-its-at PERF 3SG plant
> 'the man planted a tree in the middle of the garden'

In Motu, as in Papuan languages, the verb appears clause-finally, with all nominals preceding it. The locative oblique noun *imea* 'garden' is marked by a postposition *bogarai* 'middle', to which is suffixed a locative affix *-i* 'at'. In all these features Motu is typical of a Papuan language, rather than of the Austronesian family to which it belongs. It seems obvious that these Austronesian languages like Motu, which have Papuan typological features, have borrowed these from neighbouring Papuan languages (in the case of Motu, from the neighbouring Koiarian family languages). This structural diffusion is the result of language interference over a couple of millennia.

There also seem to be cases of linguistic interference working in the opposite direction – with Papuan languages taking on the typological features diagnostic of Austronesian. This has occurred in the east Bird's Head area of Irian Jaya, an area in which Austronesian languages are widespread. The languages of the East Bird's Head family, a group of Papuan languages, have the structural features exemplified above by Tolai, which are typical of Austronesian languages. Consider these examples from Mantion (Voorhoeve 1975b):

> *le-na   le-sa   hose koji*
> those-men 3PL-spear fish big
> 'those men speared a big fish'

> *le-čičuk   se Lei*
> 3PL-return to Lae
> 'they returned to Lae'

While Mantion is undoubtedly a Papuan language, having no significant cognates with Austronesian languages, it nonetheless has the typological features of SVO word-order and prepositions characteristic of them. This is the result of diffusion (again over at least a couple of millennia) from the neighbouring Austronesian languages, especially Wandamen. Another area in which Papuan languages have taken on Austronesian structural characteristics is northern Halmahera (Voorhoeve 1982).

In some cases the degree of linguistic contact may be so intense, and the resulting linguistic diffusion so extensive, that a language becomes difficult to classify as either Austronesian or Papuan. Two famous cases of this are in Papua: Magori of the south coast and Maisin of the Oro Province. Dutton (1976) has done a very careful comparative study of Magori with neighbouring Austronesian and Papuan languages. Dutton concludes that Magori is an Austronesian language, but one that has come to resemble neighbouring Papuan languages because of massive borrowing at all levels of vocabulary and structure. Speakers of Magori are fluent in Magi, the dominant Papuan language in the area, and this situation must have held in pre-contact times. This extensive bilingualism of Magori in a Papuan language resulted in massive 'Papuanization' of their language, with the result that the actual genetic affiliation of their language has been a point of contention among linguists (Strong 1911; Ray 1911; Dutton 1976).

Similar controversy surrounds the status of Maisin of coastal Oro Province (Strong 1911; Capell 1976b). This language has not been subject to as rigorous a comparative study as Magori, but Capell (1976b) concludes that it is a Papuan language with a very heavy influence from neighbouring Austronesian languages. More detailed research will be necessary to ascertain exactly the affiliation of Maisin, but if this turns out to be correct, then Maisin represents the opposite historical development from Magori – a Papuan language which has been 'Austronesianized'.

The Magori and Maisin cases are important in that they recapitulate the 'unity in diversity' theme which has run throughout this book. In both cases, languages have converged towards neighbouring languages, but have stopped short of actual identity. Throughout New Guinea there are strong forces of convergence, both linguistic and cultural, that diffuse from group to group. On the other hand, the opposing forces of village and in-group solidarity resist the homogenizing influence of diffusion. The whole dynamic interplay results in each community of language presenting 'an aggregation of widely diffused traits peculiar to it' (Mead 1938: 151). Each community constructs its identity by drawing on the available pool of cultural and linguistic traits. Each language will converge toward its neighbours by borrowing linguistic features; but to converge too much, to become identical, is to lose language as an important marker of a community's unique identity. Thus, the inherent contradiction in the theme 'unity in diversity' is one that speakers of a Papuan language have struggled with for many millennia and, it is to be hoped, one they will continue to grapple with for many to come.

REFERENCES

Abbreviations used in references for journals and serials:

AA	*American Anthropologist*
AEL	*Acta Ethnographica et Linguistica*
AnL	*Anthropological Linguistics*
BijdrTLV	*Bijdragen tot de Taal-, Land- en Volkenkunde*
JPS	*Journal of the Polynesian Society*
JRAI	*Journal of the Royal Anthropological Society of Great Britain and Ireland*
LD, AP	*Language Data, Asian–Pacific Series*
Lg	*Language*
MBA	*Micro-Bibliotheca Anthropos*
MSOS	*Mitteilungen des Seminars für Orientalische Sprachen*
NGS	*Nieuw Guinea Studien*
OL	*Oceanic Linguistics*
OLM	*Oceania Linguistic Monographs*
PL	*Pacific Linguistics*
SJA	*Southwest Journal of Anthropology*
VBG	*Verhandelingen van het Koninklijk Nederlandse Akademie van Wetenschappen, afdeeling Letterkunde*
VKI	*Verhandelingen van Koninklijke Instituut voor Taal-, Land- and Volkenkunde*
WPNGL	*Workpapers in Papua New Guinea Languages*
WZKM	*Wiener Zeitschrift für die Kunde des Morgenlandes*
ZES	*Zeitschrift für Eingeborenen-Sprachen*
ZEthn	*Zeitschrift für Ethnologie*

Abbott, S. 1977. Nor-Pondo lexicostatistical survey. Unpublished manuscript, Summer Institute of Linguistics, Ukarumpa, Papua New Guinea.
1978. Murik verb morphology. Unpublished manuscript, Summer Institute of Linguistics, Ukarumpa, Papua New Guinea.
Abbott, S. and J. Abbott 1978. Murik grammar: clause to word. Unpublished manuscript, Summer Institute of Linguistics, Ukarumpa, Papua New Guinea.
Alungun, J., R. Conrad and J. Lukas 1978. Some Muhiang grammatical notes. *WPNGL* 25: 89–130.
Anceaux, J. 1965. The Nimboran language. *VKI* 44.
Anderson, N. and M. Wade 1981. Ergativity and control in Podopa. Unpublished manuscript, Summer Institute of Linguistics, Ukarumpa, Papua New Guinea.

Aufenanger, H. 1952. Vokabular und Grammatik der Gende-Sprache in Zentral-Neuguinea. *MBA* 1.

Austing, J. F. and J. Austing 1977. Semantics of Ömie discourse. *LD*, *AP* 11.

Bailey, D. 1975. The phonology of the Abau language. *WPNGL* 9: 5–58.

Bateson, G. 1936. *Naven*. Cambridge: Cambridge University Press.

Becker, A. 1975. A linguistic image of nature: the Burmese numerative classifier system. *Linguistics* 165: 109–121.

Bee, D. 1965. Usarufa distinctive features and phonemics. *P.L* A6: 39–68.

1972. Phonological interference between Usarufa and Pidgin English. *Kivung* 5: 69–95.

1973. Usarufa: a descriptive grammar. In McKaughan 1973: 225–323.

Bellwood, P. 1978. *Man's conquest of the Pacific*. Auckland: Collins.

Bergmann, W. 1953. *Grammar of the Kuman language*. Chimbu: Lutheran Mission.

Berndt, C. 1954. Translation problems in three New Guinea Highlands languages. *Oceania* 24: 289–317.

Biggs, B. G. 1963. A non-phonemic central vowel type in Karam, a 'Pygmy' language of the Schrader Mountains, Central New Guinea. *AnL* 5/4: 13–17.

Bloomfield, L. 1933. *Language*. New York: Holt.

1946. Algonkian. *Viking Foundation Publication in Anthropology* 6: 85–129.

Blowers, B. L. 1970. Kaugel phonemic statement. *PL* A26: 1–12.

Blowers, B. L. and R. Blowers 1970. Kaugel verb morphology. *PL* A25: 37–60.

Boelaars, J. 1950. *The linguistic position of south-western New Guinea*. Leiden: Brill.

Boxwell, H. and M. Boxwell 1966. Weri phonemes. *PL* A7: 77–93.

Boxwell, M. 1967. Weri pronoun system. *Linguistics* 29: 34–43.

1980. Identification and movement of participants in Weri narrative discourse. *PL* A56: 1–34.

Brandson, R. ms a. Strange bedfellows: internal reconstruction and the comparative method, a case study. Unpublished manuscript, University of Manitoba.

ms b. Verb morphology in the East-Central language family. Unpublished manuscript, University of Manitoba.

in preparation. A grammar of Gende. PhD dissertation, University of Manitoba.

Bromley, H. M. 1961. The phonology of Lower Grand Valley Dani: a comparative structural study of skewed phonemic patterns. *VKI* 34.

1965. The phonology of Lower Grand Valley Dani. *VKI* 34.

1967. The linguistic relationships of Grand Valley Dani: a lexicostatistical classification. *Oceania* 37: 286–308.

1981. A grammar of Lower Grand Valley Dani. *PL* C63.

Brookfield, H. and D. Hart 1971. Melanesia: a geographical interpretation of an island world. London: Methuen.

Brown, H. 1968. A dictionary of Toaripi. *OLM* 11.

1973. The Eleman language family. *PL* C26: 279–375.

Brown, P. 1962. Non-agnates among the patrilineal Chimbu. *JPS* 71: 57–69.

Brown, R. 1981. Semantic aspects of Waris predications. In K. Franklin, ed., *Syntax and semantics in Papua New Guinea languages*, 93–124. Ukarumpa, Papua New Guinea, Summer Institute of Linguistics.

Bruce, L. Jr 1974. Alamblak passivity. *Kivung* 7: 178–96.

1975. Alamblak alveopalatals – dead portmanteaus. *PL* A40: 91–102.

1979. A grammar of Alamblak (Papua New Guinea). Unpublished PhD dissertation, Australian National University.

1984. The Alamblak language of Papua New Guinea (East Sepik). *PL* C81. Published version, with deletions, of Bruce 1979.

Bulmer, R., B. Biggs and A. Pawley, in preparation. Kalam dictionary.

Bunn, G. 1974. Golin grammar. *WPNGL* 5.

Bunn, G. and R. Bunn 1970. Golin phonology. *PL* A23: 1–7.

Capell, A. 1948–9. Distribution of languages in the central highlands, New Guinea. *Oceania* 19: 104–29, 234–53, 349–77.

1956. A new approach to Australian linguistics. *OLM* 1.

1969. The structure of the Binandere verb. *PL* A18: 1–32.

1976a. Features of Austronesian languages in the New Guinea area in contrast with other Austronesian languages of Melanesia. *PL* C39: 235–82.

1976b. Austronesian and Papuan 'mixed' languages: general remarks. *PL* C39: 527–79.

Chowning, A. 1977. *An introduction to the peoples and cultures of Melanesia*. Menlo Park, California: Cummings.

Conrad, R. 1978a. Some notes on attitudes toward language and language choice in May River Iwam. *WPNGL* 24: 31–46.

1978b. A survey of the Arapesh language family of Papua New Guinea. *WPNGL* 25: 57–77.

Cowan, H. 1951–2. Notes on Sentani grammar. *Oceania* 21: 214–28, 302–9; 22: 53–71, 315–16.

1952. Drie verhalen in Sentani-taal. *BijdrTLV* 108: 347–64.

1965. Grammar of the Sentani language. *VKI* 47.

Davies, H. J. 1980a. Kobon phonology. *PL* B68.

1980b. The phonological status of the semivowel in Kobon. *PL* A56: 197–214.

1981a. The syntax of the simple sentence in Kobon. *PL* A61: 1–70.

1981b. Kobon. *Lingua Descriptive Series* 3.

Dawson, M. and M. Dawson 1974. Kobon phrases. *WPNGL* 6: 119–82.

De Bruyn, J. and J. Pouwer 1958. Anthropological research in Netherlands New Guinea since 1950. *Oceania* 29: 132–71.

Deibler, E. Jr 1976. Semantic relationships of Gahuku verbs. Summer Institute of Linguistics, *Publications in Linguistics*, 48.

Dempwolff, O. 1933–8. Vergleichende Lautlehre des austronesischen Worktschatzes. *ZES*, Beihefte 15, 17, 19.

Dixon, R. 1971. A method of semantic description. In D. Steinberg and L. Jakobvits, eds., *Semantics*, 436–71. Cambridge: Cambridge University Press.

1977. *A grammar of Yidiny*. Cambridge: Cambridge University Press.

1979. Ergativity. *Lg* 55: 59–138.

1980. *The languages of Australia*. Cambridge: Cambridge University Press.

1982. Noun classifiers and noun classes. In *Where have all the adjectives gone? and other essays in semantics and syntax*, 211–34. The Hague: Mouton.

Doble, M. 1960. *Kapauku–Malayan–Dutch–English Dictionary*. The Hague: Nijhoff.

1962. Essays on Kapauku grammar. *NGS* 6: 152–5, 211–18, 279–98.

Drabbe, P. 1950. Twee dialecten van de Awju-taal. *BijdrTLV* 106: 93–147.

1952. *Spraakkunst van het Ekagi, Wisselmeren, Nederlands Nieuw Guinea*. The Hague: Nijhoff.

1953. *Spraakkunst van de Kamoro-taal*. The Hague: Nijhoff.

1954. Talen en dialecten van Zuid-West Nieuw-Guinea. *MBA* 11.

1955. Spraakkunst von het Marind. *Studia Instituti Anthropos* 11.

1957. *Spraakkunst van het Aghu-Dialect van de Awju-Taal*. The Hague: Nijhoff.

1959a. *Grammar of the Asmat language*. Syracuse, Indiana: Our Lady of the Lake Press.

1959b. *Dictionary of the Asmat language*. Syracuse, Indiana: Our Lady of the Lake Press.

1959c. *Kaeti en Wambon: Twee Awju-Dialecten*. The Hague: Nijhoff.

1963. Drie Asmat-dialekten. *VKI* 2.

Dubert, R. and M. Dubert 1973. Biangai phonemes. *WPNGL* 2: 5–35.

Dutton, T. 1969. The Koiarian languages of Central Papua: a historical and descriptive linguistic study. Unpublished PhD dissertation, Australian National University.

ed. 1975. Studies in languages of central and south-east Papua. *PL* C29.

1976. Magori and similar languages of south-east Papua. *PL* C39: 581–636.

1980. Queensland Canefields English of the late nineteenth century. *PL* D29.

Dutton, T. and H. A. Brown 1977. Hiri Motu: the language itself. *PL* C40: 759–93.

Dyen, I. 1956. The Ngadju Dayak 'old speech stratum'. *Lg* 32: 83–7.

Emeneau, M. 1956. India as a linguistic area. *Lg* 32: 3–16.

Fabian, E., G. Fabian and C. Peck 1971. The morphophonemics of Nabak. *Kivung* 4: 147–60.

Fahner, C. 1979. The morphology of Yali and Dani: a descriptive and comparative analysis. Unpublished PhD dissertation, University of Leiden.

Farr, C. and C. Whitehead 1981. This, that, and the other: a study of Korafe demonstratives. *Language and Linguistics in Melanesia* 13: 64–80.

Farr, J. and C. Farr 1974. A preliminary Korafe phonology. *WPNGL* 3: 5–38.

1975. Some features of Korafe morphology. *PL* C29: 731–69.

Feldman, H. 1983. A grammar of Autuw. Unpublished PhD dissertation, Australian National University.

Ferguson, C. 1959. Diglossia. *Word* 15: 325–40.

1966. Assumptions about nasals: a sample study in phonological universals. In J. Greenberg, ed., *Universals of language*, 53–60. Cambridge, Mass: MIT Press.

Firchow, I. and J. Firchow 1969. An abbreviated phoneme inventory. *AnL* 11/9: 271–6.

Flierl, W. and H. Strauss 1977. Kâte dictionary. *PL* C41.

Foreman, V. 1974. Grammar of Yessan-Mayo, *LD, AP* 4.

Foreman, V. and H. Marten 1973. Yessan–Mayo phonemes. *WPNGL* 2: 79–108.

Fortune, R. 1942. Arapesh. *Publications of the American Ethnological Society* 19.

Franklin, K. 1965. Kewa clause markers. *Oceania* 35: 272–85.

1967. Names and aliases in Kewa. *JPS* 76: 76–81.

1968. The dialects of Kewa. *PL* B10.

1971. A grammar of Kewa, New Guinea. *PL* C16.

1972. A ritual pandanus language of New Guinea. *Oceania* 43: 61–76.

ed. 1973. The linguistic situation in the Gulf District and adjacent areas, Papua New Guinea.

1974. A diachronic note on Mendi vowels. *Kivung* 7: 167–77.

1975a. Comments on Proto-Engan. *PL* C38: 263–75.

1975b. Nasalisation in Kewa dialects. Kivung 8: 72–86.

1975c. A Kewa religious argot. *Anthropos* 70: 713–25.

1981. Existentials and pro-verbs in Kewa. In K. Franklin, ed., *Syntax and semantics in Papua New Guinea languages*, 153–74. Ukarumpa, New Guinea: Summer Institute of Linguistics.

Franklin, K. and J. Franklin 1962. Kewa I: phonological asymmetry. *AnL* 4/7: 29–37.

1978. A Kewa dictionary, with supplementary grammatical and anthropological materials. *PL* C53.

Frantz, C. 1973. Gadsup phoneme and toneme units. In McKaughan 1973, 406–43.

Freudenburg, A. 1976. The dialects of Boiken. *WPNGL* 16: 81–90.

Freudenburg, A. and M. Freudenburg 1974. Boiken phonemes. *WPNGL* 4: 97–128.

Freyburg, P. 1977. Missionary lingue franche: Bel (Gedaged). *PL* C40: 855–64.

Geary, E. 1977. Grammatical studies in Kunimaipa. *WPNGL* 23.

Gerstner, A. 1963. Grammatik der Alübansprache. *MBA* 37.

Geurtjens, H. 1926. Spraakleer der Marindineesche taal. *VBG* 68/2.

1933. Marindineesch-Nederlandsch Woordenboek. *VBG* 71.

Golson, J. 1977. No room at the top: agricultural intensification in the New Guinea highlands. In J. Allen *et al.*, eds., *Sunda and Sahul: prehistoric studies in Southeast Asia, Melanesia and*

Australia, 601–38. New York: Academic Press.

1982. The Ipomoean revolution revisited: society and the sweet potato in the upper Wahgi valley. In A. Strathern, ed., *Inequality in the New Guinea highlands*, 109–36. Cambridge: Cambridge University Press.

Greenberg, J. 1966. Some universals of grammar with particular reference to the order of meaningful elements. In J. Greenberg, ed., *Universals of language*, 73–113. Cambridge, Mass: MIT Press.

Griffin, M. 1970. Buin directionals. *PL* A26: 13–22.

Grimes, J. 1972. *The thread of discourse*. The Hague: Mouton.

Haantjens, H., J. Mabbutt and R. Pullen 1965. Anthropogenic grasslands in the Sepik plains. *Pacific Viewpoint* 6: 215–19.

Haas, M. 1944. Men's and women's speech in Koasati. *Lg* 26: 142-9.

Haiman, J. 1978. Conditionals are topics. *Lg* 54: 564–89.

1980. *Hua: a Papuan language of the Eastern Highlands of New Guinea*. Amsterdam: Benjamins.

Hale, K. 1976. Phonological developments in particular Northern Paman languages. In P. Sutton, ed., *Languages of Cape York*, 7–49. Canberra: Australian Institute of Aboriginal Studies.

Hartzler, D. 1976. A study of Sentani verb structure. *Irian* 5/2: 18–38.

Hartzler, M. 1976. Central Sentani phonology. *Irian* 5/1: 66–81.

Haviland, J. 1979. How to talk to your brother-in-law in Guugu–Yimidhirr. In T. Shopen, ed., *Languages and their speakers*, 161–239. Cambridge, Mass: Winthrop.

Healey, A. 1964a. Telefol phonology. *PL* B3.

1964b. A survey of the Ok family of languages. Unpublished PhD thesis, Australian National University.

1970. Proto-Awyu-Dumut phonology. *PL* C13: 997–1063.

1974. A problem of Telefol verb classification. *WPNGL* 7: 167–75.

Healey, P. M. 1964. Telefol quotative clauses. *PL* A3: 27–34.

1965a. Telefol clause structure. *PL* A5: 1–26.

1965b. Telefol verb phrases. *PL* A5: 27–53.

1965c. Telefol noun phrases. *PL* B4.

1966. Levels and chaining in Telefol sentences. *PL* B5.

ed. 1981. Angan languages are different: four phonologies. *LD, AP* 12.

Healey, P. M. and A. Healey 1977. Telefol dictionary. *PL* C46.

Healey, P. M., A. Healey and W. Steinkraus 1972. A preliminary vocabulary of Tifal with grammar notes. *LD, AP* 5.

Henderson, J. and A. Henderson 1979. Essentials of Yele grammar. Manuscript, Summer Institute of Linguistics, Ukarumpa, Papua New Guinea.

Hope, G., J. Golson and J. Allen 1983. Palaeoecology and prehistory in New Guinea. *Journal of Human Evolution* 12: 37–60.

Huisman, R. 1973. Angaataha verb morphology. *Linguistics* 110: 43–54.

Huisman, R. and J. Lloyd 1981. Angaatiha tone, stress, and length. In P. M. Healey, ed., *Angan languages are different: four phonologies. LD, AP* 12.

Hurd, C. 1977. Nasioi projectives. *OL* 16: 111–78.

Hurd, C. and P. Hurd 1966. *Nasioi language course*. Port Moresby: Department of Information and Extension Services.

1970. Nasioi verbs. *OL* 9: 37–78.

Irwin, B. 1974. Salt–Yui grammar. *PL* B35.

James, D. ms. A grammar of Siane. Unpublished manuscript, Summer Institute of Linguistics, Ukarumpa, Papua New Guinea.

Jones, R. 1979. The fifth continent: problems concerning the human colonization of Australia. *Annual Review of Anthropology* 8: 445–66.

Kerr, H. 1966. A preliminary statement of Wiru grammar. Unpublished MA thesis, University of Hawaii, Honolulu.

Keysser, C. 1925. Wörterbuch der Kâte-Sprache gesprochen in Neuguinea. *ZES*, Beiheft 7.

King, C. 1927. *Grammar and dictionary of the Binandere language, Mamba River, North Division, Papua*. Sydney: Ford.

Kirk, R. 1980. Population movements in the southwest Pacific: the genetic evidence. In J. J. Fox *et al.*, eds., *Indonesia: Australian perspectives*, 45–56. Canberra: Australian National University, Research School of Pacific Studies.

Klaffl, J. and F. Vormann 1905. Die Sprachen des Berlinhafen-Bezirks in Deutsch-Neuguinea. *MSOS* 8: 1–138.

Kolk, J. van de and P. Vertenten 1922. *Marindineesch woordenboek. Weltevreden*. Batavia: Landsdrukkerij.

Lang, A. 1973. Enga dictionary, with English index. *PL* C20.

1975. The semantics of classificatory verbs in Enga (and other Papua New Guinea languages). *PL* B39.

Langness, L. 1964. Some problems in the conceptualization of Highlands social structures. In J. Watson, ed., *New Guinea: the Central Highlands*. *AA* 66.4(2): 162–182.

Larsen, R. and M. Larsen 1977. Orokaiva phonology and orthography. *WPNGL* 19: 5–28.

1980. Orokaiva: language lessons and grammar notes. *WPNGL* 30.

Larson, G. and M. Larson 1972. The Ekagi–Wodani–Moni language family of West Irian. *Irian* 1/3: 80–95.

Larson, M. and G. Larson 1958. Preliminary studies in the Moni language. *BijdrTLV* 114: 406–31.

Lawrence, M. 1983. Viewpoint in Oksapmin. Paper presented at the Congress of the Linguistic Society of Papua New Guinea, Port Moresby, July 1983.

Laycock, D. 1965. The Ndu language family (Sepik District, New Guinea). *PL* C1.

1966. Papuans and Pidgin: aspects of bilingualism in New Guinea. *Te Reo* 9: 44–51.

1969. Sublanguages in Buin: play, poetry, and preservation. *PL* A22: 1–23.

1973a. Sepik languages – checklist and preliminary classification. *PL* B25.

1973b. Sissano, Warapu, and Melanesian pidginization. *OL* 12: 245–77.

1975. The Torricelli phylum. *PL* C38: 767–80.

1977a. Special languages in parts of the New Guinea area. *PL* C40: 133–49.

1977b. Me and you versus the rest: abbreviated pronoun systems in Irianese/Papuan languages. *Irian* 7: 33–41.

forthcoming. Basic materials in Buin: grammar, texts and dictionary. To appear in *PL*.

Laycock, D. and S. Wurm 1977. Observations on language change in parts of the New Guinea area. *PL* C40: 195–205.

Laycock, D. and J. Z'graggen 1975. The Sepik–Ramu Phylum. *PL* C38: 731–66.

Leeden, A. van der, 1956. *Hoofdtrekken der sociale struktuur in het westelijke binnenland van Sarmi*. Leiden: Brill.

1960. Social structure in New Guinea. *BijdrTLV* 116: 119–49.

Lincoln, P. 1978. Reef–Santa Cruz as Austronesian. *PL* C61: 929–67.

Litteral, R. 1978. Changes in the Bibriari communicative system. *WPNGL* 24: 25–30.

1980. Features of Anggor discourse. Unpublished PhD dissertation, University of Pennsylvania.

Litteral, S. 1972. Orientation to space and participants in Anggor. *PL* A31: 23–44.

Lloyd, R. 1973. The Angan language family. *PL* C26: 31–110.

Lloyd, R. and A. Healey 1968. Baruya phonemes – a problem in interpretation. *Linguistics* 60: 33–48.

Loeweke, E. and J. May 1980. General grammar of Fasu (Namo Me). *WPNGL* 27: 5–106.

Longacre, R. 1972. *Hierarchy and universality of discourse constituents in New Guinea languages* (2 volumes). Washington: Georgetown University Press.

Loving, R. 1973a. Awa phonemes, tonemes, and tonally differentiated allomorphs. In McKaughan 1973, 10–18.

1973b. An outline of Awa grammatical structures. In McKaughan 1973, 65–87.

Loving, R. and A. Loving 1975. Awa dictionary. *PL* C30.

Loving, R. and H. McKaughan 1973. Awa verbs I: the internal structure of independent verbs. In McKaughan 1973, 36–55.

Luzbetak, L. 1954. *The Middle Wahgi dialects, vol. 1: Banz grammar*. Banz, New Guinea: Catholic Mission.

1956. Middle Wahgi phonology. *OLM* 2.

Lynch, J. 1981. Austronesian 'loanwords' (?) in Trans-New Guinea phylum vocabulary. *PL* A61: 165–80.

1983. On the Kuman 'liquids'. Unpublished manuscript, University of Papua New Guinea.

McCarthy, J. 1965. Clause chaining in Kanite. *AnL* 7/5: 59–70.

McElhanon, K. 1967a. Preliminary observations on Huon Peninsula languages. *OL* 6: 1–45.

1967b. Selepet vocoid clusters. *PL* A12: 1–18.

1970a. Selepet phonology. *PL* B14.

1970b. Selepet verb morphology. *PL* A25: 19–35.

1970c. Selepet pronominal elements. *PL* A26: 23–48.

1970d. Stops and fricatives: non-unique solutions in Selepet. *Linguistics* 60: 49–62.

1970e. Lexicostatistics and the classification of Huon Peninsula languages. *Oceania* 40: 214–31.

1971. Classifying New Guinea languages. *Anthropos* 66: 120–44.

1972. Selepet grammar, part I: from root to phrase. *PL* B21.

1973. Towards a typology of the Finisterre–Huon languages, New Guinea. *PL* B22.

1975. North-Eastern Trans-New Guinea Phylum languages. *PL* C38: 527–68.

McElhanon, K. and N. McElhanon 1970. Selepet–English dictionary. *PL* C15.

McElhanon, K. and C. Voorhoeve. 1970. The Trans-New Guinea Phylum: explorations in deep-level genetic relationships. *PL* B16.

McGregor, D. and A. McGregor 1982. Olo language materials. *PL* D42.

McKaughan, H., ed., 1973. *The languages of the Eastern Family of the East New Guinea Highland Stock*. Seattle: University of Washington Press.

McVinney, P. and L. Luzbetak 1954. *Tabare dialect, vol. 1: grammar*. Alexishafen: Catholic Mission.

Manning, M. and N. Saggers 1977. A tentative phonemic analysis of Ningil. *WPNGL* 19: 49–72.

Martens, M. and S. Tuominen 1977. A tentative phonemic statement of Yil in West Sepik Province. *WPNGL* 19: 29–48.

Mead, M. 1935. *Sex and temperament in three primitive societies*. New York: Morrow.

1938. The Mountain Arapesh: an importing culture. *American Museum of Natural History, Anthropological Papers* 36: 139–349.

Mecklenburg, C. 1974. Phonology of Faiwol. *WPNGL* 7: 143–66.

Mihalic, F. 1971. *The Jacaranda dictionary and grammar of Melanesian Pidgin*. Brisbane: Jacaranda Press.

Mintz, M. 1971. *Bikol grammar notes*. Honolulu: University of Hawaii Press.

Mosel, U. 1981. Tolai and Tok Pisin: the influence of the substratum on development of New Guinea Pidgin. *PL* B73.

Mühlhäusler, P. 1977a. The history of New Guinea Pidgin. *PL* C40: 497–510.

1977b. Sociolects in New Guinea Pidgin. *PL* C40: 559–66.

Nekitel, O. 1979. A sketch of nominal concord in the Abu' dialect of Mountain Arapesh. BA subthesis, University of Papua New Guinea.

Neuendorf, A. 1977. Missionary lingue franche: Gogodala. *PL* C40: 875–80.

Newman, P. 1965. *Knowing the Gururumba*. New York: Holt.

Nilles, J. 1969. *Kuman–English dictionary*. Kundiawa: Catholic Mission.

Oates, W. and L. Oates 1968. Kapau pedagogical grammar. *PL* C10.

Oatridge, D. and J. Oatridge 1973. Phonemes of Binumarien. In McKaughen 1973, 517–22.

Olson, M. 1975. Barai grammar highlights. *PL* C29: 471–512.

1981. Barai clause junctures: towards a functional theory of interclausal relations. Unpublished PhD thesis, Australian National University.

Oosterwal, G. 1961. *People of the Tor*. Assen, Netherlands: Van Gorcum.

Pagotto, L. 1976. The noun phrase in Chambri. *Department of Language, University of Papua New Guinea, Occasional Papers* 5.

Pain, C. and G. Scott 1981. Highland–lowland interactive systems in Enga Province, Papua New Guinea. *Mountain Research and Development* 1: 71–8.

Palmer, F. 1954. *The Latin language*. London: Faber and Faber.

Parker, J. and D. Parker 1974. A tentative phonology of Baining. *WPNGL* 4: 5–44.

Parlier, J. 1964. Managalasi verb inflection. *Te Reo* 7: 28–35.

Parlier, J. and J. Parlier 1980. *Managalasi dictionary*. Ukarumpa, Papua New Guinea: Summer Institute of Linguistics.

Pawley, A. 1966. The structure of Kalam: a grammar of a New Guinea Highlands language. Unpublished PhD dissertation, University of Auckland.

1975a. Verb reduction in the Kalam pandanus language. Unpublished manuscript, University of Auckland.

1975b. Kalam classification of body and mental processes. Unpublished manuscript, University of Hawaii.

1980. On meeting a language that defies description by ordinary means. Paper presented at the Congress of the Linguistic Society of Papua New Guinea, Lae, September 1980.

Pawley, A. and R. Green 1973. Dating the dispersal of the Oceanic languages. *OL* 12: 1–68.

Payne, A. and D. Drew 1966. *Kamano language course*. Ukarumpa, Papua New Guinea: Summer Institute of Linguistics.

Pence, A. 1966. Kunimaipa phonology: hierarchical levels. *PL* A7: 49–67.

Phillips, D. 1976. Wahgi phonology and morphology. *PL* B36.

Piau, J. 1985. The verbal syntax of Kuman. Unpublished MA thesis, Australian National University.

Pilhofer, G. 1928. Formenlehre von zehn Mundarten und Nachbarsprachen des Kâte. *ZES* 18: 196–231, 298–315.

1929. Wörterverzeichnis aus zwölf Mundarten und Nachbarsprachen des Kâte. *ZES* 19: 41–69.

1933. Grammatik der Kâte Sprache in Neuguinea. *ZES*, Beiheft 14.

Posposil, L. 1966. *The Kapauku Papuans of West New Guinea*. New York: Holt.

Pouwer, J. 1960. Loosely structured societies in Netherlands New Guinea. *BijdrTLV* 116: 109–18.

Rausch, J. 1912. Die Sprache von Sudost-Bougainville, Deutsche Salomonsinseln. *Anthropos* 7: 105–34, 585–616, 964–94.

Ray, S. 1911. Comparative notes on Maisin and other languages of eastern Papua. *JRAI* 41: 397–405.

1912. A grammar of the Fuyuge language. In R. Williamson, ed., *The Mafulu: mountain people of British New Guinea*, 307–31. London: Macmillan.

1923. The languages of the Western Division of Papua. *JRAI* 53: 332–60.

1933. *A grammar of the Kiwai language, Fly delta, Papua*. Port Moresby: Government Printer.

Read, K. 1959. Leadership and consensus in a New Guinea society. *AA* 61: 425–36.

Reesink, G. 1983. Switch reference and topicality hierarchies. *Studies in Language* 7: 215–46.

Renck, G. 1975. A grammar of Yagaria. *PL* B40.

1977a. Yagaria dictionary with English index. *PL* C37.

1977b. Missionary lingue franche: Kâte. *PL* C40: 839–46.

Riley, E. and S. Ray 1930–31. Sixteen vocabularies from the Fly River, Papua. *Anthropos* 25: 173–94, 831–50; 26: 171–92.

Ross, M. 1980. Some elements of Vanimo, a New Guinea tone language. *PL* A56: 77–109.

Ross, M. and J. Paol 1978. A Waskia grammar sketch and vocabulary. *PL* B56.

Rule, W. 1977. A comparative study of the Foe, Huli and Pole languages of Papua New Guinea. *OLM* 20.

Salisbury, R. 1962. Notes on bilingualism and language change in New Guinea. *AnL* 4/7: 1–13.

Sanders, A. and J. Sanders 1980a. Defining the centres of the Marienberg language family. *PL* A56: 171–96.

1980b. Phonology of the Kamasau language. *PL* A56: 111–36.

1980c. Dialect survey of the Kamasau language. *PL* A56: 137–90.

Sankoff, G. 1977. Multilingualism in Papua New Guinea. *PL* C40: 265–307.

Sapir, E. 1949. Internal linguistic evidence suggestive of the northern origin of the Navaho. In R. Mandlebaum, ed., *Selected writings of Edward Sapir*, 213–24. Berkeley: University of California Press.

Schmidt, J. 1953. Vokabular und grammatik der Murik-Sprache in Nordost-Neuguinea. *MBA* 3.

Schmidt, W. and F. Vormann 1900. Ein Beitrag zur Kenntnis der Valman-Sprache. *ZEthn* 32: 87–104.

Schneuker, C. 1962. *Kâte language handbook*. Madang: Lutheran Mission Press.

Scorza, D. 1974. Sentence structure of the Au language. *WPNGL* 1: 165–246.

in press. Au morphology and syntax. To appear in *PL*.

Scott, G. 1978. The Fore language of Papua New Guinea. *PL* B47.

1980. Fore dictionary. *PL* C62.

Seiler, W. 1983. From verb serialization to noun classification. Unpublished paper, Australian National University.

1984. Grammar of the Imonda language. Unpublished PhD dissertation, Australian National University.

Shaw, R. and K. Shaw 1977. Samo phonemes. *WPNGL* 19: 97–135.

Shibatani, M., ed., 1976. *The grammar of causative constructions*. (*Syntax and Semantics*, vol. 6.) New York: Academic.

Silverstein, M. 1976. Hierarchy of features and ergativity. In R. M. W. Dixon, ed., *Grammatical categories in Australian languages*, 112–71. Canberra: Australian Institute for Aboriginal Studies.

Smith, J. 1977. Mianmin sentence structure. *WPNGL* 22: 5–53.

Smith, J. and P. Weston 1974a. Mianmin phonemes and tonemes. *WPNGL* 7: 5–34.

1974b. Notes on Mianmin grammar. *WPNGL* 7: 35–142.

Souter, G. 1963. *New Guinea: the last unknown*. Sydney: Angus and Robertson.

Spölgen, N. and W. Schmidt 1901. Beitrage zur Kenntnis der Valman-Sprache. *WZKM* 15: 335–66.

Staalsen, P. 1966. The phonemes of Iatmul. *PL* A7: 69–76.

1969. The dialects of Iatmul. *PL* A22: 68–84.

1972. Clause relationships in Iatmul. *PL* A31: 45–69.

1975. The languages of the Sawos region. *Anthropos* 70: 6–16.

n.d. a. Iatmul grammar essentials for translation. Unpublished manuscript, Summer Institute of Linguistics, Ukarumpa, Papua New Guinea.

n.d. b. The pronouns of Iatmul. Unpublished manuscript, Summer Institute of Linguistics, Ukarumpa, Papua New Guinea.

Stap, P. van der, 1966. Outline of Dani morphology. *VKI* 48.

Steinkraus, W. 1969. Tifal phonology showing vowel and tone neutralization. *Kivung* 2: 57–66.

Steltenpool, J. 1969. Ekagi–Dutch–English–Indonesian dictionary. *VKI* 56.

Steltenpool, J. and P. van der Stap 1959. *Leerboek van het Kapauku*. Hollandia: Office of Aboriginal Welfare.

Strange, D. 1973. Indicative and subjunctive in Upper Asaro. *Linguistics* 110: 82–97.

Strange, G. 1965. Nominal elements in Upper Asaro. *AnL* 7/5: 71–9.

Strathern, A. 1972. *The rope of moka*. Cambridge: Cambridge University Press.

Strauss, H. n.d. Grammatik der Medlpa-Sprache. To be published in *PL* in an English translation.

Strong, W. 1911. The Maisin language. *JRAI* 41: 381–96.

Stucky, A. and D. Stucky 1973. Nii phonology. *WPNGL* 2: 37–78.

Swadling, P. 1981. *Papua New Guinea's prehistory: an introduction*. Port Moresby: Papua New Guinea National Museum.

1984. Sepik prehistory. Paper prepared for Wenner-Gren symposium 95: Sepik research today: the study of Sepik cultures in and for modern Papua New Guinea. Basel, Switzerland, August.

Swick, J. 1966. Chuave phonological hierarchy. *PL* A7: 33–48.

Thorne, A. 1980. The longest link: human evolution in Southeast Asia and the settlement of Australia. In J. J. Fox *et al.*, eds., *Indonesia: Australian perspectives*, 35–44. Canberra: Australian National University, Research School of Pacific Studies.

Thurman, R. 1975. Chuave medial verbs. *AnL* 17/7: 342–52.

Trefry, D. 1969. A comparative study of Kuman and Pawaian–Non-Austronesian languages of New Guinea. *PL* B13.

Tuzin, D. 1974. Social control and the tambaran in the Sepik. In A. Epstein, ed., *Contention and dispute: aspects of law and social control in Melanesia*, 317–51. Canberra: ANU Press.

1977. Kinship terminology in a linguistic setting: a case study. *PL* C40: 101–29.

Van Valin, R. 1977. Aspects of Lakhota syntax. Unpublished PhD dissertation, University of California, Berkeley.

Vincent, A. 1973. Tairora verb structure. In McKaughan 1973, 561–87.

Voorhoeve, C. 1965. The Flamingo Bay dialect of the Asmat language. *VKI* 46.

1969. Some notes on the linguistic relations between the Sentani and Asmat languages of New Guinea. *BijdrTLV* 125: 466–86.

1970a. The languages of the Lake Murray area. *PL* A25: 1–18.

1970b. Some notes on the Suki–Gogodala subgroup of the Central and South New Guinea Phylum. *PL* C13: 1245–70.

1971. Miscellaneous notes on languages in West Irian, New Guinea. *PL* A28: 47–114.

1975a. Central and western Trans-New Guinea Phylum languages. *PL* C38: 345–459.

1975b. East Bird's Head, Geelvink Bay Phyla. *PL* C38: 867–78.

1977. Ta-poman: metaphorical use of words and poetic vocabulary in Asmat songs. *PL* C40: 19–38.

1980. The Asmat languages of Irian Jaya. *PL* B64.

1982. The Makian languages and their neighbours. *PL* D46.

Vormann, F. and W. Scharfenberger 1914. *Die Monumbo-Sprache: Grammatik und Wörterverzeichnis.* Wien: Anthropos Linguistic Library.

Wacke, K. 1931. Formenlehre der Ono-Sprache (Neuguinea). *ZES* 21: 161–208.

Watson, J. 1970. Society as organised flow: the Tairora case. *SJA* 26: 107–24.

Webb, T. 1974. Urii phonemes. *WPNGL* 4: 45–96.

Weimer, H. and N. Weimer 1975. A short sketch of Yareba grammar. *PL* C29: 667–730.

Wells, M. 1979. Siroi grammar. *PL* B51.

West, D. 1973. Wojokeso sentence, paragraph, and discourse analysis. *PL* B28.

Weston, P. 1977. Mianmin interrogatives. *WPNGL* 22: 55–69.

White, J. and J. O'Connell 1982. *A prehistory of Australia, New Guinea and Sahul.* Sydney: Academic.

Whitehead, C. 1981. Subject, object and indirect object: towards a typology of Papuan languages. *Language and linguistics in Melanesia.* 13: 32–63.

Wilden, J. 1976. Simplicity and detail in Kemtuk predication. *Irian* 5.2: 59–84.

Wilson, D. 1969a. The Binandere language family. *PL* A18: 65–86.

1969b. Suena grammar highlights. *PL* A18: 95–110.

1974. Suena grammar. *WPNGL* 8: 1–170.

Wilson, P. 1973. Abulas sentences. *WPNGL* 1: 21–164.

1976. Abulas dialect survey. *WPNGL* 16: 52–79.

1980. Abulas grammar. *WPNGL* 26.

Wurm, S. 1951. Studies in the Kiwai languages, Fly Delta, Papua New Guinea. *AEL* 2.

1961. The linguistic situation in the Highlands Districts of Papua and New Guinea. *Australian Territories* 1/2: 14–23.

1964. Australian New Guinea Highlands languages and the distribution of their typological features. *AA* 66/4(2): 79–97.

1973. The Kiwaian language family. *PL* C26: 219–60.

ed., 1975. New Guinea area languages and language study, vol.1: Papuan languages and the New Guinea linguistic scene. *PL* C38.

1977a. Missionary lingue franche: Kiwai. *PL* C40: 893–906.

1977b. The nature of New Guinea Pidgin. *PL* C40: 511–32.

1978. Reefs–Santa Cruz: Austronesian, but ...! *PL* C61: 969–1010.

1982. The Papuan languages of Oceania. *Acta Linguistica* 7. Tübingen: Gunter Narr.

Wurm, S. and D. Laycock 1961. The question of language and dialect in New Guinea. *Oceania* 32: 128–43.

Wurm, S., C. L. Voorhoeve and K. A. McElhanon 1975. The Trans-New Guinea phylum in general. *PL* C38: 299–322.

Young, R. 1971. The verb in Bena-Bena: its form and function. *PL* B18.

Z'graggen, J. 1977. Missionary lingue franche: Boiken. *PL* C40: 947–52.

LANGUAGE INDEX

Where the affiliation of a language is discussed in section 7.3, on Papuan language families, the family name is listed immediately following the language name, with the location of the discussion. Other topics discussed for that language follow.

SUBJECT INDEX

Because this book discusses linguistic features systematically, with a number of languages being used to illustrate the variety of treatments of a concept, this index has been largely confined to general terms. For example, since allative, locative and ablative cases are discussed together for several pages, instead of including separate listings for *allative*, *ablative* and *locative* with the same page references, there is only one entry, for *locational cases*; and instead of entries for *nominative*, *accusative* and *ergative* cases, there is one entry for *core relations*.